Praise for *Come Let Us Rebuild*

"Writing from a practical and rich pasto
addresses concerns and challenges being faced in matt...
world's newest state . . This nation-building will require the patience
and patriotism of Nehemiah, his participatory leadership, his persever-
ance and persistent prayers. It is becoming clear that waging the war of
liberation is different from leading and building a civilized nation on a
foundation of good governance, peace, reconciliation, unity and toler-
ance. All these issues make it absolutely important to hear and respond
to the positive message of Nehemiah, conveyed to us by Bishop Poggo.
I highly commend this book to you. Read it, examine it and use it in
your life and work as you play your role in nation-building."

Dr. Isaiah Majok Dau
General Overseer (Presiding Bishop) Sudan Pentecostal Church
Author, Suffering and God: A Theological Reflection on the War in Sudan

"Bishop Anthony Poggo's new book enlarges and enriches the resources available to South Sudan's people as they seek to build a new nation
in justice and freedom. Bishop Anthony's life, and that of his family,
traverses the modern story of South Sudan's struggle for independence.
He himself has been deeply immersed in it in thoughtful reflection,
through his involvement in development and community work, and in
his ministry as a Christian priest and bishop. Few are better placed to
observe, guide and inspire South Sudan's new citizens. In this book he
brings together mature biblical reflection on the ancient story of Nehemiah, his extensive personal experience in development and reconciliation, and a deep love for his people. May the message of 'Come Let Us
Rebuild' be widely heard."

Rev. Canon Andy Wheeler, D.D.
World Mission Advisor, Diocese of Guildford
Author, editor and co-editor, Faith in Sudan series

Emmanuel Cathedral, Kajo-Keji

Come Let Us Rebuild

Lessons from Nehemiah

Bishop Anthony Poggo

Edited by Tim Flatman

millipede books

Published by
Millipede Books
8 Ebenezer Court
Hertford SG14 1LT

ISBN: 978-0-9530369-3-6
EAN: 9780953036936

Set in Monotype Sabon MT
Printed by Lightning Source

Contents

Foreword

BISHOP ANTHONY DANGASUK POGGO, who was formerly the Executive Director of ACROSS in Kenya, is one of the few we have in his generation. He relinquished his high-paid job and felt led to become Bishop of Kajo Keji, rolling up his sleeves in the course of rebuilding our nation ruined in the last 55 years of war.

The strength to make such a bold move he found in the experiences of Nehemiah, who was in exile and burdened with the task of rebuilding the walls of Jerusalem, despite numerous discouragements and mockeries hurled at him by the opposition and enemies to frustrate his effort.

The life of Nehemiah became a lived experience to Bishop Anthony. Out of it emerged his reflections in the form of this book, which he intends to benefit not only this generation, but also coming generations and those beyond the national borders of the Republic of South Sudan.

From what he shared with me, Bishop Anthony was convinced that the way to build people spiritually is to build worship and learning centres. Upon returning home, like Nehemiah, he started multiple construction projects within a short timespan: Emmanuel Cathedral in Kajo Keji, 40 churches and Canon Benaiah Poggo College.

He was true to his conviction. Now leaders are being made or trained in the college, and lives traumatised as a result of long war, are being transformed to face life with sober attitudes. As it is commonly said, 'like father like son', Bishop Anthony learned wisdom from his dear late Father, Rev. Canon Benaiah Duku Poggo, whose leadership was highly cherished and desired by us all.

When Bishop Gwynne College (BGC) was relocated to Juba from Mundri, at the peak of the civil war in South Sudan, many questions surrounded the decision. Fortunately, BGC was being relocated together with a visionary leader and creative thinker. Canon Benaiah seised the moment to purchase a good number of houses for BGC, when most of the residents in Juba were fleeing the war. He foresaw the future, and yet he did not live to see it unfolded. It is surprising to learn that when he was campaigning to buy these houses, people with less foresight went to the extent of calling him 'Crazy Principal'. In a way, that was true; he was crazy for the vision he had for the College and the Church.

After the Comprehensive Peace Agreement (CPA), BGC became a self-supporting institution and is now in the process of gaining the status of a university.

I have a hope that Bishop Anthony will do the same as his father. South Sudan needs visionary leaders like him for the rebuilding of this new nation. Our nation faces challenges of corruption, nepotism, tribalism, division, and lack of appreciation and embracing one another in love.

May this book stir up your heart to love South Sudan, and sharpen your inner eyes to see the vision that brings this nation onwards.

Peace and Grace of God to you all!

Dr. Daniel Deng Bul Yak
Archbishop & Primate of the Episcopal Church of South Sudan/Sudan
Bishop, Juba Diocese

September 2013

Acknowledgements

I would like to thank God for making it possible for me to produce this book. The process of writing began about ten years ago, when I first heard someone preach on the book of Nehemiah. He connected it to the situation of South Sudan. I took an interest in the book, and began to teach and preach from it myself.

Although I have long hoped to write a book on Nehemiah, it was not possible to bring this hope to fulfilment until I took a sabbatical at Ridley Hall in early 2013. The sabbatical was a time of what I called '5 Rs': rest, reading, (w)riting, relaxation, and reflection. The preparation for and writing of this book occupied the lion's share of my time during my sabbatical.

I would like to thank the Rev. Andrew Norman, Principal of Ridley Hall, Cambridge, whom I first met when he worked for the Archbishop of Canterbury. We met again at the Lausanne Congress in Cape Town in 2010, where he invited me to consider Ridley Hall as one possibility for my sabbatical when the right time came. I made many friends there, especially among the staff and students on E Staircase.

I would like to thank His Grace the Most Rev Dr Daniel Deng Bul Yak, Archbishop of the Episcopal Church of Sudan ECS, for granting me permission to undertake my sabbatical.

I am grateful to my family for releasing me for the sabbatical, and for their patience as I carried out the remaining part of the work after my return. My wife Jane and children Grace, Faith and Joy have been very understanding when I spent a great deal of time behind a computer.

A number of people encouraged me in this project. They include Mike and Ruth Wall of All Nations Christian College, Ware, and the Rev. Derek and Jane Waller in Rushden, Northampton, whose house has been a second home to me.

I would like to thank Tim Flatman for reading through and editing the manuscript. I first met Tim about in 2004 when he was a university student and was doing a paper on Sudan. God had laid a burden for Sudan in Tim's heart many years prior to our meeting. We travelled together to Yei and Kajo-Keji later the same year. More recently, Tim has been travelling regularly to Abyei. He can be contacted at tflatman@gmail.com

I would like to thank many other people who played different roles in bringing this book to fruition. Many have read different parts of the book and have made very helpful suggestions.

Thank you all.

Anthony Poggo
Kajo-Keji
September 2013

Introduction

Why Nehemiah?

Studying the book of Nehemiah, I have been struck by its relevance to the new nation of South Sudan.

Many South Sudanese were exiled like Nehemiah and can readily identify with him. Most of these exiles were refugees in the former Sudan's nine neighbouring countries. Others settled in the USA, UK, Australia, Europe and the Arab world. Between 1983 and 2005, an estimated 4.4 million South Sudanese people were displaced either as refugees or as Internally Displaced Persons.

To appreciate the full relevance of the book of Nehemiah, it is worth reminding ourselves of the circumstances in which the new nation of South Sudan was born.

Before South Sudan became an independent nation, it had been the main battlefield of a long civil war. The first period of war had already begun by the time the former Sudan declared its independence on 1 January 1956. There was a brief period of peace when the Addis Ababa agreement was signed in 1972. Fighting broke out again in 1983 until the signing of the Comprehensive Peace Agreement (CPA) on 9 January 2005. This marked the end of a 21-year-long second civil war, during which over two million people were estimated to have died.

The CPA, signed in 2005, specified an interim period of six years, after which the people of South Sudan would choose between unity with and secession from North Sudan in a referendum. This referendum was held from 9 January 2011. On 7 February 2011, the referendum commission published the final results, with 98.83% voting in favour of independence. As a result, the Republic of South Sudan came into being on 9 July 2011.

Now we South Sudanese face a new challenge: building our new nation. We can identify not only with Nehemiah the exile, but with the Nehemiah who rebuilt the walls of Jerusalem.

Reconstruction

Nehemiah was responsible for the reconstruction of Jerusalem. Jerusalem had been destroyed by invading armies from the North, who had taken its people as slaves and stolen its economic resources.

Reconstruction is a concept familiar to us in South Sudan. What little infrastructure we had was destroyed by the many years of war. We have had to begin afresh, from a very low base. The late John Garang used to say that after peace we would start from below zero, not from zero or from scratch! Much of what we have been doing in South Sudan is therefore construction rather than reconstruction. Both concepts are relevant and need defining.

Mugambi defines these terms as follows:

> The terms construction and reconstruction belong to the engineering vocabulary. An engineer constructs a complex according to specifications in the available designs. Sometimes modifications are made to the designs, in order to ensure that the complex will perform the function for which it is intended. Reconstruction is done when an existing complex becomes dysfunctional, for whatever reason, and the user still requires using it. New specification may be made in the new designs, while some aspects of the old complex are retained in the new.[1]

South Sudan has an opportunity to draw a new design for our shared life as a national community. However, South Sudan has also emerged from a particular set of circumstances and embodies a diverse range of existing cultures. Some aspects of the 'old complex' should, and will inevitably, be retained in the new. We can learn many lessons from Nehemiah, himself the director of a national reconstruction project, as we construct and reconstruct our nation.

Nehemiah's message of reconstruction also has a wider relevancet to Africa. This is because "the slave trade deprived the continent of Africa of its human and economic resources, and colonisation often had a devastating effect on the structure and functioning of traditional African society."[2] The books of Ezra and Nehemiah contain the needed guidelines for the spiritual, social and economic reconstruction of Africa.[3]

Land

In his seminal study on land, Brueggemann argues that Nehemiah documents "an attempt to order life, community and land in covenantal ways"[4] in the light of the "powerful memory of land-loss".[5]

Land is a crucial issue for us in South Sudan. The civil war was, in part, about land. Some leaders were reported to have claimed the land of South Sudan with or without the people. At the time of writing, the border between South Sudan and Sudan has not been demarcated along its whole length. A procedure for resolving the status of the disputed region of Abyei has not yet been agreed by both countries.

Within South Sudan, there have also been conflicts over land and disagreements about county borders. Many returnees have found that 'their' land was occupied by others, and have had to either forfeit the land or undertake legal recourse to recover it. Brueggemann points out that just as Joshua found the promised land filled with Canaanites, Haggai, Zechariah, and Zerubbabel found it surrounded by Samaritans, Edomites and 'Arabs'.[6] This is the context in which the landless exiles came to Jerusalem where the purification and reconstruction under Nehemiah and Ezra was to be undertaken. A detailed study of Nehemiah may yield lessons about how to understand, distribute and manage land.

Africa and the Old Testament

Africans identify strongly with the Old Testament. From my own experience, I can affirm Mugambi's assertion that a number of independent churches in Africa refer more to the Old Testament than the New Testament.[7] He notes that the first generation of African heads of state were symbolically likened to Moses, who led his people from bondage to freedom.[8] Many of these leaders were involved in the liberation struggle in Africa in the 1960s and 1970s.

The South Sudanese leader Dr John Garang died in a helicopter crash, three weeks after becoming Sudan's Vice President and President of then Southern Sudan. The Episcopal Church of Sudan (ECS) Archbishop of the day, Joseph Marona, likened him to Moses, who died before he could lead the people of Israel to the promised land. Archbishop Marona then referred to John Garang's successor, Salva Kiir Mayerdiit, as Joshua, who was to complete the process of leading the people of South Sudan to the promised land. This came to pass in July 2011 when South Sudan became an independent nation after six years of a challenging interim period. President Salva Kiir Mayerdiit, South Sudan's 'Joshua', led the people well through the challenging six years leading up to the January 2005 referendum.

The South Sudanese people have drawn deeply from the Exodus story. However, we are left with an impoverished gospel if we treat the Exodus motif in isolation. Mugambi writes that:

> Christian theology in Africa, particular during the 1960s and 1970s, emphasised very much the theme of liberation as Exodus from colonial bondage, without highlighting the transformative and reconstructive dimensions. The Exodus motif was so dominant that there were hardly any other biblical texts that could be associated with the African Christian theology. In the New Testament, Luke 4:16-22, which echoes Isaiah 61:1-2, was the passage most frequently associated with African Christian theology.[9]

The solution is to look to other biblical texts: "Whereas the theology of liberation focused on the Exodus and Moses, the theology of reconstruction focuses on Ezra and Nehemiah in their post-exilic leadership roles."[10] Nehemiah can thus help us to rearticulate our theology and affect a shift from liberation to reconstruction.

The content of the book of Nehemiah

The book of Nehemiah describes how God used Nehemiah to undertake the specific task of building the walls of Jerusalem. Nehemiah accomplishes the work by the help of God, bringing "healing and reassurance to the returned exiles."[11] The name Nehemiah means 'the Lord comforts'. Unlike Ezra, a priest, Nehemiah was a layperson who was working as a cupbearer to the Persian king.

The work of repairing and rebuilding Jerusalem's walls and gates was completed in just 52 days (Nehemiah 6:15). Packer summarises the content of Nehemiah pithily: "Nehemiah through God built walls; God through Nehemiah built saints"[12] and divides up the book as follows:

Chapter 1 to 6 (building of the wall)
Chapter 8-10 (renewal of worship in Jerusalem)
Chapter 11 to 12 (repopulation of the city of Jerusalem)
Chapter 13 (the renewing of Jerusalem's renewal)[13]

Nehemiah also speaks of poverty alleviation, and documents the easing of an economic crisis that came as a result of high taxes and interest rates. Nehemiah worked for justice, preventing the exploitation of the poor by the wealthier members of society. Nehemiah also gives a record and genealogy of all the nobles, officials and people who were then living in Judah.

Allen and Laniak describe Ezra-Nehemiah as "the Old Testament equivalent of the Acts of the Apostles."[14] The book of Acts "opens with the outpouring of the Holy Spirit (Acts 1:4-5; 2:16-21, 3)" while Ezra 1:1 opens with "the fulfilment of 'the word of the LORD spoken by Jeremiah'".[15] Allen and Laniak note that early church history is narrated in Acts through the key figures of Peter, Stephen, Philip and Paul, and in Ezra-Nehemiah the "re-establishment of the people of God after the exile is presented in a series of phases associated with the names of Sheshbazzar, Zerubbabel, Ezra and Nehemiah."[16]

The book of Nehemiah as historical and literary document

This book is geared towards practical application, and is not intended as a contribution to the debate about the origins of the book of Nehemiah and its relation to Ezra and Chronicles. However, it is important to highlight a few of these issues for the benefit of the reader unfamiliar with the debate. Blenkinsopp writes that

> Together with Chronicles, Ezra-Nehemiah belongs to the second great historical corpus in the Hebrew Bible. The first consists in the books of Genesis to 2 Kings and covers the history from creation to the catastrophe of the destruction of Jerusalem and its temple followed by exile... The second historical corpus... continues beyond the point at which the first concludes to take in the constitution of the new community around a rebuilt sanctuary.[17]

It is said that the books of Ezra and Nehemiah were originally one long book and were later separated. Childs writes that:

> The books of Ezra and Nehemiah formed a single book in the Hebrew canon and preceded Chronicles in the order established for the Writings. The separation into two books was a relatively late development – it did not appear in the Hebrew Bible until the fifteenth century – and apparently arose in Christian circles, first attested in Origen, through the influence of a development within LXX.[18]

Most scholars argue for two key sources for Nehemiah. Nehemiah 8–10 is considered part of the so-called 'Ezra Source' (which includes Ezra 7–10), while Nehemiah 1–7 and 11–13 are from a separate source that scholars call the Nehemiah Memoir.

The Nehemiah Memoir is written in the first person and recounts details of Nehemiah's life, including his actions as governor. Williamson argues that the following passages are Nehemiah's first-hand account:

- Nehemiah 1 & 2 (preparation and return to Jerusalem)
- Nehemiah 4-6 (rebuilding of the walls in spite of difficulties)
- Nehemiah 7:1-5 (defence of the city and move to repopulate Jerusalem)
- Parts of Nehemiah 12:31-43 (dedication of the wall)
- Nehemiah 13:4-31 (Nehemiah's second term as governor)[19]

There are substantial disagreements between scholars as to the authorship, composition and dating of Ezra-Nehemiah. Questions include: were there three authors including a 'chronicler'? If not, to what extent did the author of Chronicles shape the present form of Ezra and Nehemiah? When did the events recorded in Nehemiah take place? Did Ezra return from exile before Nehemiah arrived, or were the two contemporaries? If they were contemporaries, why do they not refer to each other? Childs poses a series of questions:

> . . . how is one to explain the large number of apparent anomalies in the structure of the two books? For example, Ezra arrives in Jerusalem in Ezra 8 with a mandate to teach his statutes and ordinances in Israel, but after a brief mission seems to disappear until he reappears abruptly some twelve years later in Neh. 8. Has there been a literary displacement? Again, Neh. 7 introduces the topic of enrolment of the populace for the settlement of Jerusalem, but the execution of the project is delayed until ch. 11. Finally, the parallel genealogies in Ezra 2 and Neh. 7 and the similarity between the introductions of Ezra 3.1 and Neh. 7.73 are difficult to understand.[20]

The lack of agreement as to whether Ezra-Nehemiah was originally one book, separate books, or part of Chronicles, highlights the limitations of the historical-critical approach that aims to reconstruct the history behind the text. In contrast, a canonical approach focuses on the text of the biblical canon itself as a finished product which, by its construction, testifies to theological concerns: in this case, "to describe the restoration as a theological model for the obedient and holy people of God".[21]

Throughout the discussion that follows, I have taken the traditional view that Ezra preceded Nehemiah. However, resolving all the questions highlighted above is beyond the scope of this book. With Throntveit, I will "usually avoid an overly historical approach to the text that seeks to determine 'what really happened'".[22] On the basis of current research, it is not possible to establish an accurate historical sequence with certainty, and the attempt to do so, as Childs points out, risks disregarding the theological intent of Ezra-Nehemiah.[23]

A personal appreciation

I have over the years preached and taught from the book of Nehemiah. I have used it in leading pastors' seminars and as one of the main texts in leadership sessions during retreats for the ordination of priests and consecration of bishops.

The more I studied Nehemiah, the more I came to appreciate and identify with it. I appreciated the strategies Nehemiah used in undertaking his national reconstruction project. I appreciated the ways he dealt with the problems he encountered. I came to see how Nehemiah used many concepts outlined in modern management books, including teamwork and planning. I saw in Nehemiah a participatory leader who was patriotic; prayerful; a planner; patient; involved in poverty alleviation, and who persevered.

During a recent sabbatical, I have had the opportunity for further study and reflection on the book of Nehemiah and its significance for South Sudan. This book represents the results of those reflections. I hope it will be of use within South Sudan as a resource for pastoral teaching, and also relevant to the South Sudanese diaspora and to those interested in African theology.

---

1   Jesse Mugambi, From Liberation to Reconstruction: African Christian Theology after the Cold War (Nairobi: East African Educational Publishers, 1995), 12.

2   Nupanga Weanzana, "Ezra," in Africa Bible Commentary, ed. Tokunboh Adeyemo (Nairobi: WordAlive Publishers, 2006), 532.

3   Ibid.

4   Walter Brueggemann, The Land: Place as Gift, Promise, and Challenge in Biblical Faith, Overtures to Biblical Theology 1 (Philadelphia: Fortress Press, 1977), 158.

5   Ibid.

6   Ibid., 151.

7   Jesse Mugambi, "Africa and the Old Testament," in Interpreting the Old Testament in Africa: Papers from the International Symposium on Africa and the Old Testament in Nairobi, October 1999, ed. Mary N. Getui, Knut Holter, and Victor Zinkuratire, vol. 2, Bible and Theology in Africa (New York: Peter Lang Publishing, 2001), 16.

8   Ibid., 18.

9   Mugambi, From Liberation to Reconstruction, 39.

10 Mugambi, "Africa and the Old Testament," 17.

11 Nupanga Weanzana, "Nehemiah," in Africa Bible Commentary, ed. Tokunboh Adeyemo (Nairobi: WordAlive Publishers, 2006), 543.

12 J I Packer, A Passion for Faithfulness: Wisdom from the Book of Nehemiah (London: Hodder & Stoughton Ltd, 1995), xxvii.

13 Ibid.

14 Leslie C Allen and Timothy Laniak, Ezra, Nehemiah, Esther, New International Biblical Commentary 9 (Carlisle: Hendrickson Publishers; Paternoster Press, 2003), 3.

15 Ibid.

16 Ibid.

17 Joseph Blenkinsopp, Ezra-Nehemiah, Old Testament Library (London: SCM Press Ltd, 1989), 36.

18 Brevard S Childs, Introduction to the Old Testament as Scripture (London: SCM Press Ltd, 1979), 626.

19 Hugh G M Williamson, Ezra and Nehemiah, Old Testament Guides (Sheffield, England: Sheffield Academic Press, 1987), 15.

20 Childs, Introduction to the Old Testament as Scripture, 627.

21 Ibid., 637.

22 Mark A Throntveit, Ezra-Nehemiah, Interpretation, a Bible Commentary for Teaching and Preaching (Louisville: John Knox Press, 1992), 3.

23 Childs, Introduction to the Old Testament as Scripture, 630.

CHAPTER ONE
Nehemiah the patriotic exile

Nehemiah 1:1-3

Nehemiah 1:1-3 sets the scene. Before we learn of Nehemiah's position as a senior civil servant (1:11), we are introduced to him as an exile desperate to hear news of the situation back home. The situation of the surviving Jews is also outlined. Their condition is linked to the physical condition of Jerusalem.

1:1a *The words of Nehemiah son of Hacaliah.*

I have already referred to the debate over the origins of the book of Nehemiah in the introduction. Resolving these questions is beyond the scope of this book. However, it is worth noting that the first sentence gives us a hint as to how the whole book of Nehemiah should be read. The phrase 'The words of', especially when combined with the immediate switch to the first person in 1:1b, encourages us to read Nehemiah as a first-hand account. However, the presence of the phrase, written in the third person, indicates the involvement of an editor or editors. The text therefore presents itself as containing the first-hand account of Nehemiah himself, with materials structured to help readers understand the theological significance of the events that took place. Respect for the text leads me to adopt this approach in my own reading of Nehemiah.

The name Nehemiah means 'Jehovah comforts'. Evers writes that Nehemiah's name "aptly sums up his ministry to the troubled Jews living among the rubble of Jerusalem, the capital city of Judah."[1] Nehemiah's name is an indication that God's purpose for him was bigger than merely rebuilding walls. Although the focus of the first six chapters of Nehemiah is on rebuilding walls, there are hints (eg 1:9; 5:1-19) that physical reconstruction is linked to the wider purpose of reconstructing a covenantal community. Security measures, including the rebuilding of the walls from Chapter 3 onwards, and the specific measures detailed in Chapter 4, go hand-in-hand with repopulation. After the reconstruction of the walls is completed in 6:15, the focus switches to repopulation and reconstruction of a covenantal community.

Nehemiah did comfort the people of Jerusalem. The meaning of his name evokes Isaiah 40:1-2: *"Comfort, O comfort my people, says your God. Speak tenderly to Jerusalem, and cry to her that she has served her term, that her penalty is paid, that she has received from the LORD's hand double for all her sins."* This passage seems especially relevant given the emphasis in Nehemiah on confession of sins (1:6-7; 9:2-3), the focus on Jerusalem (eg 1:2-3, 12, 17; 7:1-5; 11:1-2) and the correlation between return and having 'served her term'. Comfort is thus linked to reconstruction, repopulation, and restoration of relationship with God.

Nehemiah's name is therefore significant. Like Nehemiah's father Hacaliah, parents today should give their children names that have a positive meaning. The names we give our children will be used for life to identify them. In many parts of West and Southern Africa, Christian parents give names that carry a positive message, or that reflect their wishes and prayers for their child. Such names include Goodluck, Blessing and Moreblessing. Parents should think twice before giving a child a name like Suffering. Does this name reflect what they would wish and pray for their child?

New names are often given at baptism. In the past, churches in Africa would give biblical or European-sounding names at baptism. Some of these European-sounding names were not remotely biblical. I have heard stories of people who were asked to change their names to Napoleon and Bismarck! Things have now changed and it is now possible to receive an African name – Wani, or Matur, or Wambui, for example – at baptism.

A proper understanding of baptism helps to put the acquisition of a new name in perspective. Baptism can be understood as an outward sign of an inward change. The acquisition of a name is not the purpose of baptism; rather a new name acts as a reminder of the rite of baptism. This underlines the importance of taking a name that is positive and has a meaning.

Some believers have rejected the traditional practice of naming children after their grandparents. They argue that children named after their grandparents could inherit their ways. They fear that if the owner of the name was violent, the child may follow in his footsteps. Readers will have different theological views on this subject but should agree that when facing situations like these, an effective pastoral response which recognises the power of God is required. I have often asked those who pray during such naming ceremonies to say a prayer of blessing and sanctification over names some family members may have concerns about.

1:1b *In the month of Chislev, in the twentieth year, while I was in Susa the capital*

The reference to Susa shows Nehemiah was part of the exilic community in Persia. The events of the exile are described in 2 Chronicles 36:11-21. The Israelite exiles were first taken to Babylonia, where they suffered very much until that kingdom was conquered by the Persian empire. Some of the exiles were then allowed to return to their own country (2 Chronicles 36:22-23). Evidently Nehemiah's family were among those taken away to Persia.

The exile was not simply the consequence of power struggles between opposing nations and empires. The background to the exile can be traced to a number of warnings given to the Israelites by God. Deuteronomy 28 is a prime example.[2] The passage declares that if the children of Israel obeyed God's commandments, He would bless them, but if they disobeyed He would curse them. Among the curses listed in the passage is the threat of exile (Deuteronomy 28:25, 36-37, 64). Despite repeated warnings and opportunities to repent (Nehemiah 9:29-30), the Israelites continually disobeyed God and were sent into exile for a long period.

While at first there may have been many competing explanations among the exiles as to why God allowed his chosen people to be removed from the land he had promised them, the understanding reflected in Jeremiah 4:18a came to be the dominant one: "Your ways and your doings have brought this upon you." More specifically, Judah triggered the exile by transgressing God's law (Jeremiah 7:9), oppressing the alien, orphan and widow (Jeremiah 7:6, cf. 2:34) and serving foreign gods (Jeremiah 7:18). The book of Nehemiah reflects this understanding, both in the general sense that the people of Israel were blamed for neglecting their part in the covenant God made with them (Nehemiah 1:6-9; 9:26-30) and in its concern to avoid the specific errors listed above (Nehemiah 5:13; 10:28-39; 13:1-31).

The South Sudanese can readily identify with Nehemiah, as many have lived in exile as refugees. The life of a person in exile is not easy. In many countries, refugees live in camps and are forced into dependence on relief agencies for food. Refugees are not allowed to leave the camps without special passes. They are given plastic sheets to make shelter for their families. Education is provided in refugee schools. In many countries, refugees are blamed when things go wrong, such as increases in crime or rises in the cost of commodities.

The 1951 Refugee Convention (as amended by the 1967 Protocol) defines a refugee as someone who, "owing to a well-founded fear of being persecuted for reasons of race, religion, nationality, membership of a particular social group or political opinion, is outside the country of his nationality, and is unable to, or owing to such fear, is unwilling to avail himself of the protection of that country."[3] War and ethnic, tribal and religious violence are identified as the leading causes of refugee flight.[4] Internally Displaced Persons (IDPs) may have faced similar problems, but have been displaced within their country of origin and have not crossed an internationally recognised border.[5]

The distinctions between refugees, IDPs and other migrants are more relevant in Western countries where they form part of a complex system of immigration controls. The 1951 definition acts as the basis of legal criteria, determining who may stay in a country not of his or her origin. I use the term refugee to describe those who consider themselves exiles from their homeland for any reason, including IDPs. Likewise, I use returnees to include those who have been IDPs, those who have been awarded refugee status in Western countries, and those who have migrated without gaining official recognition. For the purposes of this book, it is the lived experience of the exile that is important, and not his or her status. The experience of an IDP is not always different to the experience of a refugee: IDPs can find themselves living in camps, dependent on relief agencies and separated from local communities in the same way as refugees. Nehemiah may not have fallen into any of these official categories. In modern language Nehemiah's family could be described as 'trafficked'. I shall therefore use the terms refugee, exile and diaspora interchangeably.

The Bible tells the stories of a number of refugees. Mugambi writes that Egypt is depicted as "the country of refuge and bounty for Abraham and his descendants."[6] Abraham migrated to Egypt when there was famine in Canaan (Genesis 12:10-20). Joseph, the son of Jacob, was a refugee in Egypt, after initially being trafficked there. He was used by God to rescue his family and the Egyptians from starvation. The children of Israel were then refugees in Egypt for 300 years. They were badly treated by the host population, as many refugees are today. The memory of their time in Egypt was used as the basis for the commandment to treat foreigners as native-born (Leviticus 19:34, NIV). Our Lord Jesus Christ was a refugee early in his life when his earthly parents, Joseph and Mary, fled to Egypt to prevent King Herod from killing him (Matthew 2:13-23).

Many of the people of the former Sudan have experienced refugee life. I was a refugee in Uganda as a child from 1964 to 1973. My family returned to Sudan after the signing of the Addis Ababa agreement in 1972, which ended the first civil war. When war broke out again in 1983, many South Sudanese people fled the country. Most sought refuge in neighbouring countries, including Egypt. Many of these refugees began to return when the CPA was signed between the Government of Sudan and the Sudan People's Liberation Movement/Army (SPLM/A) in 2005. It is estimated that war displaced 4.5 million people, either as refugees or IDPs, in Sudan.

Many citisens of Sudan and South Sudan are still refugees. In the year 2011, thousands of Sudanese crossed over to South Sudan as refugees. During the war, many South Sudanese lived in Khartoum, in Uganda and in Kenya. At the present time, Sudanese, Ugandans and Kenyans are coming to live in South Sudan. Sadly there have been reports of such foreigners being targeted and beaten in South Sudan.

Israel is arguably unique in that it grew from a family into a nation while in exile. Yet in some respects, a comparison can be drawn between Israel and South Sudan. South Sudan grew from an assortment of tribes into a nation during the years of war while many were in exile. Leaders from different tribes and factions became united by the experience of living in one diaspora community in countries like the UK. Perhaps South Sudanese could paraphrase Leviticus 19:34: "The Sudanese, Kenyan and Ugandan among you must be treated as your native-born. Love them as yourself, for you were refugees in Khartoum, in Kenya and Uganda." In this way, in South Sudan as in Israel, memory of times of exile could be used as the basis for godly hospitality and love for the stranger.

1:2 one of my brothers, Hanani, came with certain men from Judah; and I asked them about the Jews that survived, those who had escaped the captivity, and about Jerusalem.

Although Nehemiah worked as a senior civil servant in the king's palace (1:11), he was deeply concerned about life back in Jerusalem. When his brother Hanani visited, he asked for news about home. The strength of his reaction (1:4) shows that his request was not a fleeting concern but born from patriotism: a deep love of his country.

One of the most difficult things about being a refugee is being away from home. Most refugees are eager to hear about home. Refugees know better than most the meaning of the saying "East or West, home is best". Many refugees are also defensive of their home country, especially while they are separated from it. Sir Winston Churchill, who rallied Great Britain as its Prime Minister in wartime, has been quoted as saying: "When I am abroad, I always make it a rule never to criticise or attack the government of my own country. I make up for lost time when I come home." South Sudanese express similar sentiments, with an equally dry sense of humour, when we say: "You cannot talk ill of your mother's cooking. Even if your mother is the worst cook, you will not talk about it outside your own home!"

Patriotism is often judged by simple external acts like the knowledge and singing of the national anthem. Few South Sudanese learned how to sing the national anthem of their former country, Sudan, between the independence of Sudan in 1956 and the independence of South Sudan in 2011. Yet in the weeks leading up the independence of South Sudan, South Sudanese made a great effort to learn and practice the words of the new national anthem. This included, on the eve of independence, a group of ECS Bishops together with Baroness Caroline Cox, who has been an advocate for the marginalised people of South Sudan, Darfur, Nuba Mountains, Blue Nile and Eastern Sudan. For any South Sudanese who have not yet learned the words of the national anthem, I include them here.

Oh God
We praise and glorify you
For your grace on South Sudan,
Land of great abundance
Uphold us united in peace and harmony.

Oh motherland
We raise rising flag with the guiding star
And sing songs of freedom with joy,
For justice, liberty and prosperity
Shall forever more reign.

Oh great patriots
Let us stand up in silence and respect,
Saluting our martyrs whose blood
Cemented our national foundation,
We vow to protect our nation

Oh God, Bless South Sudan.[7]

However, patriotism means more than learning to sing a national anthem. A patriot can be defined as one who makes sacrifices for the sake of his country. Like Christian love, love for one's country involves sacrifice. For Nehemiah, patriotism meant leaving his senior position at the king's palace to undertake basic construction work in insecure and difficult conditions in Jerusalem.

Nehemiah is not the only biblical figure who became eminent while in exile. Others include Joseph, Daniel and Mordecai. Neither is Nehemiah the only biblical figure who returned from exile to contribute toward his nation's development. Key examples include Zerubbabel, who led the first wave of returnees from exile before Ezra and Nehemiah followed him, and Israel's first leader, Moses.

Moses was raised in exile as a prince. Mugambi writes that Moses was "a leader whose values were formed under Egyptian high culture"[8] and that he "internalised the moral and religious values of his Egyptian foster parents before he became a liberator of his own people."[9] Mugambi aims to show the debt that the nation of Israel, and the Old Testament, owe to Africa. While it is true that Moses had high status as a prince, it is also important to remember that God did not use Moses to lead his people out of slavery until Moses had been humbled. Moses was rejected by his own people after killing the Egyptian (Exodus 2:11-15). He became a refugee from the place of exile when he fled from Pharaoh and was therefore doubly displaced!

History is full of examples of refugees who, like Nehemiah, went on to become prominent people in their countries of refuge. It is said that the United States of America is a nation built by immigrants. One such prominent person is the former Secretary of State, Madeleine Albright. She was born in Prague, Czechoslovakia (now in the Czech Republic). In 1939, when she was two years old, her family fled to London. Although they returned in 1945, they once again had to flee in 1948 and were granted political asylum in the United States. Before her appointment as Secretary of State, Albright was US Permanent Representative to the United Nations.

Another example is that of the Most Rev Dr John Sentamu, who became the first black African Archbishop of York. Sentamu fled from Uganda to Britain as a refugee in 1974. He was a colleague of my late father, Canon Benaiah Duku Poggo, at Ridley Hall where he trained for ordination. He was ordained in 1979 and appointed Bishop for Stepney in 1996. He went on to become Diocesan Bishop of Birmingham in 2002 and then Archbishop of York in 2005. In this role, he is Primate of England and Metropolitan, a member of the House of Lords and a Privy Councillor. As Archbishop of York he holds the second most high-ranking position within the worldwide 77 million member Anglican Church, after the Archbishop of Canterbury.

We should not be surprised to find among the South Sudanese diaspora, those who have risen to positions of prominence, gained impressive qualifications or taken on roles of great responsibility. In one of my visits to England, I was pleased to encounter a South Sudanese man with a PhD in Engineering overseeing work on a water system installation project in one of the major cities of Britain. He told me that he had previously overseen the construction of a major shopping mall in another city. Such people need to be encouraged to return home. Doing so will, like Nehemiah, require sacrifice on their part. However, the Government of South Sudan should also do what it can to develop polices to facilitate their homecoming and (re)integration into existing communities.

Many South Sudanese refugees have already returned home following the signing of the CPA, and especially after South Sudan became a new nation on 9 July 2011. Others have been considering whether to return to South Sudan or to remain in exile. Some will only consider returning home when basic services like schools and hospitals are in existence.

The availability of education is a key factor for families considering whether to return home or remain in exile. Some refugees chose to stay in the refugee camps of northern Uganda and Kenya, because educational services in the camps were better than those in many parts of South Sudan. Many South Sudanese schools were schools 'under trees' without buildings. The situation has improved since South Sudan became an independent nation, but there is a long way to go to raise the general quality of education in South Sudan to an acceptable level. Necessary tasks include the provision of scholastic materials, training of teachers, and construction of classrooms.

When I speak to the South Sudanese diaspora, I often say that improving basic services is a task for the South Sudanese. Outsiders may help, but South Sudanese need to take the lead. All South Sudanese, including the diaspora, have a role to play. If Nehemiah had waited for infrastructure or services to be put in place before returning to Jerusalem, he would not have rebuilt the city walls. South Sudan needs Nehemiahs who are ready to sacrifice the comforts and even the necessities they have become accustomed to, in order to play their part in the reconstruction and rehabilitation of our country. To wait until "all is ready" may mean years of delay in returning home, and will deprive the nation of the skills and experience that they have learned and gained in exile.

When I discussed return with the diaspora in Canada, there were complaints that whenever some of them return home, they find it very hard to get employment. Nepotism, especially within the civil service, was raised as one of the factors that makes securing employment difficult. I suggested to the Canadian diaspora that they could put their resources together and invest in the country. Instead of coming back as employees they could come back as employers, just as Nehemiah did. Too many exiles expect to get jobs working for the government as civil servants. Yet not everyone can or should work for the government. I do not condone nepotism, a subject I shall return to later. Nonetheless, none of us should use the sins of others as an excuse for failing in our own patriotic duty.

One way that the diaspora could contribute is by instituting, developing and working in good-quality schools. This is important, as many middle-class South Sudanese parents send their children to boarding schools in neighbouring countries. Such schools would also raise the profile and status of teachers in South Sudan. Currently, too many see the role of teacher as a stepping stone to a local government job. The role of school teacher is undervalued. Often teachers are not paid on time; sometimes teachers go for months without being paid. This does not encourage teachers to commit to their jobs. Some teachers take other jobs as a precaution, meaning they are not always present in the classroom. This is unacceptable; a teacher who regularly fails to turn up, leaving a classroom of students without a teacher, should not keep his or her job. However, government should show that teachers are valued by making sure their salaries are paid just as regularly as civil servants, even when government finances are tight. The diaspora can help by funding, supporting and coming back as teachers, instead of demanding or waiting for invitations to take up government jobs.

We should not condemn those who opt to live or work aboard. Many countries benefit from financial remittances sent by nationals living or working aboard. South Sudan should also benefit from such remittances. The most important thing is not where someone is living, but how they are contributing. Nonetheless, the best way that many exiles could show their love for their country is by returning home to contribute their skills and experience at the grassroots level.

While South Sudanese cannot rely on or wait for outsiders to construct and reconstruct our nation, other nations do have a responsibility to South Sudan and to Africa in general. I have already outlined the contributions that refugees have made to their new countries. Mugambi argues that Africa has faced a brain drain because of slavery, the resettlement of refugees, and the enticement of highly trained personnel to fill vacancies in the Western world.[10] It is not popular to admit this in Western countries, where there is often a lot of negativity toward refugees. The people of Western countries tend to think that refugees owe a debt to them for providing a place of refuge, rather than the other way round. The reality is that Western countries have prospered from the labour and skills of Africans. South Sudan has also benefited from the assistance of Western countries. This includes the involvement of the Troika in the CPA. The actions of Western countries in plundering Africa in the past, and our current mutual interdependence, underline our responsibilities toward each other. In the case of Western countries, this could involve supporting the initiatives of refugees living in their own countries who wish to return and make a contribution.

Poor living conditions, inadequate basic services and difficulty in securing employment are not the only difficulties returnees face when they arrive back home. There is often misunderstanding between those who remained and those who went into exile. Some of those who stayed feel that returnees are bringing new ways of doing things without properly understanding the situation they are coming into. When unaddressed, this tension can turn into hostility. Returnees are labelled "cowards who ran away" or "*jallaba* who stayed with the enemy". A division is made between those who fought and liberated the nation, and those who did not.

This is a dangerous and misleading distinction. Once we start to give certain groups the credit for liberation and accuse other groups of non-involvement, we divide our nation. We must give the ultimate credit for liberation to God, rather than to human leaders or institutions. Our national anthem does this in praising God first before speaking to the land and acknowledging martyrs who shed their blood during the war. The national anthem is right to pay homage to martyrs. However, it is not only soldiers who shed their blood during the war, or who made sacrifices for their nation. With 2.2 million dead, there cannot be a single South Sudanese who did not lose a close relative during the war.

The war of liberation was fought in many ways. Some fought bravely; others provided food for the soldiers; others sent assistance; others undertook advocacy to bring the world's attention to the suffering masses of South Sudan. South Sudanese from every tribe, and in every diaspora community around the world, participated in the referendum whose result triggered independence. All sections of South Sudan took part in the independence struggle in some way; credit for independence is not the preserve of a select group.

Those who stayed in South Sudan should not therefore insult diaspora or assume they did not contribute to independence because they left the country. However, refugees who have lived in the West should not assume that its technical knowledge is always superior to the local knowledge possessed by people who stayed. As we saw when looking at Mugambi's definition of reconstruction, new specifications are required, but "some aspects of the old complex" must be retained in the new.

The Committee for National Healing, Peace and Reconciliation headed by Archbishop Daniel Deng Bul has included Diaspora and Reconciliation as one of the thirteen components of the National Programme for Healing, Peace and Reconciliation in its working paper. Recognising the role that the diaspora has to play in reconstruction, it argues that:

> South Sudanese in the Diaspora have played a pivotal role throughout the history of the conflict and civil war as well as the post-war reconstruction efforts at home. There's much political awakening amongst South Sudanese in the Diaspora. The war has contributed to the sharp increase in the Diaspora community from different sides of the divide. The Diaspora communities remain active in South Sudan's political landscape. In order for the Diaspora community to continue to serve as a vital resource for post-war state building, there is a need to foster reconciliation and unity among them and also between the Diaspora communities and those in South Sudan.[11]

There is therefore widespread recognition that reducing the tensions between the diaspora and those who remained is key to the reconstruction of South Sudan. Both groups have an opportunity, especially through the national reconciliation process, to appreciate each other's knowledge and strengths, and imagine ways of co-operating. Again, there are relevant lessons to be learned from the book of Nehemiah. Later, I will show how Nehemiah used the skills and resources of those already living in Jerusalem and the wider area, in combination with the skills he had learned in exile and the resources he was able to mobilise from Persia. At this stage, I will simply outline some of the challenges he faced, which strike a surprising parallel with the challenges the South Sudanese diaspora face in returning.

The first wave of returnees under Zerubbabel faced opposition from an existing population who did not welcome them. Ezra 4:4 refers to the existing population as *the people of the land*, to distinguish them from *the people of Judah*, viewed as the rightful occupants of the land.[12] Some of the people of the land may have been Samaritans: close relations of the people of Judah. It has been suggested that ethnic conflicts over Jerusalem during the time of Nehemiah marked the beginning of the later Samaritan-Jewish split.[13] The books of Ezra and Nehemiah make it clear that the returnees were rightful occupants of the land; but they do not pretend the land was empty, or exclude other groups from rights to the land. Some scholars argue that the land of Israel "had always been shared with others".[14] The situation was complicated by the existence of a group of Israelites who had never been taken into exile, but who were certainly rightful occupants of the land.

Return may have been even more difficult for Nehemiah than it had been for Zerubbabel and the first wave of returnees. Brown writes that

> Nehemiah realised that that now he too must follow their steps, but there were insuperable obstacles. Those earlier returnees had left not only with the permission but encouragement of the Persian king. They were at liberty to make the long journey, but Nehemiah was not a free agent. He was employed by the king and court at Susa. Yet, if God had spoken so clearly in Scripture about gathering his people from the farthest horizon, promising to bring them to the place he has chosen as a dwelling place in his Name, then he was capable of fulfilling his promise in the personal experience of Nehemiah, whatever the human obstacle, political problems and natural difficulties.[15]

It was less clear for Nehemiah than for Zerubbabel whether the authorities would approve of plans to return and to reconstruct. Local opposition from rival groups was just as vehement for Nehemiah as it was for Zerubbabel, as shown in Chapters 2, 4 and 6 of Nehemiah. Local opposition aimed to exploit the ambiguous attitude of the authorities toward return and reconstruction. Local authorities were suspicious of Nehemiah's intentions and concerned that his work would threaten their own power.

Ethnic and political conflict were complicated by social conflict. During the exile, those permitted to remain were *"the poorest people of the land"*

(2 Kings 23:14). The *"elite of the land"* (v.15) were carried off. Blenkinsopp suggests that the poor expropriated the land of the exiles "on the grounds that the deportees had, in effect, been expelled from the Yahwistic cult community and had therefore forfeited title to property (Ezek. 11:15-16)",[16] citing Jeremiah 39:11 in support. The exiles were hardly likely to be persuaded by this logic, and must have demanded their land back on their return.

Blenkinsopp also argues that most of the exiles who returned "must have been relatively well off by the very fact of being able to return"[17] and points to Ezra 2:68-69; 8:26-27; and Zechariah 6:9-11 to back up his claim. The exiles, who had gained wealth while in exile, expected those who remained poor while remaining in and looking after the land, to surrender land to the returnees on their arrival. Nehemiah 5 suggests that when they did not, the wealthier returnees exploited conditions of famine and high taxation to gain land, slaves and other resources on the cheap from the poor who had remained.

The parallels with South Sudan should be obvious. Returnees may risk becoming embroiled in ethnic disputes they had forgotten while in exile. Local officials may be suspicious of them and jealous of their qualifications and experience, fearing them as a threat to their own power. Many returnees find their claims to land contested by others and difficult to prove. These cases are complicated by the lack of clear demarcation between many villages, *payams* and counties. Yet ethnic, political and social conflicts such as these did not prevent Nehemiah from returning. He even became a mediator, willing to act (Nehemiah 5:11) against those who, as diaspora like Nehemiah, might have expected him to take their side.

I will take up many of these themes in greater detail as they appear in the biblical text. It has been worth highlighting the similarities between the situation Nehemiah faced and the situation faced by many diaspora considering return at this stage, so that readers can see the relevance of the book of Nehemiah and the personal example of Nehemiah as I move through the text. There is no problem faced by South Sudanese refugees in returning—poor living conditions, absence of basic infrastructure and services, instability, resentment and division—that Nehemiah did not also face. At this stage, what is significant is that the patriotism we first see in Nehemiah in 1:2 was strong enough to motivate him to return despite all of these challenges.

1:3 *They replied, "The survivors there in the province who escaped captivity are in great trouble and shame; the wall of Jerusalem is broken down, and its gates have been destroyed by fire.*

In response to his request for news from home, Nehemiah's brother and his associates told him about the deplorable condition of the returned exiles, and of Jerusalem itself. Jerusalem was in ruins and no wall surrounded it. The emphasis given to the condition of the wall and gates reflects the importance of city walls for security at the time.[18] This is still the case in many of our cities in Africa today. Tall walls are built around houses and estates to maintain and act as a symbol of security. In Kenya, these walls often bear signs saying "Mbwa kali" ("fierce dog"), whose job, like those Nehemiah instructed to be appointed in 7:3, is to guard the gates and walls!

The report from Hanani raises important historical questions. Firstly, there is the apparent inconsistency with Ezra 9:9, which speaks of a wall: *"... our God has not forsaken us in our slavery, but has extended to us his steadfast love before the kings of Persia, to give us new life to set up the house of our God, to repair its ruins, and to give us a wall in Judea and Jerusalem."* Some argue that Nehemiah had already built the wall by the time Ezra arrived. While acknowledging that we cannot be totally certain about the order, I have taken the view that Ezra preceded Nehemiah. How then can I account for Ezra 9:9? As I have shown above, walls signified security. Clines writes that it is possible the word wall is used metaphorically in Ezra 9:9 to refer to the protection given by the Persian government; "for a city-wall could hardly be a called a wall in Judea and Jerusalem."[19] While a plain reading is usually preferable, it is obvious that there was no wall around the whole region of Judea. Clines' interpretation is helpful.

Secondly, there is the question of when the events referred to in Nehemiah 1:3 took place. It is unlikely that Hanani was referring to the destruction of Jerusalem by Nebuchadnezzar. Williamson writes that

> Nehemiah's reaction to the news (v 4) is so strong that this report cannot refer to the destruction of Jerusalem by Nebuchadnezzar some 140 years previously. A recent event, as yet unconfirmed in Susa, must be intended, and for this the destruction mentioned briefly in Ezra 4:23 presents itself as the ideal, and indeed only possible, candidate.[20]

An earlier attempt to restore the city walls, frustrated by external opponents, is documented in Ezra 4:6-23. The *"people of the land"* wrote a letter to King Artaxerxes and gained his consent to prevent the stop work on the walls *"by force and power"* (4:23). This phrase suggests the likelihood that they also destroyed what work had already been done on the partially rebuilt walls. This is what is referred to in Nehemiah 1:3.

This incident also highlights the importance for Nehemiah of gaining the support of the king. A previous attempt to rebuild the walls had failed in part because the ultimate human authority in the land had not approved it. Getz writes that "Humanly speaking, only one person could make it possible for Nehemiah to help the Jews in Jerusalem – the king he served."[21] The link between Nehemiah 1:3 and Ezra 4:23 thus helps us to understand Nehemiah's actions in Nehemiah 2.

The situation outlined in Nehemiah 1:3 resonates with the South Sudanese story in obvious ways. One of the effects of war is the destruction of infrastructure, including walls and gates. In the years from 1983 to 2005, South Sudan lost everything, including what little infrastructure was built during the eleven years of relative peace from 1972 to 1983. If Hanani were to have come to South Sudan, he would have given a similar report, saying, "South Sudan is in ruins".

The report given to Nehemiah links the condition of the returned exiles (*"in great trouble and shame"*) to the physical condition of Jerusalem (*"the wall of Jerusalem is broken down, and its gates have been destroyed by fire"*). This is more likely to surprise readers from the West, characterised by a sense of rootlessness and the division of people and place, than readers in Africa where people and place are very closely connected.

The parallel between the physical condition of Jerusalem and the emotional, psychological and spiritual condition of the people of Judah is expressed poetically in Lamentations. The shame Hanani refers to in Nehemiah 1:3 is characterised as humiliation (Lamentations 2:1); Jerusalem is unable to protect herself from or respond to the mocking taunts of her enemies (1:7-8; 2:15-16). Although God is in fact near (3:56-57), there are times when it feels as if he is absent (1:16) or has even become like an enemy (2:5). In such times, as during the time of war in South Sudan, it is the task of the Church to reveal God's presence; to offer hope and the possibility of release from shame.

The social effects of war and destruction on South Sudan are many and interlocking. A lack of education has perpetuated a high level of illiteracy. The reliance of refugees and IDPs on food aid from non-governmental organizations (NGOs) has led to dependency. I heard a story of someone who was told to go and dig in one of the refugee camps. He replied by asking, "Has it stopped raining in Geneva?" (Geneva is where the UNHCR headquarters are based.) Trauma is widespread. A trauma survey conducted by Kush Inc. among the displaced population of Abyei in 2012 found that 38% met the criteria for post-traumatic stress disorder, rising to 51% among women. The working paper of the Committee for National Healing and Reconciliation comments that:

> The string of political violence and disruptions in the history of South Sudan as well as the nature of the violations during the civil war have contributed to deep and widespread psychological trauma across all communities in South Sudan. Most communities are stuck in the past and are desperate to find closure. It will take a long process for deeply traumatised societies to heal and recover. While this framework does not make full healing a precondition for reconciliation, it recognises that without some measures of psychosocial healing, individuals and their communities will find it difficult to move on and to establish civic and social trust critical to recovery.[22]

It is easy to see how a lack of education, the erosion of the traditional value of hard work, and desensitisation to violence reinforce each other. Communities can get stuck in a cycle of vengeance, focused only on short-term survival, finding it difficult to reason together or to see things from the perspective of the other.

The emotional, psychological and spiritual condition of the people and the physical condition of the land are, in South Sudan as in Nehemiah 1:3, inexorably connected. Nehemiah's task, shown throughout the book of Nehemiah and especially in the later chapters, was not merely to reconstruct walls, but to reconstruct a community characterised by obedience to God's commands and a sense of social solidarity (including the "civic and social trust" the working paper above refers to). That is also the task of construction and reconstruction in South Sudan.

Nehemiah 1:4-11

In Nehemiah 1:1-3 we are introduced to Nehemiah as a patriotic exile. Nehemiah's reaction to the report given in 1:3 shows him to be a prayerful man. Nehemiah showed concern, listened to the people who brought him the sad news from home, and acted appropriately. He first wept, then fasted, talking and listening to God in prayer before taking further action.

The importance of prayer is a regular theme in Nehemiah. Nehemiah's prayers, as is clear from 1:4-10, were "saturated with the Word of God".[23] Nehemiah claimed the promises of God in Scripture. We should also do this. However, this requires spending time studying the word of God which contains these promises!

Prayer and Bible reading are important aspect of a Christian's life, especially for a Christian leader. They help deepen our vertical relationship with God. We speak to him in prayer and he communicates to us through the Bible. Brown writes that listening to God by reading his word and responding to him in prayer are "twin aspects of every believer's experience. There can be no spiritual growth or development in Christian maturity without the regular cultivation of this dual privilege and discipline."[24] They form the first two of five principles of spiritual growth identified by Bill Bright, the founder of Campus Crusade for Christ.[25]

Christian families should have a time of Bible reading and prayer. This is sometimes referred to as the "family altar". The evening time, when the family is together, may be the best time. Morning times can be challenging, as parents may be rushing to work and children preparing to go to school. Children brought up in the fear of the Lord will remember the biblical grounding they have been given when they have grown up. This is what is written in Proverbs 22:6: *"Train up a child in the way he should go: and when he is old, he will not depart from it"* (KJV).

1:4 *When I heard these words I sat down and wept, and mourned for days, fasting and praying before the God of heaven.*

Nehemiah wept. Some people have said that Christians should not weep or cry when they hear bad news. It is fine to do so. Jesus, the perfect model of what it means to be a human being, himself wept when he heard the news of the death of his friend Lazarus (John 11:35). He wept even though he knew that he had the authority to raise Lazarus from the dead. Famously this verse, *"Jesus wept"*, is the shortest verse in the Bible.

Weeping is not only one valid response to bad news; sometimes it is the best response. There are times when we are commanded to weep. Romans 12:15 instructs us to *"Rejoice with those who rejoice, weep with those who weep."* This is an expression of love to our neighbour. It also suggests that for the Christian, orthopathos (right feeling) is just as important as orthodoxy (right belief) and orthopraxis (right action). Ecclesiastes tells us that there is *"a time to weep, and a time to laugh; a time to mourn, and a time to dance"* (3:4), a theme taken up by Jesus in his criticism of the Pharisees (Luke 7:31-32). When Jesus was asked why his disciples do not fast, he replied that it was not the appropriate time for fasting. They would fast when Jesus was taken away from them (Matthew 9:15).

Rejoicing and weeping at the appropriate time is a mini-theme in Nehemiah. In 1:4, it is appropriate for Nehemiah to weep. However, in 8:9-12, the people are told that weeping is not appropriate for a day of celebration, and rejoice instead. In 8:17, during a festival celebration, there is *"great rejoicing"*. In 9:1, the people adopt the outward signs of mourning, dressing in sackcloth and putting earth on their heads as they mourn their sin. At the dedication of the wall, rightly a time of celebration, there is *"rejoicing, with thanksgivings and with singing, with cymbals, harps, and lyres"* (12.27). Nehemiah could be said to be a case study in the application of Romans 12:15!

The expression of grief through crying or weeping is part of a process of healing and comfort. Brueggemann, discussing Jeremiah (known as the "Weeping Prophet"), argues that sometimes only grief can break through denial:

> ... the coming joy depends on the present grief. The new gift is premised on the relinquishment. The sorrow of death permits the joy of new birth. But the new birth 'from above' and the rush of the spirit only appears in the hurt and loss of the old dying (John 3:3-15)... If the healing comes only when the wound is acknowledged, if the new comes only in the presence of explicit grief, then new possibility turns up only in the candor of loss. When life has become a massive denial, there is too much at stake and the new possibility, the new age, the new community cannot be risked.[26]

Brueggemann argues that God's own grief on hearing the nations mock his humiliated chosen people prompted him to heal them, citing Jeremiah 31:17 in support.[27] Before the Israelites were able to receive God's comfort they first had to weep by the canals of Babylon (Psalm 137:1). So it was for Nehemiah. Nehemiah first wept, then confessed his sin and the sin of his people, and was then able to contribute to the reconstruction of his nation.

The first national event of the National Programme for Healing, Peace and Reconciliation, was a day of prayer and fasting, held on 8 July 2013. The theme was lamentation. The choice of theme recognised the expression of grief through crying or weeping as part of a process of healing and comfort. For Nehemiah, the process of reconstructing community began with weeping. Perhaps the power of grief can break through and permit renewal where societies are deeply traumatised and stuck in the past. The timing of the event, on the day before the second anniversary of independence, was deliberate. South Sudanese were encouraged to weep on the 8th, and rejoice on the 9th. We are again reminded of Ecclesiastes 3:4 and Romans 12:15.

1:5-6a *I said, "O LORD God of heaven, the great and awesome God who keeps covenant and steadfast love with those who love him and keep his commandments; let your ear be attentive and your eyes open to hear the prayer of your servant that I now pray before you day and night for your servants, the people of Israel,*

There are many models of prayer in the Bible. One model that many Christians find helpful is the ACTS model. ACTS is an acronym, standing for Adoration, Confession, Thanksgiving, and Supplication. Nehemiah's prayer in verses 5 to 11a appears to follow this model, with one exception: there is no 'thanksgiving' section. Instead, Nehemiah reminds God of his covenantal promises.

Nehemiah began in **adoration**. Nehemiah praised God as a great, awesome and covenant-keeping God. The mention of covenant is not accidental. Covenant is an important theme in Nehemiah. It is highly significant that the first reference to covenant is to God's part in it. We are reminded that the possibility of return rests in God's character. 1:5 also sets up a contrast between the faithful God, who keeps covenant, and the unfaithful people of Israel, who have failed to keep his commandments (1:7). Implicit in verse 6a is a recognition that God hears and answers prayers day and night, 24/7.

The Bible commands us to praise and adore God. Hebrews 13:15 instructs us to praise God continually: *"Through him, then, let us continually a sacrifice of praise to God, that is, the fruit of lips that confess his name."* A popular chorus sung in South Sudan and elsewhere puts it simply:

> *Praise him, praise him,*
> *Praise him in the morning,*
> *Praise him in the noontime,*
> *Praise him, praise him,*
> *Praise him when the sun goes down.*

Starting with adoration, as Nehemiah did, ensures that our focus is first on God rather than ourselves, and helps us to pray in line with God's will. We might find that the requests we make of God are different when we start praying by praising him for who he is and what he has done, rather than starting with our own requests. Adoration also helps to humble ourselves before God, reminding us that he is Creator and we are created. Declaring the glory of God can lead us naturally into confession, as we recognise that we have fallen short of the glory of God (Romans 3:23).

1:6b-7 *confessing the sins of the people of Israel, which we have sinned against you. Both I and my family have sinned. We have offended you deeply, failing to keep the commandments, the statutes and the ordinances that you commanded your servant Moses.*

Nehemiah acted as a representative of the people in *confessing* their sins. This was Nehemiah's first act of leadership. In using the word "we", Nehemiah acknowledged his own part in the sin of the nation. He did not set himself apart from the nation. Nehemiah led, but as one of the people, not in isolation from them.

The book of Nehemiah affirms the importance of collective repentance. In the same way, when Jesus taught his disciples the Lord's Prayer, he taught them to pray *"forgive us our sins"* (Luke 11:4a), not "forgive *me my* sins". We should all take the initiative in pleading with God to forgive our nation. Instead of complaining about what our leaders are doing or not doing, it is better to pray for them and confess their weaknesses to God. Like Nehemiah, we should also confess our own part in the sins of the nation. For example, where there is corruption, it may be that we have protested more when members of another tribe have been accused than when questions have been raised about members of our own tribe.

Although Nehemiah acted as a representative of the people in 1:6b-7, there was still a need for the people themselves to repent. They did so later, in Nehemiah 9, following Nehemiah's example in confessing their own sins and the sins of their ancestors. In confessing the sins of their ancestors, the people of Israel marked themselves out from their ancestors and showed their determination not to repeat their mistakes.

It is important for us in South Sudan to confess the sins of our ancestors. While God holds each of us accountable for our own sin (Ezekiel 18:20), the sins of ancestors can affect us in ways we do not always realise. In South Sudan, ancestors are revered. It can be taboo to admit that our ancestors did things that were wrong. This makes us especially vulnerable to repeating their mistakes. In South Sudan, then, it is especially important that we include confession of the sins of our ancestors in collective repentance. We can still respect and honour our ancestors (Exodus 20:12) while admitting they were not perfect.

Nehemiah confessed the sins of his ancestors in detail: the failure to keep their side of God's covenant by obeying the commandments, statues and ordinances God gave to Moses. In acknowledging the specific sins of the people of Israel, the way was open for them to learn the lessons of the past. Reconstructing a community based on covenantal norms was then possible. This is made even clearer in Nehemiah 9 and 10. This is why acknowledging the harm that we have done to others is such an important part of reconciliation. It opens up the possibility of behaving in new ways in the future.

1:8-10 *Remember the word that you commanded your servant Moses, "If you are unfaithful, I will scatter you among the peoples; but if you return to me and keep my commandments and do them, though your outcasts are under the farthest skies, I will gather them from there and bring them to the place at which I have chosen to establish your name. They are your servants and your people, whom you redeemed by your great power and your strong hand.*

Throntveit characterises this section as Nehemiah's *appeal* to God to remember the promise of return.[28] Nehemiah 1:8-9 paraphrases Deuteronomy 30:1-5, suggesting Nehemiah knew Scripture well. Nehemiah reminded God of the promise he made to Moses that if the children returned to him, he would restore them. He reminded God that the people of Israel are God's people. While there is no explicit *thanksgiving* element in Nehemiah's prayer, it could be said that these verses imply gratitude at being chosen as God's elect. Alternatively, these verses could reflect the influence of the lament form of prayer, especially in light of the references to weeping and mourning in 1:4.

It is clear that the people of Israel could not earn the right to return. The possibility of returning was rooted in God's faithfulness. He would keep the promises he had made. Confession and repentance were necessary, but they could not earn God's favour. God describes Himself as *"He who blots out your transgressions for my own sake"* (Isaiah 43:25). All Nehemiah could do was appeal to the promises God had made.

We too can appeal to the promises God has made. However, we should remember that, like the Israelites who expected the Messiah to be a military leader who would overthrow the Romans, our ideas as to how God will fulfil his promises may be mistaken. While it is valid for us to use scripture as Nehemiah did here, we must be open to God's correction.

1:11a *O Lord, let your ear be attentive to the prayer of your servant, and to the prayer of your servants who delight in revering your name. Give success to your servant today, and grant him mercy in the sight of this man!*

Finally, we come to the **supplication** element in Nehemiah's prayer. Nehemiah's prayer takes up seven verses, but the request Nehemiah made of God takes up only one verse. Nehemiah devoted far more time to adoring God, confessing his own sins and the sins of his people, and recalling God's promises. This is a challenge to us. It is easy to rush through adoration, confession and thanksgiving and spend most of our time praying in supplication.

In verse 11a, Nehemiah requested God's intervention in relation to his plan to petition the king. Williamson argues that Nehemiah was aware that he would effectively be asking the king to overrule a previous decree (Ezra 4:21).[29] Making such a request was highly dangerous. Yet Nehemiah did not relent. It is likely that this was because of his faith in the God he prayed to in 1:5-11. Acknowledging God's faithfulness and appealing to God's promises can only have strengthened Nehemiah's faith and resolve.

1:11b *At the time, I was cupbearer to the king.*

This statement concludes our introduction to Nehemiah. It is significant that we are introduced to Nehemiah as a patriotic exile, and as a prayerful leader well-versed in scripture, before we learn anything about his position or title. God had placed Nehemiah in his job for a purpose, but his qualities were more important than his status.

The statement is also the beginning of our story. It explains how Nehemiah had access to the king. Nehemiah served the king as a wine steward. It is said that one of the roles of a cupbearer was to taste the wine before the king drank it. If the wine was poisoned, it would be the cupbearer who would die. Being given this role showed the high level of trust the king had in Nehemiah.

In many parts of South Sudan, there is also a great fear of people who are reported to poison others, including witch doctors, providers of traditional medicine, wizards, and sorcerers. The church must acknowledge the existence of evil and demonic forces but encourage believers that the God they serve is more powerful than these forces, and so they do not need to fear such people. The Bible tells us that he that is in us is greater that he that is in the world (1 John 4:4).

Cupbearers were also expected to guard the royal apartment. Again, this demonstrates the trust the king had in Nehemiah. Since Nehemiah was a refugee, not one of the king's own people who could be expected to be loyal, Nehemiah must have been especially trustworthy. God uses trustworthy people like Nehemiah.

As cupbearer, Nehemiah was very close to the king at all times. This meant that he was in a position to offer occasional informal advice, which gave him considerable influence in the palace. Today, such people are sometimes referred to as the 'kitchen cabinet'. Williamson writes that in addition to serving wine, royal cupbearers were "also expected to be convivial and tactful companions to the king. Being much in his confidence, they could thus wield considerable influence by way of informal counsel and discussion."[30] Pharaoh took his cupbearer's advice seriously enough to send for Joseph to interpret his dream (Genesis 41:14).

Getz summarises the role of cupbearer and the implications for Nehemiah's character well:

> This important position in the king's court gives insight into Nehemiah's life and character. A mighty monarch such as the king of Persia would select for that position a man who was wise and discreet, and consistently honest and trustworthy. Nehemiah's position alone reveals much about his intellectual capabilities, his emotional maturity, and his spiritual status.[31]

We need many more Nehemiahs, whose character inspires trust to the extent they are selected for roles of influence by those outside their own ethnic group.

Conclusion

Nehemiah 1 introduces Nehemiah as a patriotic exile, a prayerful leader and a trustworthy servant appointed to a position of influence. The bulk of the chapter focuses on Nehemiah's prayer, demonstrating his dependence on God in everything that he did. The chapter also introduces us to the situation of the returned exiles in Jerusalem, linking their condition to the physical condition of the city walls and gates. Finally, the chapter introduces the theological themes of the book. Nehemiah's prayer introduces the theme of covenant, positing the failure of the people to keep covenant as the reason for the exile. It contrasts the faithful God who keeps covenant with the unfaithful people who do not, and appeals to the covenantal promises of God in scripture. The focus on covenant, and the association between the physical condition of Jerusalem and the spiritual, emotional and psychological condition of the community, hint that physical reconstruction of the city and spiritual reconstruction of a covenantal community must go hand in hand.

1   Stan K Evers, *Doing a Great Work: Ezra and Nehemiah Simply Explained* (Darlington: Evangelical Press, 1996), 100.

2   Gene M Getz, "Nehemiah," in *The Bible Knowledge Commentary: An Exposition of the Scriptures*, ed. John F Walvoord and Roy B Zuck (Wheaton: Victor Books, 1985), 673.

3   UNHCR, "Convention and Protocol Relating to the Status of Refugees" (UNHCR communications and public information service, December 2010), 16, cf. 46, http://www.unhcr.org/3b66c2aa10.html.

4   USA for UNHCR, "What Is a Refugee?," *USA for UNHCR, the UN Refugee Agency*, n.d., accessed August 12, 2013.

5   Ibid.

6   Mugambi, "Africa and the Old Testament," 8.

7   Government of the Republic of South Sudan, "State Symbols," *Government of the Republic of South Sudan*, July 12, 2011, http://www.goss-online.org/magnoliaPublic/en/about/symbols.html.

8   Mugambi, "Africa and the Old Testament," 8.

9   Ibid.

10 Ibid., 21.

11 Archbishop Daniel Deng Bul, "A Working Paper of the Committee for National Healing, Peace and Reconciliation: Comprehensive Strategic Dimensions for Healing, Peace and Reconciliation for All South Sudanese: The Way Forward," July 2013, 15.

12 Philip Satterthwaite and Gordon McConville, *The Histories*, Exploring the Old Testament 2 (London: SPCK, 2007), 246.

13 Ibid., 263.

14 Joseph Blenkinsopp, "The Bible, Archaeology and Politics; or The Empty Land Revisited," *Journal for the Study of the Old Testament* 27, no. 2 (December 2002): 174.

15 Raymond Brown, *The Message of Nehemiah: God's Servant in a Time of Change*, The Bible Speaks Today (Leicester: Inter-Varsity Press, 1998), 39.

16 Blenkinsopp, *Ezra-Nehemiah*, 60.

17   Ibid., 68.

18   Jacob M Myers, *Ezra, Nehemiah*, The Anchor Bible 14 (Garden City: Doubleday, 1965), liii.

19   David J A Clines, *Ezra, Nehemiah, Esther*, The New Century Bible Commentary (Grand Rapids; Basingstoke: Wm B Eerdmans Publishing Company; Marshall Morgan and Scott, 1984), 124.

20   Hugh G M Williamson, *Ezra, Nehemiah*, Word Biblical Commentary 16 (Waco: Word Books, 1985), 124.

21   Getz, "Nehemiah," 675.

22   Deng Bul, "A Working Paper of the Committee for National Healing, Peace and Reconciliation," 11.

23   Evers, *Doing a Great Work*, 107.

24   Brown, *The Message of Nehemiah*, 141.

25   Bill Bright, "Five Principles of Growth," *Cru (Campus Crusade for Christ)*, accessed August 9, 2013, http://www.cru.org/training-and-growth/classics/10-basic-steps/1-the-christian-adventure/03-five-principles-of-growth.htm.

26   Walter Brueggemann, *Hopeful Imagination: Prophetic Voices in Exile*. (London: SCM Press Ltd, 1992), 45.

27   Ibid., 39–42.

28   Throntveit, *Ezra-Nehemiah*, 65.

29   Williamson, *Ezra, Nehemiah*, 173.

30   Ibid., 174.

31   Getz, "Nehemiah," 674.

CHAPTER TWO

Nehemiah the planner

Nehemiah 2:1-5

In Nehemiah 1, Nehemiah wept, fasted and prayed. In Nehemiah 2, we see him taking action.

There comes a time when we have prayed, and need to take action. I have had to remind those asking for prayer over medical problems, that prayer and seeking medical attention are not alternatives and should complement each other.

This is not a problem that is confined to Africa. Many years ago I heard a story about a pastor from Europe who visited Nigeria in the 1960s during the civil war. This pastor was disturbed by the suffering of people in the Biafra region. He reported back to his church council and asked them to raise support to provide food and clothing to those affected by war. His council responded by offering to pray. The pastor retorted, "These people don't eat prayers."

Although God has the power to do miracles, he likes to partner with us to bring change. Weanzana has written that

> Though God has the power to do anything by simply speaking the word, he will not come down in person to build hospitals, repair roads, bring an end to tribal conflicts and wars, stop the HIV/AIDS epidemic, and so on. God needs men and women of this continent who will take the initiative in his name to mobilise the entire community to work to rebuild Africa. A theology that simply waits to see miracles is harmful. Ezra and Nehemiah were men of prayer and men of faith and holiness (7:10, 27-28; 9:3; 10:6; Neh 1:5-11; 2:4-5), but they were also and especially men of action. The African church needs men and women of their calibre today.[1]

Nehemiah translated his concern for the returned exiles into action. We too need to put our faith into action: faith without works is dead (James 2:26). Packer writes that the Hebrew noun for "work" appears frequently in the book of Nehemiah (2:16, 18; 4:11, 16, 17, 19, 21; 5:16; 6:9, 16, etc.). Work is "much more than what we do for money or gain, what we call our job or our employment. In the Bible, work as such means any exertion of effort that aims at producing a new state of affairs".[2] Nehemiah did not become a leader for personal gain. He became a leader because God laid a burden in his heart for the returned exiles and the city of Jerusalem. Because Nehemiah acted, the wall of Jerusalem was built.

2:1a *In the month of Nisan, in the twentieth year of King Artaxerxes, when wine was served him, I carried the wine and gave it to the king.*

Nisan, equivalent to the month of April,[3] was fourth months after Nehemiah met the delegation from Jerusalem. Why wait for four months? The Bible does not give an answer. It is possible that Nehemiah needed this time to pray, plan and prepare for an opportune time to speak to the king. Nehemiah was patient all this time. His response to the news from Jerusalem and his prayer show that he felt God's call to do something about the situation there. Nonetheless, Nehemiah did not relinquish his position as cupbearer or set out for Jerusalem straight away. He recognised that God's timing is always best. Williamson argues that

> This period of waiting upon God is not to be regarded as a sign of weakness on his part. From the later narrative, we know that he was a dynamic man of action. But if a true vocation has been received from God, such a testing time of waiting is often to be expected; prayer during such a period will be an indication of whether the call has been genuine and whether commitment to it is unwavering.[4]

2:1b-2 *Now, I had never been sad in his presence before. So the king said to me, 'Why is your face sad, since you are not sick? This can only be sadness of the heart.' Then I was very much afraid.*

During the four months, Nehemiah went on with his work, but his concern for his people continued to disturb him. As Nehemiah served the king, the king noticed Nehemiah's sadness and asked him what the problem was. Nehemiah had taken a risk. People were not supposed to appear sad in front of the king. When the king laughed, his servants also laughed. A gloomy face could have been seen as evidence Nehemiah was plotting against the king.[5]

South Sudanese will identify with this situation. Especially during the war, plots and rumours of plots against leaders were common. Some leaders were paranoid. Their suspicions could be raised at the slightest pretext.

In peacetime, this needs to change. We need to learn to trust each other. Leaders must allow and encourage their junior workers to take the initiative. Otherwise, whenever a leader is away, work stops, as workers are too afraid to take action without receiving an instruction from their boss. However, this kind of cultural change takes time. In the meantime, South Sudanese workers can learn from Nehemiah's example of how to make requests of their bosses and how to get things done.

2:3a *I said to the king, "May the king live forever!"*

Rather than answer the king's question immediately, Nehemiah began his response with a formal salutation, in accordance with the etiquette expected of him. Nehemiah took a strategic risk in appearing sad, in order to draw the king's attention. Once he had gained the king's attention, he observed the proper protocols so as to avoid offending him.

It is important to know the way a person expects to be addressed at formal functions. Presidents and ambassadors should be addressed as Your Excellency; kings and queens as Your Majesty; mayors as Your Worship; members of parliament as Honourable. Failure to use the expected form of address can cause offence. Other common protocols include the salutation of all dignitaries at a function, and the introduction of the guest of honour by the second most senior person.

However, we should not take pride in our titles. When South Sudan attained independence, there was a surfeit of people who claimed the title of 'Your Excellency' or 'Honourable' but who were not ambassadors or members of parliament. This phenomenon has even crept into the church. Those of us with positions in the church should set an example. We should be humble, never insisting on being addressed by our respectful titles but leaving it to others to decide how to address us.

We in the Episcopal Church of the Sudan have now agreed that bishops should not be addressed as Your Lordship. The origin of this form of address was linked to bishops in England and Wales, some of whom are members of the House of Lords. Other countries do not use this title. In the US, no citisen is legally permitted to use a title of nobility. 'My Lord' and 'Your Grace' are technically illegal. Bishops play no formal part in government and have their life and dignity entirely within the church, whose only Lord is Christ. The title 'Your Lordship' has been forbidden in the ecclesiastical constitution of the US Episcopal Church since 1789.

In my diocese, Kajo-Keji, the Master of Ceremonies (MC) recognises and acknowledges all dignitaries at functions. We discourage speakers from making their own acknowledgements at the beginning of their speeches. This saves time and prevents a situation arising where people get the 'pecking order' wrong and offend some of the dignitaries. The MC, rather than the second most senior guest, introduces the guest of honour. Again, this saves time.

2:3b *'Why should my face not be sad, when the city, the place of my ancestors' graves, lies waste, and its gates have been destroyed by fire?'*

Kidner suggests Nehemiah did not mention Jerusalem by name to avoid touching a sensitive political nerve.[6] Nehemiah described the situation in personal rather than political terms, emphasising that his ancestors' graves were in ruins. This approach enlisted the sympathy of the king, who went on to ask Nehemiah what he wanted. Knowing that the king was sympathetic, Nehemiah was able to proceed.

It is important to make requests to senior people at the appropriate time. We need to gauge their mood before making requests. Nehemiah's care in using the proper protocol when addressing the king, and gauging the king's mood before making his request, suggests the risk he took in displaying his sadness was a strategic risk, rather than a reckless one.

2:4-5 *Then the king said to me, 'What do you request?' So I prayed to the God of heaven. Then I said to the king, 'If it pleases the king, and if your servant has found favour with you, I ask that you send me to Judah, to the city of my ancestors' graves, so that I may rebuild it.'"*

We know from Nehemiah 1:4-11 that Nehemiah had already spent a good deal of time in prayer in preparation for this moment. However, he still offered a quick 'arrow prayer' before he answered the king. Evers calls this kind of prayer a 'fax prayer'.[7] Perhaps a modern equivalent would be an SMS prayer, or a Twitter prayer. I know of people who when in need of prayer send out an SMS. In an instant, many people uphold them in prayer. One of our international partners tweets daily prayers for different parts of our province. Evers points out that "Nehemiah's 'fax prayer' is one of eight brief petitions recorded in his memoir (4:4-5; 5:19; 6:9,14; 13:14, 22,29)". It has been said that Nehemiah "walked with God because he talked with God".[8]

Nehemiah 2:6-8

It is clear from my treatment of Nehemiah 2:1-5 that Nehemiah prepared well for his meeting with the king. He prayed and waited on God; he chose his moment carefully; he knew the right protocol to use in addressing the king; he gauged the mood of the king before making his request; and he raised the issue in a politically sensitive manner. Nehemiah 2:6-8 demonstrates that he had also thought through the details of the project itself. Nehemiah was able to answer the king's questions, and because he had planned in advance, he knew what specific requests to make of the king, avoiding delays at a later stage. Although Nehemiah was very practical, the reference to prayer in 2:4 and the statement in 2:8b makes it clear that God's hand was in all of this. There is no conflict between good planning and allowing God's Spirit to work, providing we listen to God and do everything in an attitude of prayer.

2:6a   *The king said to me (the queen also was sitting beside him)*

2:6 contains the only mention of the queen in the entire book. The queen's presence is an indication of the intimate and private nature of the occasion.[9] Clines argues that the king probably wanted to appear generous before the queen.[10] The king's sympathetic response in 2:4 may have been influenced by her presence. If so, Nehemiah may have chosen this occasion deliberately to raise his request, guessing he would be more likely to receive a favourable response. Again, this suggests the risk Nehemiah took in displaying his sadness to the king was a strategic risk.

A wife can have a significant influence on her husband. The wife of one of our leaders was heard to say that people often ask her to speak to her husband on certain issues, especially where he had taken a strong position and may need to soften it. This underscores the importance of a Christian leader marrying a committed, prayerful spouse, so that any influence will be positive rather than negative.

Some writers have suggested that Nehemiah must have been a eunuch, or he would not have been allowed to serve in the presence of the queen. This is difficult to reconcile with his position as a Jewish leader: Deuteronomy 23:1 excludes eunuchs from the assembly of the Lord. Some scholars argue that if Nehemiah was a eunuch, he would have been disqualified from leadership. However, Clines reckons that Isaiah 56:3-6 demonstrates the rule was relaxed in the post-exilic dispensation.[11]

2:6b *'How long will you be gone, and when will you return?' So it pleased the king to send me, and I set him a date.*

The king was concerned to hear how long Nehemiah would be away from the palace. No employer wants to lose a good worker. We do not know what response Nehemiah gave. At this stage, Nehemiah may not have asked for the twelve years referred to in 5:14 and 13:6.[12] If Nehemiah had told the king he would be away for such a long time, it is likely his request would have been rejected. In any case, Nehemiah may not himself have expected to spend so long in Jerusalem. He may have come back to update the king after the wall was built, fulfilling the promise made in verse 6b, before returning once again to Jerusalem.

An alternative suggestion is that the king promoted Nehemiah immediately, and he went to Judah as governor. It is good for an employer to give staff opportunities for professional progress. Giving capable people challenging roles helps them gain experience, motivates them, and ensures their skills are used well for the benefit of the organisation.

2:7 *Then I said to the king, 'If it pleases the king, let letters be given me to the governors of the province Beyond the River, that they may grant me passage until I arrive in Judah;*

Nehemiah was a good planner. He knew exactly what he wanted, and worked all the details out before he went to see the king. He was able to respond immediately to the king's question about the duration of his absence. He knew that he needed human and material resources to accomplish this task, and made specific requests for the necessary resources. It was important for Nehemiah to have concrete plans. If he did not, it would have shown that his project was not well thought out.

Some projects in Africa fail because they lack a convincing plan. No donor will fund a project which has not been properly thought out. Many businesses fail because they lack an adequate business plan; some building projects have not been completed because no proper architectural plan or costings have been done. Often inflation is not factored in. In many parts of Africa, building materials are subject to price fluctuations. Weather, especially tropical rain, very often affects the transportation and cost of materials.

Nehemiah anticipated the obstacles that rivals might put in his path. He knew that previous attempts to rebuild the city walls had failed because of local opposition (see my comment under 1:2, above). They had been able to exploit a lack of clarity about whether the plans had been authorised at the highest level. Nehemiah learned the lessons of history and made sure he had letters of authorisation to ensure that the governors of the province Beyond the River would have no excuse to prevent him reaching his destination.

In a country like South Sudan, where communications infrastructure is patchy and messages do not always get through, letters of authorisation can be very important. Without them, officials may be unsure as to whether their seniors wish them to co-operate with a person, leading to significant delays while they seek advice. Without a letter, the personal agenda of local officials can take pre-eminence. Letters of authorisation from a senior person can also reduce the likelihood of being asked for a bribe. For us as for Nehemiah, planning a project properly means anticipating the obstacles people might put in our way and gathering evidence of support from senior persons that can overcome such obstacles.

2:8a *...and a letter to Asaph, the keeper of the king's forest, directing him to give me timber to make beams for the gates of the temple fortress, and for the wall of the city, and for the house that I shall occupy.'*

As a law-abiding citisen, Nehemiah asked the king's permission to cut the timber he required for the gates of the temple fortress, the wall of the city, and for his own house. No doubt he could have used his position as a palace worker (and especially his subsequent position as governor) to instruct workers to cut the timber. However, Nehemiah was keen to follow protocols and set a good example for others. Sadly, many South Sudanese cut timber without following due processes and with little awareness of the environmental consequences.

One of the effects of a long war is an ingrained disregard for the environment. War tends to promote a short-term perspective. People are focused on survival. They do not know whether they will be able to stay in their homeland or they will have to flee. Armed groups may destroy vegetation as part of a 'scorched earth' policy. They therefore plunder the land while they can. Traditional values of care and respect for the land are eroded. During the 21 years of war in South Sudan, large areas of forest in South Sudan were felled, to sell the timber and as a source of fuel for cooking. No efforts were made to plant more trees.

I remember my early years at school when we were exhorted to plant two trees for every one tree we cut down. We were made to value forests as a vital part of the larger environment, and taught that they must be carefully managed if they are to be sustainable. I have given regular teaching on the importance of trees for our timber needs, produce and protection of the environment, since becoming bishop of Kajo-Keji diocese in 2007. I have encouraged parishes to plant timber and fruit trees. I have even argued that planting trees is one way they can pay their workers. If each of our 57 parishes planted 200 trees per year, we would have 114,000 trees in 10 years.

I have not only taught this but also put it into practice. In Kajo-Keji, the church has made a deliberate effort to intensify tree planting. Whenever we dedicate a new church, we plant trees. At the bishop's residence, I have planted lemon, orange, mango and jackfruit trees. In my own private residence, I have planted over 100 teak trees.

A number of churches and individuals have also put this teaching into practice, including Chaplain Sunamurye, one of the leaders of the Revival Movement. Recently he wrote to thank me for my teaching on this subject. He told me he has planted 400 eucalyptus trees and that 206 have survived and are doing well. He has also planted teak trees and citrus fruit trees. I am glad that at least someone was listening to my teaching!

Of course, it is unlikely Nehemiah would have been aware of the climate change that is exacerbated by the destruction of forests. Climate change in South Sudan is noticeable. When I was growing up in Kajo-Keji, annual seasons were regular and predictable. We had our rainy season from March/April to October/November. This is not the case any more.

Changes in the climate have also affected the availability of water. Some of the rivers that used to retain water during the dry season no longer do so. There is a river in my village called Linyakure (literally meaning 'finisher of thirst') that used to remain swollen but now recedes quickly during the dry season. What we are witnessing in my village appears to represent a general phenomenon in Sub-Saharan Africa. Doing nothing is not an option. The church can play a significant role in enlightening the people about the causes of this phenomenon. The church meets more people from a wider range of backgrounds, face to face every week, than any other institution or group. It was a significant actor in educating people at the grassroots about the referendum on independence. It should do the same on other issues like climate change.

Climate change could become a significant factor driving conflict. As water becomes scarcer along the South Sudan-Sudan border, the likelihood of conflict between seasonal Sudanese migrants and the settled South Sudanese population increases. The scarcity of grazing land has the potential to cause inter-tribal conflicts, which could escalate and degenerate into a war over resources between South Sudan and Sudan.

2:8b *And the king granted me what I asked, for the gracious hand of God was upon me.*

Some scholars have asked why a Persian king would sponsor the project of rebuilding the walls of Jerusalem. They argue that a Persian king would not finance, oversee and carry out such a project through one of their own trusted civil servants if it did not serve their own strategic and military interests. Howard-Brook has likened the Persian king's actions to the United States building naval bases at Pearl Harbour or in South Korea.[13]

Regardless of what the Persian king had in mind, 2:8b makes it clear that God was sovereign in this situation. "Ezra-Nehemiah does not deny imperial involvement" in the project but shows that the "Persian authority is an expression of YHWH's will."[14]

Nehemiah went to a pagan king and asked for permission to build the walls of Jerusalem. If God used a donkey to speak to Balaam (Numbers 22:21-35), he can use a pagan king. He redeems our mixed motives. The Persian king may have had his own reasons for taking the actions he did, but God worked everything into his plan.

There are other examples of God using people who did not know him in the Old Testament. Isaiah 45 describes Cyrus, another Persian king, as his 'anointed' (45:1). God equipped him, even though he did not know the Lord (45:5), because his actions would show others that "I am the Lord, and there is no other" (45:6). In the same way, God used King Artaxerxes to reveal his glory to others by contributing to the rebuilding of the city of Jerusalem, even though Artaxerxes did not know him.

The Lord even described Nebuchadnezzar, the king of Babylon, as his servant (Jeremiah 25:9; 27:6; 43:10), because the king of Babylon served his purposes in humbling Israel. However, being used by God can be dangerous when we do not know him! Nebuchadnezzar did not give God the credit for his successes. He believed his success demonstrated his own power and glory rather than God's. He overstepped the mark in his treatment of God's people, and was made to drink the cup of God's wrath as a consequence (Jeremiah 25:26; 51:1-64).

In South Sudan, God is using not only his own people, but also secular NGOs, to bring development and relieve poverty. Because they do not know God, secular NGOs may lack understanding in some areas. For example, many do not have a proper understanding of the role of the local church as God's chosen instrument. Certainly, NGOs serve their own interests. Nonetheless, God is capable of redeeming mixed motives and working everything into his plan, using secular NGOs to do good in South Sudan, even if they do not know him.

Nehemiah gave God the credit for his success, even though the Persian king did not. It is part of the Church's role to demonstrate God's involvement in the good that takes place in our world. As discussed above under 1:2, South Sudan's national anthem gives God the credit for the liberation of South Sudan, rightly speaking of his grace on South Sudan before testifying to the sacrifice made by martyrs and others. We are called to be witnesses to what God has done, especially to what he has done through the death and resurrection of Christ (Luke 24:48; Acts 1:8; 3:15; 5:32; 10:39, 41). This includes what he is doing in our communal life, as well as the transformation he has brought in our personal lives.

2:8b makes it clear that the king's favourable response was an answer to Nehemiah's prayer for success and to be granted mercy in the king's sight (1:11). Nehemiah's prayer did not absolve him from the responsibility to plan or to act. It did ensure that God was present in his planning and in the carrying out of his plans. Because he had prayed, Nehemiah was able to recognise God's involvement and give him the credit for the king's response. We are best able to see how God is working when we have prayed, because we recognise God's answers to our prayers in the events of our lives.

Nehemiah 2:9-20

Having gained the support of the king, thanks to the gracious hand of God, Nehemiah 2:9-20 shows how Nehemiah gained the support of the returned exiles, despite serious opposition from local officials.

Nehemiah continued to take action, rooted in prayer and careful preparation. He took strategic risks but also took precautionary measures to minimise those risks wherever possible.

The importance of planning is emphasised: Nehemiah inspected the city wall in secret to survey the damage and map out what work needed to be done. However, the passage also makes it clear that Nehemiah's plans were God-centred. It is God who called Nehemiah to rebuild Jerusalem; the testimony that convinces the returned exiles to begin work emphasises that God was behind Nehemiah's plans and was already at work. Nehemiah's ultimate answer to his opponents was that God would grant him success.

In this Nehemiah concurs with the wisdom expressed in Proverbs 16:1-9. This passage emphasises the importance of planning, but leaving ultimate ownership of our plans to the Lord. The Lord is referred to in eight of nine verses. The passage begins with the proverb: *"The plans of the mind belong to morals, but the answer of the tongue is from the LORD"* (16:1) and ends with the similar wisdom that *"The human mind plans the way but the LORD directs the steps"* (16:33). All plans should be God-centred. God will establish such plans (16:3).

2:9 *Then I came to the governors of the province Beyond the River, and gave them the king's letters. Now the king had sent officers of the army and cavalry with me.*

Nehemiah had good strategic reasons for accepting an armed escort. Arriving with an armed escort would indicate that Nehemiah had the support of the king[15] and strengthen the impact of the letters of authority he carried.

Nehemiah's willingness to accept an armed escort marks him out from Ezra. Ezra had been reluctant to ask for an armed escort, as he had told the king that God would protect him (Ezra 8:22). He subsequently fasted and prayed to God for protection, and God honoured his request. However, we should not make a principle out of Ezra's example as some have done. Some have even refused to rear guard dogs, arguing that having a guard dog is saying that God does not protect us.

Nehemiah's example should caution us from making Ezra 8:22 into a universal principle. We need to take precautionary measures for our security. There is a saying that has falsely been attributed to the Bible, that God helps those who help themselves. I am reluctant to use this saying so that people do not attribute it to the Bible. However, there is an element of truth in it.

Who we accept an armed escort from, and when, is a strategic decision requiring wisdom and careful discernment after prayer. God honoured both Ezra and Nehemiah in their decisions. The importance of precautionary measures, and the impact that association with different kinds of armed personnel will have on others, are relevant factors in making a prayerful decision about such matters.

2:10 *When Sanballat the Horonite and Tobiah the Ammonite official heard this, it displeased them greatly that someone had come to seek the welfare of the people of Israel.*

2:10 introduces us to the two of the three leaders of the opposition. Sanballat was the governor of Samaria. Nehemiah does not refer to him as governor, but rather as 'the Horonite'. This may have been Nehemiah's way of refusing to recognise Sanballat's authority over Jerusalem.

It was obvious that Nehemiah had come to seek the welfare of the people of Israel, but Sanballat and Tobiah did not yet realise the full extent of Nehemiah's intentions (2:12, 16).

2:11-16 *So I came to Jerusalem and was there for three days. Then I got up during the night, I and a few men with me; I told no one what my God had put into my heart to do for Jerusalem. The only animal I took was the animal I rode. I went out by night by the Valley Gate past the Dragon's Spring and to the Dung Gate, and I inspected the walls of Jerusalem that had been broken down and its gates that had been destroyed by fire. Then I went on to the Fountain Gate and to the King's Pool; but there was no place for the animal I was riding to continue. So I went up by way of the valley by night and inspected the wall. Then I turned back and entered by the Valley Gate and so returned. The officials did not know where I had gone or what I was doing; I had not yet told the Jews, the priests, the nobles, the officials, and the rest that were to do the work.*

Nehemiah's excellent planning skills and his realistic attitude to opposition are apparent in this passage. It was inevitable that Sanballat and Tobiah would find out what Nehemiah was up to eventually. However, this was a delicate time. Further preparation needed to be done before mobilising the public behind his vision. Nehemiah needed to see the condition of the walls for himself so he could map out exactly what had to be done. If Sanballat and Tobiah had become aware of Nehemiah's intentions before he had finished inspecting the walls, they may have started to spread rumours, discourage the people and mobilise opposition before Nehemiah had opportunity to present a credible plan to them.

Although Nehemiah had good reason for conducting his activities in secret, he did not inspect the walls alone. He took with him a select number of trusted aides. It is important to share one's initial vision with a few people and get their input and advice before making it public. Once we have mapped out what needs to be done, we can make our vision and plan known to others.

As we have seen, Nehemiah was conscious of his security. In 2:9, this meant accepting an armed escort. During his night-time expeditions, Nehemiah travelled without a large convoy or security detail to avoid alerting officials. The purpose of Nehemiah's security detail was not to impress others with his importance; it was a practical measure to help accomplish the task God had given him. When the task required him to adapt, he did so.

2:12 confirms what until now the text has only implied: it was God who laid a burden on Nehemiah's heart to rebuild Jerusalem. The Bible shows that God calls people to specific tasks in very different ways. God spoke to Moses through a burning bush. David was called through the prophet Samuel. Elijah was sent by God to effect Elisha's call, throwing a cloak around him to designate him his successor. Isaiah had a vision from God. Jeremiah was called before he was born! Paul received his calling on his way to Damascus, but God used Barnabas to confirm the call.

Many of these people felt inadequate and unable to live out the callings God gave them. Jeremiah told God he was too young, and did not know how to speak (Jeremiah 1:6). All Christian leaders have weaknesses, whether physical, emotional, intellectual or spiritual. Paul had a "thorn in the flesh" (2 Corinthians 12:7). God deliberately chooses the weak to shame the strong, "so that no human being might boast in the presence of God" (1 Corinthians 1:29). If we understand that we are weak, we will rely on God. Whatever weaknesses God has allowed in our lives, we must accept them and rely on his grace.

God encouraged Jeremiah not to focus on his age (Jeremiah 1:7) and reassured Jeremiah that he would be with him (1:8). He touched Jeremiah's mouth and told him he had put his words into his mouth (1:9). When God chooses and appoints us, he always equips us for the task that he has before us. The most important equipping for any Christian is the presence of the Holy Spirit. The Holy Spirit apportions spiritual gifts to each believer (1 Corinthians 12:4-11) for building up the body of Christ, the Church. When God calls, he also provides everything we need to live out the calling he gives us.

Jeremiah was ultimately obedient to God's call, even though it meant a life of suffering and sacrifice. Peter left everything when Jesus called him to be one of his disciples. Elisha slaughtered and burnt his oxen, using his ploughing equipment as fuel to cook the meat. This was to show that he had broken with his vocation as a farmer to take up a new vocation as a prophet. Sometimes a person may be called from a profession where he is earning a reasonable income. Obedience for Nehemiah meant leaving his job as a cup-bearer in order to fulfil his call to rebuild the walls of Jerusalem. We all need to know God's purpose for our lives and live it out in obedience.

One of the ways God calls us is by laying a burden on our heart and making us restless until we fulfil what he wants us to do. This was the case for Nehemiah. There is no description of a call like that of Isaiah or Jeremiah in the book of Nehemiah. However, in Nehemiah 1 we see Nehemiah struggling with a burden for the city of Jerusalem and the returned exiles over a prolonged period of time. In Nehemiah 2 we see him do something about it, and in 2:12 we learn that it was God who laid the burden on his heart.

If we are not sure what God has called us to do, one way of thinking about this is to prayerfully consider what concerns or bothers us about the situation in our churches, countries or world, and whether that could be a burden God has given us. Some of these issues might include:

- Young people – do they appear to be out of control? Do they refuse to listen to their parents, teachers and elders?
- Teenage pregnancies, early marriages and infant/maternal mortality: in the year 2011, 207 primary school girls left their studies in Kajo-Keji county in South Sudan. In many cases this was due to pregnancy. Many of these young girls face problems during delivery. South Sudan has exceptionally high levels of infant and maternal mortality.
- Violence, including war, robbery, abuse and rape.
- Poverty.
- Lack of health care.
- Governance issues, including corruption.

If you felt God moving your heart as you read through these issues, it might be worth pausing to pray and ask God whether his calling on your life relates to any of these issues. God needs people to 'rebuild the walls' in South Sudan, undertaking different roles in the Church and living out different callings in society. Some of us may be called to be teachers, midwives, health workers, tax collectors or politicians. Unless God specifically calls us out of our jobs, those of us who have jobs should consider them as our Christian calling and do them as unto the Lord. We should 'eat to live' rather than 'live to eat', and always keep the big picture – contributing to the growth of the Kingdom of God – in mind.

2:17 *Then I said to them, 'You see the trouble we are in, how Jerusalem lies in ruins with its gates burned. Come, let us rebuild the wall of Jerusalem, so that we may no longer suffer disgrace.'*

Once Nehemiah had an idea of the extent of the damage and the work that needed to be undertaken, it was time to share his plan with a larger group of people. Tollefson and Williamson write that communication with all stakeholders is important for the success of any plan:

> Any significant plan must be shared with some community in order to become effective. Nehemiah shared his plan first with the king, in an effort to obtain material along with a building permit; and he shared it second with the people, in an effort to acquire their support and labour.[16]

Nehemiah began by identifying with the predicament of the returned exiles. He showed he understood the problems the people faced and how they felt. This is a sensible communications strategy. As a senior civil servant in the royal palace, who had almost certainly grown up outside his country, Nehemiah might have been perceived by the returned exiles as more connected with the king than with their own community. Nehemiah knew he had to prove himself to them. He emphasised his membership of the community, using 'we' twice in two sentences, and showed that he shared their pain.

In his exhortation to action, Nehemiah also included himself: "let us rebuild". This is an indication that Nehemiah was a team player, and would take part in the work of rebuilding. As we shall see in our discussion of Nehemiah 3, Nehemiah exemplified a participatory style of leadership.

The condition of Jerusalem and the condition of the returned exiles are linked even more strongly here than in Nehemiah 1. The ruins of Jerusalem are linked to "the trouble we are in". There is a causal relationship between rebuilding the wall and no longer suffering disgrace.

2:18 *I told them that the hand of my God had been gracious upon me, and also the words that the king had spoken to me. Then they said, 'Let us start building!' So they committed themselves to the common good.*

Identifying with the people and their predicament was not enough on its own to persuade them to take action. Nehemiah went on to give testimony of what God had already done to make his vision a reality, using a similar form of words to 2:8b.

Rather than calling on the returned exiles to initiate something new, Nehemiah revealed what God had already begun and invited them to join in. This is what we should do whenever we encourage people to get involved in mission, since God's Spirit is always working in a situation before us!

The testimony of God's protection and provision would have encouraged the people. The words the king had spoken to Nehemiah would have increased their fragile faith that this project might succeed where others had failed. Nehemiah believed in "the power of persuasive testimony"[17] that can "enrich others by widening their horizons and inspiring their confidence."[18]

We should not underestimate the power and importance of sharing testimony of what God has done in our personal lives and our communities. God uses our testimony to strengthen the faith of believers and to bring non-believers to Christ.

Witnessing is the fourth of Bill Bright's five principles for spiritual growth.[19] Jesus told his disciples they would be witnesses (Acts 1:8). The most important qualification for a witness is that they must testify about what they have seen or heard (testimony). This means that a witness for Christ must himself or herself be a believer. The witness must be connected to Jesus Christ. Bill Hybels and Mark Mittelberg have written about 'contagious Christianity'.[20] Christians must share their faith with non-believers.

The Bible gives many examples of how to do this effectively. Paul even used the occasion of his arrest as an opportunity to give testimony of what God had done in his life (Acts 21:37-22:21). Paul used an appropriate language, Hebrew in this case, to draw the attention of the crowds. He introduced himself. He told the crowd what his life had been like, how it changed and what his life was like now. These are important components when sharing Christian testimony with non-believers. I have adapted Paul's speech and distilled it into four headings to use when giving testimony to non-believers ourselves:

- Introducing ourselves: who we are and what we were like before God intervened.
- How God intervened in our lives, with reference to concrete events and specific details.
- What God told us.
- The change that has happened in our lives.

Soon afterwards, Paul had another chance to share his testimony. He changed the content, to make it relevant to a different audience and a different situation. Likewise, we must be prepared to give testimony of different things that God has done in our lives and in our communities, emphasising different aspects depending on the situation and the needs of the listener.

Nehemiah's testimony was persuasive. He designed his testimony with the specific aim of motivating the returned exiles to rebuild the walls of Jerusalem. 2:18b shows he was successful: *"Then they said: 'Let us start building!'"* It is noteworthy that the response of the people was to commit themselves *"to the common good."* When people experience trauma, as the returned exiles must have done when the partially rebuilt walls were destroyed *"by force and power"* (Ezra 4:23), they can often turn in on themselves and focus on individual survival. Focusing on God and playing our part in implementing his plans has the opposite effect. It builds social solidarity and leads to fellowship.

Three factors contributed to the success of Nehemiah's testimony. Two of them are mentioned in 2:18: the hand of God, and the support Nehemiah received from the king. Finally, God also used Nehemiah's own giftings to rally the returned exiles to support the project, including his charisma, and his ability to identify with the people.

2:19-20 *But when Sanballat the Horonite and Tobiah the Ammonite official, and Geshem the Arab heard of it, they mocked and ridiculed us, saying, 'What is this that you are doing? Are you rebelling against the king?' Then I replied to them, 'The God of heaven is the one who will give us success, and we his servants are going to start building; but you have no share or claim or historic right in Jerusalem.'*

Once again Nehemiah met with opposition. The two people who had opposed him before (2:10) were now joined by a third person: Geshem the Arab. Geshem may be the only Arab mentioned in the Bible by name, although Arabia is mentioned in passing and by implication.

The three opponents mocked and ridiculed the work that Nehemiah and the builders planned to do. No doubt this was a deliberate strategy to dishearten the returned exiles. Sanballat, Tobiah and Geshem knew that when the partially rebuilt walls of Jerusalem had been destroyed, the returned exiles had been paralysed by shame (1:3) and disgrace (2:17). They hoped to reinforce the negative self-perception of the exiles by humiliating them, making them think they were incapable of rebuilding Jerusalem. They drew on painful memories of how a lack of support from the king had jeopardised rebuilding in the past in an attempt to undermine the confidence of the builders.

Nehemiah refused to be drawn into their line of questioning. He had already demonstrated that he enjoyed the king's support. He knew that his opponents' misunderstanding was deliberate and wasted no time trying to convince them he was not rebelling against the king. Instead, he made it clear that the success of the project rested on God, not on the king's support. Equally, now that he had successfully mobilised the people there was no need to keep his plans a secret. Nehemiah openly told Sanballat, Tobiah, and Geshem that he was going to start building.

South Sudan has enemies who would like to reinforce the negative self-perception of many South Sudanese. Some, including more than a few journalists, have interests in painting South Sudan as a failed or failing state after only two years of independence. Like Nehemiah, we should not debate with them on their own terms, but rather focus on God and on the task ahead of us. Attempts to humiliate us should not be successful as we are children of God (John 1:12; Romans 8:16-21), created in his image (Genesis 1:27). God has called us to rebuild our nation. When he calls, he also equips and provides, so we need not fear we are incapable of carrying out the task.

Nehemiah drew a sharp contrast between God's servants, who would take part in the work of rebuilding, and Sanballat, Tobiah and Geshem, who had no share, claim or historic right in Jerusalem. This distinction is based on the covenantal promises Nehemiah appealed to in Nehemiah 1. In this prayer, he also referred to returnees as God's servants. Obedience to God through participation in his work of rebuilding acts to confirm this status. The share, the claim, the historic right that God's servants had in Jerusalem was solely based on God's covenantal promises. Nehemiah could confidently assert that the opponents of the rebuilding work, Sanballat, Tobiah and Geshem, had no share in Jerusalem because they were not included in these promises.

Conclusion

Nehemiah 2 shows Nehemiah taking action. Where in chapter 1, Nehemiah is presented as patriotic and prayerful, chapter 2 shows him to be a planner. He planned out his project carefully so he could answer the king's questions and knew what to ask for. He prepared extensively for his meeting with the king, ensuring he approached the king in the best possible way, to maximise the chances of success. He anticipated opposition and drew up a strategy to neutralise it. Once he arrived in Jerusalem, he spent further time in preparation, inspecting the walls and discussing his plans with a select group of trusted aides before making his plans public, mobilising supporters and confronting opposition.

Alongside the emphasis on human action and assiduous preparation is an emphasis on the sovereignty of God. Nehemiah 2 explicitly states that it is God who put Nehemiah's plans into his heart. Nehemiah was careful to give God the credit for his successful meeting with the king. It was the testimony of God's control and action that persuades the returned exiles to participate in the work of rebuilding. It is God who grants success, his servants who would do the building, and his people who share in his covenantal promises.

The dual emphasis in Nehemiah 2 on human action and planning on the one hand, and God's action and sovereignty on the other, helps guard against the twin dangers of a secular view which thinks we can solve our problems without reference to God, and a super-spiritualist view which imagines God will send down angels to solve our problems miraculously rather than working through human beings. Nehemiah 2 shows clearly that human action and God's sovereignty go hand-in-hand. We have a responsibility to take action. However, if our plans are not God-centred, they will ultimately fail.

1   Weanzana, "Ezra," 532.
2   Packer, *A Passion for Faithfulness*, 73.
3   Derek Kidner, *Ezra and Nehemiah: An Introduction and Commentary*, Tyndale Old Testament Commentaries (Leicester: Inter-Varsity Press, 1979), 77, 80.
4   Williamson, *Ezra, Nehemiah*, 175.
5   Ibid., 179.
6   Kidner, *Ezra and Nehemiah*, 80.
7   Evers, *Doing a Great Work*, 110.
8   Ibid.
9   Kidner, *Ezra and Nehemiah*, 81.
10 Clines, *Ezra, Nehemiah, Esther*, 143.
11 Ibid., 140.
12 Kidner, *Ezra and Nehemiah*, 81.
13 Wes Howard-Brook, *"Come Out My People!": God's Call Out of Empire in the Bible and Beyond* (Maryknoll: Orbis Books, 2010), 261.

14 Ibid., 263.

15 Kidner, *Ezra and Nehemiah*, 81.

16 Kenneth D Tollefson and Hugh G M Williamson, "Nehemiah as Cultural Revitalisation: An Anthropological Perspective," in *The Historical Books*, ed. J. Cheryl Exum, The Biblical Seminar 40 (Sheffield: Sheffield Academic Press, 1997), 331.

17 Brown, *The Message of Nehemiah*, 57.

18 Ibid.

19 Bright, "Five Principles of Growth."

20 Bill Hybels and Mark Mittelberg, *Becoming a Contagious Christian* (Grand Rapids: Zondervan, 1994).

CHAPTER THREE

Nehemiah
the participatory leader

Nehemiah 3:1-32

Nehemiah 3 gives a long list of the people who took part in the rebuilding of the city walls, and the work that they did. Because of the nature of the chapter, I will not comment on every verse. I will make general comments on the theological reasons for including this information in the book of Nehemiah before commenting specifically on a few clusters of verses.

Nehemiah 3 is not merely a historical record. Its inclusion in the book of Nehemiah serves theological purposes. One of these purposes is to act as a roll-call of honour. If the ruins of Jerusalem brought shame on those who lived among them (1:3), the reconstruction of its walls and gates brought honour to those who participated. The chapter acts as evidence of the civic rights of those who took part and their descendants.[1]

The chapter also demonstrates that the work of reconstruction was supported by all the people and not just those who were friends and relatives of Nehemiah.[2] People of all ages, clans and occupations; men and women; nobles and ordinary people took part. Despite this diversity, a 'unity of intention'[3] was displayed in the way the work was done. This reflects the commitment the people made in 2:18 to the common good.

This theme of unity in diversity is taken up in the New Testament, especially in sections of Paul's writings that deal with spiritual gifts. 1 Corinthians 12:4-6 and Ephesians 4:1-6 both emphasise unity but are followed by passages that speak of the diverse range of gifts given to different believers.

Individual believers have different gifts, services, and activities allotted to them (1 Corinthians 12:4-6) by the Holy Spirit (1 Corinthians 12:11). All gifts are given for the benefit of the whole church. Non-exhaustive lists of gifts are given in 2 Corinthians 12:8-10 and Romans 12:6-8. Spiritual gifts are exactly that—gifts. They are not rewards for good behaviour. They are given by the grace of God and not achieved by our own efforts. They are not the same as the natural talents we may have had before we came to faith in

Christ, although God can transform natural talents into spiritual gifts when they are used for the benefit of the Church.

Every believer has been given at least one spiritual gift. Paul warns us against being ignorant of spiritual gifts (1 Corinthians 12:1), so we have no excuse for ignoring our spiritual gifts. If we do not use our spiritual gifts the rest of the church will suffer, as the Church has been designed to work best when each member is exercising the gifts he or she has been given by God.

The Bible explains this using the picture of the human body. Each part of the body works together. When one is eating food, different parts of the body participate in the process of eating. The eye sees the food; the nose smells it; the hand takes the food and puts it into the mouth. Once the food is in the mouth, the tongue gauges whether it is too hot or has sufficient salt. If something is wrong, a message is sent to the brain requesting more salt or cooling. The tongue passes the food on to the teeth to chew and push down through the oesophagus to the stomach. I have elaborated slightly on the biblical picture, but the point is the same! The members of the body of Christ, the Church, should work together in the same manner as the members of our physical bodies.

A modern equivalent could be the picture of a football team. Each of the players has different talents; they all play in the position best suited to them. If a defender refuses to play because he is not able to score as many goals as a striker, the whole team will suffer. Unfortunately, most churches have more spectators than players. All Christians should be on the field. Non-believers should be the only spectators!

Sometimes believers are unaware of their gifts, or even believe they have not been given a spiritual gift. This can be because certain spiritual gifts are undervalued or not properly recognised as spiritual. For example, hospitality, administration and craftsmanship are not always recognised as spiritual gifts because they seem practical. However, the Bible recognises them as spiritual gifts. We should not divide the spiritual and the practical or assume the practical cannot be spiritual. If a person is unaware of their gifts, they must pray and ask for understanding. There is nothing wrong with a person asking leaders in the church what he or she can be involved in and trying something out after seeking their advice.

Having a particular spiritual gift is not an excuse for refusing to serve in another way! There are some tasks that require hard work and simply need to be done. Spiritual gifts should not be a source of pride. A humble, servant-hearted believer is likely to help clear away chairs after the church service or clean the church toilets even if they also have the gifts of prophecy, healing and working miracles. The people who participated in the rebuilding of the walls had a variety of different gifts but none shunned the hard work of reconstruction.

It is said that laziness is the mother of poverty. There are many causes of poverty in Africa. Because of the racist caricature of Africans as lazy, dating from colonial times, suggesting we need to change our attitude to work can be controversial. It is fair to point out that hard work was a traditional value in many South Sudanese tribes. However, dependence on foreign aid during the war has weakened this value. My personal experience suggests an attitude change is needed.

I have heard people argue that work is a curse, the result of the fall of humankind in Genesis 3. When I became Bishop of Kajo-Keji diocese, some people even tried to discourage me from digging on my day off! Such people forget that God asked man to work and keep the garden even before the fall (Genesis 2:15). The Bible encourages hard work. Paul writes that any person who does not work should not eat (2 Thessalonians 3:10), a verse oft-quoted by my late father, Canon Benaiah Poggo. He himself did work digging and farming despite claims by others that it was demeaning. He believed that laziness was one of the biggest causes of poverty in Africa. He was fond of saying that nobody dies because of hard work. Stress can make people ill if time is not managed well. Life is a "rhythm of work and rest"[4] and we must balance both appropriately.

The way to come out of poverty is hard work in all sectors of society. To catch up with the rest of the world, we need to change our attitude to work, seeing it as a responsibility and not a curse. We all have individual roles and responsibilities and can make useful contributions to the development of our country. We should not expect the government to do everything for us.

This will involve better time management. Before independence, we used to refer to Sudan 'local' time. This would be an acceptable expression if it referred to time applying to Sudan instead of East Africa standard time. As an expression excusing lateness as a cultural difference, it is not acceptable. African attitudes to time are not inferior to Western attitudes in every aspect. There is value in a more person-oriented attitude to time, where we welcome and offer hospitality to the stranger even if we may be late as a consequence, or help a troubled neighbour in preference to going about our own business. We do not want to be like the priest or the Levite in the parable of the Good Samaritan. However, too often, citing different cultural attitudes to time is an excuse for laziness. If a church service or function starts at 9am, there is no excuse for leaving the house at the time when the service or function is starting. Worse still is the notion that the more senior a person is, the more they should delay their arrival in order to convey their importance This attitude combines pride and laziness, and does not help us to develop our nation.

Laziness can also lead to corruption, as people look for material gain without working hard. I read a story many years ago about one of the leaders of the liberation struggles in Africa. During the struggle, this leader accused the government of the day of condoning corruption. When the liberation movement became the government, this particular person was appointed to a senior position. After his appointment, he stopped criticising his colleagues who were involved in corrupt practices. When he was asked why, he said that according to African culture, it is bad manners to talk while eating!

We all have a responsibility to speak up wherever we see corruption, at whatever level it takes place. The fight against corruption and lack of transparency should not be limited to the government, but should include individuals, the Church, NGOs and all other sectors of society. There is a need to put in place mechanisms that guard against the abuse and mismanagement of resources and to encourage transparency. We also need to encourage a culture of hard work where corruption is shamed and not tolerated as the norm.

The model of reconstruction given in Nehemiah 3 requires diverse people to work hard, together, with unity of intention. It also suggests a different model of leadership to the one found in many parts of Africa. Rather than simply issuing orders or giving assignments, Nehemiah functioned as a facilitator. He had faith in his people and delegated the reconstruction of different sections of the wall to different groups.

Nehemiah's leadership style best fits a participatory model. Participatory leadership involves team members in deciding on goals and developing strategies to achieve those goals together. It allows additional leaders to emerge, who will be able to serve the organisation at a later date. It also encourages members to have a sense of ownership over the project, ensuring they stay motivated. It often allows hidden talents to be discovered, which can then benefit the organisation. Because of the emphasis on teamwork, a sense of community is instilled.

In South Sudan, leaders may feel threatened by the possibility of new leaders emerging, especially if they have educational qualifications the existing leaders may lack. However, the participatory model of leadership is best whenever, as in Nehemiah's case, the intention is not only to deliver a project but to build community. Nehemiah aimed not only to rebuild walls, but to reconstruct a covenantal community. This required a sense of social solidarity that was strengthened by the experience of all sectors of society working hard, together, to rebuild the walls.

3:1 *Then the high priest Eliashib set to work with his fellow priests and rebuilt the Sheep Gate. They consecrated it and set up its doors; they consecrated it as far as the Tower of the Hundred and as far as the Tower of Hananel.*

3:17 *After him the Levites made repairs: Rehum son of Bani; next to him Hashabiah, ruler of half the district of Keilah, made repairs for his district.*

3:22 *After him the priests, the men of the surrounding area, made repairs.*

3:28 *Above the Horse Gate the priests made repairs, each one opposite his own house.*

I have already noted that all the people took part in the rebuilding work, no matter what their occupation. This even included priests and Levites! This is a lesson to pastors and other church leaders. We should participate in community and church work. This includes menial tasks. We lead by example. If we refuse to participate in work because we think we are too important or we have better things to do, others will follow suit.

When I became Bishop of Kajo-Keji diocese, I told local pastors and diocesan staff that my role would be that of captain of the team, rather than a manager or coach over and above the team. This meant that I would be involved in ministry with them and would not ask them to do something that I was not willing to do myself.

3:5 *Next to them the Tekoites made repairs; but their nobles would not put their shoulders to the work of their Lord.*

3:9 *Next to them Rephaiah son of Hur, ruler of half the district of Jerusalem, made repairs.*

3:14-16 *Malchijah son of Rechab, ruler of the district of Beth-haccherem, repaired the Dung Gate; he rebuilt it and set up its doors, its bolts and its bars. And Shallum son of Col-hozeh, ruler of the district of Mizpah, repaired the*

Fountain Gate; he rebuilt it and covered it and set up its doors, its bolts, and its bars; and he built the wall of the Pool of Shelah of the king's garden, as far as the stairs that go down from the City of David. After him Nehemiah son of Azbuk, ruler of half the district of Bethzur, repaired from a point opposite the graves of David, as far as the artificial pool and the house of the warriors.

I have stated that the whole community took part in the work of rebuilding. However, there was one exception. The Tekoite nobles refused to participate in the work. The likelihood is that they were proud, and viewed themselves as too important to do hard labour. As a result, they were not included in the roll-call of honour. It is clear from verses 9, 12 and 14-16 that other rulers did take part. The ordinary Tekoite people surpassed their leaders. As well as doing the work mentioned in 3:5, they repaired an additional section of the wall (3:27).

The reality in life is that you cannot get 100% agreement on anything, however good that thing may be. There are always people in society who have a different view to the majority. We must accept this. We are created to be different from one another. A plurality of views is healthy and not a threat. Many South Sudanese were surprised that the referendum of the independence of South Sudan resulted in a 98.83% vote for separation rather than a figure closer to 100%. Even on an issue as straightforward as this, there were those who had different views. They did not take up arms against the new Republic. Differences of opinion are not necessarily a physical threat. They must be tolerated. Nehemiah took no action against the Tekoite nobles. Their failure to support the project spoke for itself, brought shame on them and has been recorded permanently in God's word.

3:10a *Next to them Jedaiah son of Harumaph made repairs opposite his house.*

3:28 *Above the Horse Gate the priests made repairs, each one opposite his own house.*

3:30b *After him Meshullam son of Berechiah made repairs opposite his living quarters.*

Nehemiah's participatory style of leadership was not only principled, but strategic too! His model of delegation recognised existing clan and leadership structures, encouraging elders and political leaders to mobilise their own family members and constituencies. Where possible, he allowed people to make repairs near their own dwellings. This would have given them motivation, as the repairs would have increased their own personal security.

Tollefson and Williamson argue that Nehemiah "displayed an open style of leadership and made use of indigenous organisations whenever possible. He delegated authority to fit the task, he incorporated local loyalty groups, and he appealed to self-interest to accomplish the assignments".[5]

3:12   *Next to him Shallum son of Hallohesh, ruler of half the district of Jerusalem, made repairs, he and his daughters.*

3:12 shows that even in Nehemiah's time, women were already involved in work. Even today, many would say this kind of hard labour is not suitable for women. Yet Shallum's daughters have been included in the roll-call of honour. This is a reminder that we should not marginalise women and girls, or make a prior assumption that they cannot do a job that men could do.

Conclusion

Nehemiah acted as a representative of the people in 1:6, confessing their sin. He rallied the people in 2:17-18, mobilising them behind the plan God had put in his heart. In Nehemiah 1 and 2 we caught glimpses of Nehemiah the leader. It is not until Nehemiah 3 that we gain a clear idea of Nehemiah's leadership style. The way Nehemiah involved others in building the walls of Jerusalem shows he was a participatory leader.

The involvement of the whole community (with the exception of the Tekoite nobles) challenges us all to work hard to reconstruct our nation. We have all been called to undertake different roles. If we want to build our nation, we have to make our individual contributions to the work. No one else will do it for us. God has given us talents that are to be used for playing these roles. If we do not use our God-given talents, the nation will be missing something. It is the same in the Church. If every believer does not use his or her spiritual gifts, the Church cannot function as God intended.

Again physical reconstruction and the reconstruction of a covenantal community are linked, albeit more subtly than in Nehemiah 1 and 2. The honour of being listed in Chapter 3 is implicitly contrasted with the shame of 1:3. The social solidarity of being a covenantal community is expressed through the unity of intention displayed in the way the work is done. God used the process of building to the greater end of reconstructing a covenantal community. The lesson for South Sudan is that the kind of community we are aiming for should be expressed in the way we go about reconstructing our nation. If we want an inclusive, democratic nation with responsive and open leadership, every reconstruction project we organise should reflect those values in its design, implementation and leadership structures. We will need to be patient. Organising projects in this way may take longer, but it will be worth it. If we do this, we will see the transformation not only of our physical landscape, but of our communities.

---

1   Lester L Grabbe, *Ezra-Nehemiah*, Old Testament Readings (London: Routledge, 1998), 43.

2   Ibid.

3   Williamson, *Ezra, Nehemiah*, 211.

4   Packer, *A Passion for Faithfulness*, 74.

5   Tollefson and Williamson, "Nehemiah as Cultural Revitalisation," 332.

CHAPTER FOUR
Nehemiah's response
to opposition

In this chapter, we will look at two chapters of the book of Nehemiah: Nehemiah 4 and 6. These chapters record the way Nehemiah dealt with external opposition. The intermediate chapter shows how Nehemiah dealt with internal problems. I will return to Nehemiah 5 in the next chapter.

Nehemiah 4:1-6

Nehemiah met opposition as soon as he arrived in Jerusalem. This came in three forms: psychological warfare, physical threats and personal discouragement.[1]

The Bible is clear that behind human opposition lies spiritual opposition. Paul writes that our battle is *"against the dark spiritual forces of evil in the heavenly realms"* (Ephesians 6:12). Satan uses human agents to oppose the work of God. Evers relates this to Nehemiah.

> The apostle Paul's teaching in this verse is that behind all human antagonism to the gospel message and against ourselves as Christians is the might of Satan and his powerful regiment of demons. But the Lord who has enlisted us in his army is more powerful than the devil. Our divine Captain equips us with armour and gives us strength to conquer (Eph 6:10-11). In the language of Nehemiah, "Our God will fight for us!" God's work, then and now, is accomplished by faith – *"Our God will fight for us"* (4:20) – and hard work – '*So we continued the work*' (4:21).[2]

We were introduced to the human leaders of the opposition in 2:10 and 2:19. In Nehemiah 4:1-6, it is the first two of these opponents, Sanballat the Horonite and Tobiah the Ammonite, who attempt to disrupt the work of rebuilding. They continue and intensify the strategy of psychological warfare employed in 2:19. At this stage, there is no explicit threat of physical violence. Nehemiah prays against their attempts and focuses on continuing God's work.

4:1a *Now when Sanballat heard that we were building the wall, he was angry and greatly enraged,*

Sanballat was from Beth-Horon. His daughter was married to Eliashib, the high priest, or one of his descendants (see comment under 13:28). Sanballat was Governor of Samaria. He was one of those who settled in the central part of Israel, to replace the Israelites when they were conquered and taken away into captivity (2 Kings 17:24).

Until the time of Nehemiah, Jerusalem was under the control of the Governor of Samaria. As Governor, Sanballat benefited from the status quo. The increased autonomy of Jerusalem diminished his political and economic power and represented a threat to his control. A secure and walled Jerusalem could be a future military threat to its neighbours. Although Nehemiah was the king's servant, and had presented letters of authority, there was no guarantee he would not rebel against the king in the future. Sanballat wanted to show himself a loyal servant of the king and avoid jeopardising his relationship with the Persian rulers.[3] Tollefson and Williamson have summed up the perceived threat posed by Nehemiah as follows:

> The Jerusalem restoration project threatened both the economic and political hegemony of Samaria as well as the military stability of the surrounding region. In a series of swift and decisive actions, the leaders in Samaria are described as rapidly escalating the level of opposition from sabre-rattling speeches to the threat of an all-out military attack.[4]

If Nehemiah went to Jerusalem as governor of a new province of Judah, Sanballat's rage would be even easier to understand. Some scholars argue that the mention in 2:8 of a "house" that Nehemiah was to occupy, refers to the construction of the official residence of the governor of the new province of Judah, including Jerusalem. If this view is correct, Nehemiah's arrival would be an indication that things were going to change—a new rival governor was in town, controlling areas that used to be part of Sanballat's own territory, reporting not to Sanballat but directly to the king. Others are more ambivalent, suggesting that the house of 2:8 could equally refer to a dwelling that was to be repaired for Nehemiah's occupancy.[5]

It is easy to see why Sanballat was so angry and enraged, and why, of Nehemiah's three main opponents, he is presented as the instigator of opposition. As Governor of Samaria, Sanballat had the most to lose from the reconstruction and increased autonomy of Jerusalem.

4:1b-2 *and he mocked the Jews. He said in the presence of his associates and of the army of Samaria, 'What are these feeble Jews doing? Will they restore things? Will they sacrifice? Will they finish it in a day? Will they revive the stones out of the heaps of rubbish – and burned ones at that?'*

At first, Sanballat persisted with the strategy he adopted in 2:19. He mocked the people, attempting to shame them in the presence of others. This was part of a strategy of psychological warfare, aiming to discourage and intimidate the builders. The reference to 'burned' stones and 'heaps of rubbish' was designed to remind the builders of the recent destruction referred to in Nehemiah 1:3 and Ezra 4:23. The language is stronger than in 2:19. Sanballat aimed to destroy the confidence of the Jews and reinforce their negative self-image, describing them as 'feeble' and suggesting that their aspirations are unrealistic ("Will they finish it in a day?"). Whereas in 2:19 the insults are made directly, in 4:1b-2 they are made in the presence of others. While at this stage there is no explicit threat of violence, there must have been a danger that Sanballat's insults would incite violence against the Jews.

It is possible that internal critics used the situation to mobilise against Sanballat, painting him as weak for losing control of Jerusalem. Sanballat may have been appealing to an internal constituency of Samaritans who resented the returning Jews, in an attempt to bolster his own leadership. Hostility existed between the capitals of Jerusalem and Samaria. Feelings of enmity between Jews and Samaritans persisted for many generations and can be seen in the New Testament (Luke 10:30-37; John 4:9). It is dangerous to attempt to secure one's own leadership position by stirring up tensions between ethnic groups. Like the hostility between the Jews and the Samaritans, ethnic hatred once stirred up is not easily dissipated. Leaders who profit from such strategies often end up losing power when others turn the same strategy against them.

There is an implicit contrast between the leaderships of Sanballat and Nehemiah. Sanballat used ethnic hatred to mobilise people behind his own leadership. Nehemiah used persuasive testimony to mobilise people behind the plans God had put in his heart.

4:3 *Tobiah the Ammonite was beside him, and he said, 'That stone wall they are building – any fox going up on it would break it down!'*

Tobiah was a high-ranking official allied with Sanballat. He was not a governor like Sanballat, but aimed to ingratiate himself, using intrigue and strategic dealings to increase his personal power and status.

Tobiah is a Jewish name meaning "Yahweh is good".[6] He may have been a nominal believer. Tobiah opposed the rebuilding of the wall, but once the project had been successful, he established a close relationship with Eliashib the High Priest (13:4) and persuaded him to lease the storerooms of the temple to him so that Tobiah could profit by conducting business in the newly-constructed temple. When he was thrown out of the temple, he crossed the Jordan and built his own temple and palace.

Tobiah also used marriage to increase his political connections and influence. He married a daughter of Shecaniah, a Judahite leader, and gave his son Jehohanan in marriage to the daughter of Meshullam.

4:3 depicts Tobiah ingratiating himself to Sanballat, mocking the Jews in the same manner as the governor. Yes-men like Tobiah do not make good advisors. Instead of giving well thought-out, reasoned advice, they say whatever they imagine will please their boss, in order to improve their own standing. They are not loyal. If they think they can advance themselves by switching sides and backing an opponent of their boss, they will do so. Such people are not to be trusted.

4:4-5 *Hear, O our God, for we are despised; turn their taunt back on their own heads, and give them over as plunder in a land of captivity. Do not cover their guilt, and do not let their sin be blotted out from your sight; for they have hurled insults in the face of the builders.*

Nehemiah did not reply directly to Sanballat or Tobiah. Instead, he prayed. Rather than insulting Sanballat and Tobiah, or otherwise contributing to the mounting tension between the Jews and the Samaritans, Nehemiah took his problems to God. "Prayer was a distinct and consistent part of Nehemiah's approach to problem solving."[7]

Packer divides Nehemiah's prayer into two.[8] First, Nehemiah appealed to God to support his servants. Effectively, he prayed for the failure of Sanballat's plan to discourage the workers. Then Nehemiah called for God's judgment on his enemies.

Nehemiah prayed an imprecatory prayer: a prayer of cursing. Such prayers are controversial. Evers has detailed the ways various writers try to tone down Nehemiah's prayer. They suggest that God did not approve of Nehemiah's prayer, or that imprecatory prayers were acceptable in the Old Testament but not in the New Testament, or that many prayers described as imprecatory prayers are actually prophecies.[9] Evers is correct to describe these interpretations as "inadequate".[10] It is appropriate to pray imprecatory prayers, but only ever as a last resort.

Getz argues that Nehemiah's prayer was justifiable: by opposing what Nehemiah was doing, Sanballat and his group were effectively opposing God. "God had already pronounced judgments on Israel's enemies," so "Nehemiah was praying according to God's will."[11] Genesis 12:3 records God's promise to Abraham that God would curse those who cursed his people. Nehemiah was simply praying that God would bring about what he had promised.

Psalm 109 uses similar language. The psalmist's opponents were trying to kill him. Rather than retaliating, the psalmist appealed to God to turn his oppressors' evil back on themselves. The psalmist left justice in God's hands and did not avenge himself.

The command not to avenge ourselves is repeated throughout the Old and New Testaments. Romans 12:19b - "Vengeance is mine, I will repay, says the Lord." - quotes Deuteronomy 32:35a. Leviticus warns us not to take vengeance or bear a grudge against others but rather to love our neighbour as ourselves (Leviticus 19:18). Much of the Law was designed to prevent violence spiralling out of control. As in parts of Africa today, the accepted cultural norm was to avenge the killing of any of their kin. The cycle of vengeance could continue until the whole community was involved (Judges 19-21). Measures including the designation of cities of refuge (Numbers 35:11-29) were designed to stop these cycles of vengeance. The prescription "eye for eye, tooth for tooth" (Exodus 21:24; Leviticus 24:20; Deuteronomy 19:21) did not glorify vengeance, but aimed to stop the cycle of vengeance by ensuring the punishment was no worse than the original act, and resulted in no further violence. Jesus took this principle even further, saying "You have heard that it was said, 'Eye for eye, and tooth for tooth.' But I tell you, do not resist an evil person. If anyone slaps you on the right cheek, turn to him or her the other cheek also. And if anyone wants to sue you and take your shirt, hand over your coat as well. If anyone forces you to go one mile, go with them two miles." (Matthew 5:38-41, NIV).

I quoted many of the above passages when speaking at Emmanuel Jieng Church in Juba on the national day of prayer and fasting held on 8 July 2013 as part of the National Programme for Healing, Peace and Reconciliation. I went on to quote Mahatma Gandhi, who reportedly said that "An eye for an eye leaves the whole world blind". Finally I exhorted the congregation to put an end to the cycle of revenge.

The church has an important role to play in teaching the biblical doctrine of love for enemies and forgiveness of those who wrong us. The church also has a role to play in preventing conflicts. This is not limited to warning of the dangers of war, but should also include proposing alternative ways of resolving problems. When conflicts do occur, it is part of the mandate of the Church to facilitate reconciliation. This is something that all members of the Church should participate in. It is not for the institution of the Church alone.

I have often told Christian leaders that their role is to bless people and not to curse them. In the Bari language, the word for "ordain" is the same as the word for "bless". One who is ordained, set aside or blessed, should bless others, just as Israel was blessed in order to be a blessing (Genesis 12:2). Words of blessing should come from the mouth of one who is himself blessed. This does not mean that pastors should not rebuke or correct others. However, it should be done in accordance with biblical teaching, and out of love rather than anger.

Being a Christian does not mean we will have no enemies. Jesus said *"Love your enemies"* (Matthew 5:44). He did not say "have no enemies". If we are not of the world, the world will hate us and oppose us (John 15:19; 17:14). If we refuse to bow to cultural pressures that are inconsistent with the gospel, like the pressure of revenge, we may find that some in our own communities oppose us. We are, like Nehemiah, faced by the dilemma of what we do with our enemies. Like Nehemiah, we need to start in prayer, aligning ourselves with God's will. Packer offers useful guidelines:

> The truth is that restraining the desire for revenge and asking God to show mercy to *your* enemies by converting them, while at the same time you acknowledge that he will certainly judge *his* enemies, and even asking him to start doing that at once, are not mutually exclusive lines of prayer. Both are expressions of God-glorifying desire, both have the hallowing of God's name as their goal, and of necessity we express both in major ignorance of the details of God's plans as it relates to the destinies of individuals.[12]

There may come a time when we need to pray imprecatory prayers. We should not be in a hurry to pray such prayers. When we do pray them, our aim should be the hallowing of God's name and the fulfilment of his plans. When praying for God to judge his enemies, we should leave open the possibility that some of them will repent and be reconciled to God, even at the very last moment (Matthew 20:1-16).

4:6 *So we rebuilt the wall, and all the wall was joined together to half its height; for the people had a mind to work.*

The people's *"mind to work"* shows that Nehemiah's prayer was successful. God turned the taunt of Sanballat and Tobiah back on their own heads, and it did not affect the builders. Sanballat and Tobiah were not able to convince the people that they were feeble, or that their work would not stand. Their attempts to shame the people and remind them of previous failures had no effect.

The people were not distracted by the opposition of Sanballat and Tobiah. At this stage, the threat posed by the opposition was not explicitly violent. The people did not, therefore, focus on mounting defences or arming themselves. While keeping an eye on the situation, they focused exclusively on rebuilding the wall. As a result, they made considerable progress very quickly.

It is easy to be distracted by rumours of conflict and divert our focus at times when we should be focused exclusively on rebuilding. If we do this, we are playing into our enemy's hands. Sanballat and Tobiah would have been delighted if their taunts had distracted the Jews from rebuilding the wall, without even needing to go to war. The ultimate aim of those who oppose God is to prevent us from doing his work. If we lose our focus on God and his work, and focus on our enemies instead, we risk allowing them to succeed.

This is as true of the dark spiritual forces of evil in the heavenly places (Ephesians 6:12) as it is of our human opponents. When engaged in spiritual warfare, our focus should be on Jesus and his victory. We allow the devil to succeed if we focus too much on him to the detriment of God's work.

Nehemiah 4:7-23

This section shows the action Nehemiah took as the threat changed and became violent. Nehemiah continued to pray, but also took precautions to enable the community to defend itself if it came under attack. He took the advice of his people seriously and involved them in decision-making. He encouraged the people and reminded them that their strength was in the Lord. When his precautionary measures succeeded in avoiding violent conflict completely, he credited the success to God.

4:7-8 *But when Sanballat and Tobiah and the Arabs and the Ammonites and the Ashdodites heard that the repairing of the walls of Jerusalem was going forward and the walls of Jerusalem was going forward and the gaps were beginning to be closed, they were very angry, and all plotted together to come and fight against Jerusalem and to cause confusion in it.*

The number of enemies had now increased. While Sanballat's taunts had not succeeded in disheartening or distracting the Jews, he had managed to mobilise others who resented the returning Jews. The renewed opposition came from all four geographical sides. Sanballat represents Samaria, to the north of Judah. The Arabians were Judah's southern neighbours. The Ammonites were to Judah's east and the Ashdodites to its west.[13]

4:9 *So we prayed to our God, and set a guard as a protection against them day and night.*

This threat of invasion only served to strengthen the people's solidarity under Nehemiah.[14] For the first time in the book, it is not only Nehemiah as an individual who prays, but *"we"*, Nehemiah together with the people. In 4:1 and 4:6, *"we"* built the wall. In 4:9, *"we"* prayed. Participating in God's work and a strengthened relationship with God go hand in hand. No doubt the people learned from the example of their prayerful leader Nehemiah.

Now that the threat was physical, further action was needed. As of yet, the opposition were still plotting. They were not ready to attack. However, their intent was clear. Added vigilance was needed. For as long as possible, Nehemiah had the people focus exclusively on rebuilding. He did not ready them for battle until it was absolutely necessary. However, he was not naïve or complacent, and posted a guard, providing limited protection against a sneak attack and watching carefully for a build-up of enemy forces requiring additional action.

4:10-13 *But Judah said, "The strength of the burden bearers is failing, and there is too much rubbish so that we are unable to work on the wall." And our enemies said, "They will not know or see anything before we come upon them and kill them and stop the work." When the Jews who lived near them came, they said to us ten times, "From all the places where they live they will come up against us." So in the lowest parts of the space behind the wall, in open places, I stationed the people according to their families, with their swords, their spears, and their bows.*

Again, Nehemiah is presented as a participatory leader. Nehemiah involved the people. He listened to them and took their advice seriously. They were involved in decision-making and not only in the work itself. At this time, the threat was so severe that Nehemiah delayed the work to ensure the security of the people. He demonstrated flexibility, altering his plan and redeploying his workers.

The Jews who lived nearest to their enemies were adamant about the seriousness of the threat. They relayed their concerns to the rest of the people ten times. If Nehemiah had not acted, he could have faced desertion.[15] Certainly the unity of the people, shown in 2:18 and 3:1-32, would have been threatened. Unity is an essential precondition for the success of God's people in carrying out his work (John 17:20-23).

Listening to people, and showing that their opinions are important and valued by acting on them, is crucial for maintaining unity. While it is important to have a plan, no plan should be set in stone. All organisations should ensure that feedback is gathered throughout the duration of a project, and plans modified accordingly.

Kidner suggests that Nehemiah's choice of the "lowest parts" of the space behind the wall "was presumably dictated by the still inadequate height of the walls".[16] The partially-rebuilt wall provided a partial defence to attack. Concentrating on rebuilding rather than being distracted by taunts and rumours meant the Jews were in a better position to defend themselves when the threat was real. It is the same for us in South Sudan. Development, education, improved infrastructure, a strengthened economy, and trauma healing all contribute to security.

4:14 *After I looked these things over, I stood up and said to the nobles and the officials and the rest of the people, "Do not be afraid of them. Remember the LORD, who is great and awesome, and fight for your kin, your sons, your daughters, your wives, and your homes.*

Nehemiah continuously encouraged the people and reminded them of God's protection. The command not to be afraid of our enemies can be obeyed by remembering how great and awesome the Lord is in comparison. Jesus made a similar comparison when he commanded us not to fear those who *"kill the body, and after that can do nothing more"*, but rather to fear *"him who, after he has killed, has authority to cast into hell"* (Luke 12:4-5). Nehemiah also used the everyday things that mattered most to the people—their family and homes—to rally them.

4:15 *When our enemies heard that their plot was known to us, and that God had frustrated it, we all returned to the wall, each to his work.*

Once the immediate threat was over, the people started building again. There were no celebrations. Completion of God's work of reconstruction, not frustration of Sanballat and Tobiah's plot, would represent true victory over their enemies. Then they would celebrate.

As in 2:8 and 2:19, God is given the credit for frustrating Sanballat and Tobiah's plot. The careful judgement and decisive action shown by Nehemiah is highly impressive. Without these constant reminders of God's sovereignty and action, it would be easy to write God out of the story, crediting Nehemiah for his successes. Nehemiah himself refused to do this. For Nehemiah, taking action was not contrary to prayer or recognition of God's sovereignty.

4:16-18 *From that day on, half of my servants worked on construction, and half held the spears, shields, bows, and body-armour; and the leaders posted themselves behind the whole house of Judah, who were building the wall. The burden bearers carried their loads in such a way that each laboured on the work with one hand and with the other held a weapon. And each of the builders had his sword strapped at his side while he built. The man who sounded the trumpet was beside me.*

The people returned to work, but they did not disarm. Nehemiah's flexible approach allowed him to adapt to a fast-changing situation. As Kidner has shown, Nehemiah made four separate counter-moves against opponents of the project in Nehemiah 4, maintaining security while ensuring the maximum amount of work was done.

> He was not a man to fight new battles with old tricks. Taunts had been met with prayer and concentrated work (1-6); plots by prayer and guard-duty (7-9); stronger threats by a general call to arms and the charge to 'keep your minds on the Lord ... and fight' (10-14, cf. JB). Now the temporary lull is accepted for what it is: a chance to start building again, but not to disarm.[17]

Nehemiah did not appeal to outsiders for help. Despite the imperial backing he enjoyed, he did not send a messenger to the Persian king. Instead, he used what he had available to overcome the challenges he faced. We in South Sudan can learn from this. Too often we look to donors and development partners for all our needs. We need to find local solutions to our problems.

The tendency to seek help from outsiders reinforces the negative self-perception of many South Sudanese. Weanzana writes that many people in Africa are pessimists.[18] They assume that poverty is their fate. He calls on the Christian church to "bring hope, and renewed energy for the task of reconstruction."[19] Men and women of Nehemiah's stature can empower communities, helping them to find local solutions based on the resources and abilities they already have, restoring their dignity in the process.

In 2005, I attended a conference where General Lazarus Sumbeiywo, who mediated the Comprehensive Peace Agreement, gave a keynote address. When asked what he prayed for the people of South Sudan, he said he hoped the peace agreement would help restore the dignity of the people of South Sudan.

4:19-20 *And I said to the nobles, the officials and the rest of the people, "The work is great and widely spread out, and we are separated far from one another on the wall. Rally to us wherever you hear the sound of the trumpet. Our God will fight for us."*

As in 4:14, Nehemiah continued to encourage those he worked with, constantly reminding them of God's power and control over the situation. It is important to encourage those we work with. Such encouragement comes in many forms—a thank-you note, a mention in a formal address, a quiet word of appreciation.

Opposition had not stopped. Yet Nehemiah did not despair, or complain, or curse. He found a way of continuing the work even when workers were isolated and vulnerable to attack. He took precautions, putting in place a system for mutual support, but ultimately relying on God for protection. We all face different types of opposition, challenges and problems in our lives. We should turn to the Lord in prayer, seek support from fellow believers, but ultimately continue the work in God's strength. The devil is always looking for new ways to attack us. However, our God will fight for us.

4:21-23 *So we laboured at the work, and half of them held the spears from the break of dawn until the stars came out. I also said to the people at that time, "Let every man and his servant pass the night inside Jerusalem, so that they may be a guard for us by night and may labour by day." So neither I nor my brothers nor my servants nor the men of the guard who followed me ever took off my clothes; each kept his weapon in his right hand.*

Nehemiah and the builders showed their commitment to the rebuilding project by working all available hours, from dawn until nightfall. They remained on standby 24 hours a day. Aside from the need for security, Williamson suggests two reasons for the policy of encouraging workers to spend their nights in Jerusalem.[20] Firstly, it saved them time as workers did not need to travel to and from their homes. Secondly, it prevented workers from drifting away as things got more difficult.

Nehemiah 6:1-19

In this section, the threat changes once again. Nehemiah's opponents try to attack him personally, by setting up an attempted ambush, by smearing him, and through espionage. Nehemiah sees through their plans and avoids falling into their traps. As in 4:1-6, he does not focus unduly on dealing with his opponents, and as long as they do not present a physical threat to the completion of the project, concentrates instead on the work of reconstruction. As a result, the builders complete the work in only 52 days. Due in part to Nehemiah's earlier testimony, the nations recognise the hand of God in this extraordinary accomplishment. Completion of the work acts as a powerful witness to God's power and control.

6:1-4 *Now when it was reported to Sanballat and Tobiah and to Geshem the Arab and to the rest of our enemies that I had built the wall and that there was no gap left in it (though up to that time I had not set up the doors in the gates), Sanballat and Geshem sent to me, saying, "Come and let us meet together in one of the villages in the plain of Ono." But they intended to do me harm. So I sent messengers to them, saying, "I am doing a great work and I cannot come down. Why should the work stop while I leave it to come down to you?" They sent to me four times in this way, and I answered them in the same manner.*

Sanballat is again the instigator here (see 6:5), working this time with Geshem. The pair attempted to draw Nehemiah out into the open so they could assassinate him. Evidently they had been impressed by the leadership shown by Nehemiah, and decided the only way they could stop the building work from being completed was to strike at the head.

No doubt Nehemiah realised their intent. The plain of Ono was an open and insecure place, and bordered hostile districts. Nonetheless, Nehemiah did not escalate tensions by accusing them. Instead, he replied tactfully, saying he was busy and could not spare the time. Kidner writes that the plain of Ono was between Samaria and Jerusalem. It would have taken more than a day's travel to reach.[21] There was no reason for Nehemiah to allow his enemies to distract him from the work of reconstruction. Nehemiah displayed wisdom in saying no to this invitation.

While it might seem obvious to decline this invitation, there are many leaders today who prefer to spend their time in high-profile meetings with other leaders, even those they oppose, rather than getting on with the task of development. We can learn from Nehemiah's sense of priorities and his resolute focus on the task of reconstruction given to him by God.

We too need to be wise in our use of time. Many matters can easily be concluded over the telephone rather than making a long trip to agree a simple matter face to face. South Sudan now has mobile telephone networks working in most parts of the country. We need to take advantage of this. Of course, some matters still require face-to-face meetings. Personal counselling, for example, should be done this way.

6:5-9 In the same way Sanballat for the fifth time sent his servant to me with an open letter in his hand. In it was written, "It is reported among the nations – and Geshem also says it – that you and the Jews intend to rebel; that is why you are building the wall; and according to this report you wish to become their king. You have also set up prophets to proclaim in Jerusalem concerning you, "There is a king in Judah!" And now it will be reported to the king according to these words. So come, therefore, and let us confer together." Then I sent to him, saying, "No such things as you say have been done; you are inventing them out of your own mind" - for they all wanted to frighten us, thinking, "Their hands will drop from the work, and it will not be done." But now, O God, strengthen my hands.

Sanballat realised he would not be able to draw Nehemiah out into a place where he could do him physical harm. Instead, he aimed to sabotage Nehemiah's reputation, circulating rumours and putting them into the public domain. These serious accusations could have led to a charge of treason. Together with Tobiah's letters (6:17-19), they were meant to frighten Nehemiah.

Nehemiah was not easily intimidated. He refuted the allegations, brushing them aside as quickly as possible. He spent as little time as possible focusing on his enemies and as much time as possible doing God's work. Nehemiah continued to be rooted in prayer, offering one of his fax/arrow/sentence prayers in 6:9 (as at 1:4).

6:10 *One day when I went into the house of Shemaiah son of Delaiah son of Mehetabel, who was confined to his house, he said, "Let us meet together in the house of God, within the temple, and let us close the doors of the temple, for they are coming to kill you; indeed, tonight they are coming to kill you."*

Sanballat's direct approaches to Nehemiah had failed. Now, he operated through others. Together with Tobiah, he approached a Jew with a reputation as a prophet and bribed him to act as a double agent. Shemaiah was instructed to claim he had uncovered a plot against Nehemiah's life and urge him to seek asylum in the temple.

6:11 *But I said, "Should a man like me run away? Would a man like me go into the temple to save his life? I will not go in!"*

Sanballat and Tobiah hoped to undermine Nehemiah's reputation as a bold, decisive leader, by portraying him as a coward who fled danger. We have already seen that Nehemiah was a participatory leader. He did not ask others to do what he was not willing to do himself. Saving himself while leaving his workers in danger could have been fatal to his leadership, destroying the builders' confidence in him and leading to mutiny. Nehemiah recognised all this. He was not the sort of man to run away.

However, there was an even more sinister motive behind the suggestion Nehemiah should seek asylum in the temple. The law clearly stated that no one was to come near the altar (Numbers 3:10; 18:7). Kidner reminds us that when King Uzziah trespassed through the temple, he "had been fortunate to escape with no more than leprosy (2 Ch. 26:16ff.; cf Nu. 18:7)."[22] Only priests could enter the temple enclosure, and even then only under certain circumstances. Nehemiah was not a priest.

By accusing him of rebellion, Sanballat had tried to poison Nehemiah's relationship with the king. If he had successfully painted Nehemiah as a coward, he could have ruined his relationship with his workers. But nothing could have jeopardised Nehemiah's mission more than spoiling his relationship with God. It was God who had called him (2:12), God who answered his many prayers, and God who granted him success (2:10, 19; 4:15).

Nehemiah's knowledge of scripture helped him to see through this ruse and avoid contaminating himself. He knew that entering God's presence in an inappropriate way was so serious an offence that it was better to lose his own life, and responded accordingly: "Would a man like me go into the temple to save his life?" (6:11b).

As discussed in Chapter One, Nehemiah's aim was not simply to rebuild the city walls. Connected to this was the reconstruction of a covenantal community. Nehemiah could not help in reconstructing a covenantal community if he violated the covenant himself by breaking one of God's most important commands. There are no shortcuts to building God's kingdom. We should never be tempted to imagine we can serve God by doing something that is against his character or biblical teaching (for example, by forcing a non-believer to convert to Christianity). Any attempt to do so will backfire.

6:12-13 *Then I perceived and saw that God had not sent him at all, but he had pronounced the prophecy against me because Tobiah and Sanballat had hired him. He was hired for this purpose, to intimidate me and make me sin by acting in this way, and so they could give me a bad name, in order to taunt me.*

Getz writes that Nehemiah discerned two flaws with Shemaiah's prophecy.[23] God would not have asked Nehemiah to flee when the project of building was so close to completion. Likewise, "no true prophet would ask someone to violate God's law."[24] Shemaiah's prophecy could not therefore be from God. If it was not from God, who was it from? In the light of Sanballat and Tobiah's previous actions, the culprits were obvious.

We must be careful of false prophets. There are those who seek to make material gain or impress men by claiming to be prophets, but who are not. Some preach a gospel contrary to the true gospel. We will be better able to test prophecy if we know scripture well. No true prophecy will contradict scripture, or call on us to do something that scripture forbids.

6:14 *Remember Tobiah and Sanballat, O my God, according to these things that they did, and also the prophetess Noadiah and the rest of the prophets who wanted to make me afraid.*

Nehemiah's prayer to God to punish Tobiah and Sanballat echoes his prayer in 4:4-5. Again, Nehemiah only prays an imprecatory prayer when it is in line with God's will. Effectively, he prays that God will judge God's own enemies who have opposed God's own plan.

The mention of the prophetess Noadiah reminds us that even in the Old Testament, there were female prophets.[25] Honourable prophetesses and female leaders mentioned in the Old Testament include Miriam (Exodus 15:19-21), Deborah (Judges 4:5) and Huldah (2 Kings 22:14-20; 2 Chronicles 34:22-28), a contemporary of the prophet Jeremiah. Unlike Noadiah and Shemaiah, Miriam and Deborah "used their gifts not for sordid gain or prestige but for the glory of God."[26]

6:15-16 *So the wall was finished on the twenty-fifth day of the month Elul, in fifty-two days. And when all our enemies heard of it, all the nations around us were afraid and fell greatly in their own esteem; for they perceived that this work had been accomplished with the help of our God.*

The repairs to the wall were completed in just 52 days! This was an amazing accomplishment, especially in view of the challenges and obstacles that Nehemiah faced.

The success of the project was attributed to God's help. This was no accident. Nehemiah frequently invoked God's name (4:4, 14, 20, etc.) and credited God for his successes (2:18, 20 etc.) en route to the completion of the walls. Nehemiah's insistent recognition of God's sovereignty and his willingness to give God the glory rubbed off on others. Because Nehemiah attributed his success to God, others did too – even those outside the community of God's people. Glorifying God and witnessing to others go hand in hand.

It is part of the role of the Church to identify God's activity in the story of our communities and testify to it. Israel frequently recalled the story their community and of God's action in it as part of their worship. Special festivals helped them to remember what God had done. The power of memory is an important theme in the book of Nehemiah.[27] It is perhaps most clearly seen in Nehemiah 8 and 9, which show the people celebrating one of these festivals and reciting the story of their community.

We remember and celebrate God's action in the universal story of the Church when we read scripture and celebrate Christmas, Easter, Pentecost and other Christian festivals. However, we need to recall God's action in the particular stories of our communities as well as in the universal story of the Church. For this to be possible, the Church must first identify God's actions and give him the credit for them. Then we are in a position to recite and celebrate them.

Opposition backfired as it only served to make the accomplishment more impressive. God worked the evil actions of Sanballat, Tobiah and Geshem into his plan, using them to increase the glory of his achievement and cause the nations to see his own hand in human history. This is not an isolated occurrence in scripture. God told Moses that "... *I will harden Pharaoh's heart, and I will multiply my signs and wonders in Egypt. When*

Pharaoh will not listen to you, I will lay my hand on Egypt and bring my people the Israelites, company by company, out of the land of Egypt by great acts of judgement. The Egyptians shall know that I am the LORD, when I stretch out my hand against Egypt and bring the Israelites out from among them." (Exodus 7:3-5, see also 14:4, 18). In the case of Sanballat, Tobiah and Geshem, there is no biblical evidence to suggest God himself hardened their hearts, but the effect of opposition was the same.

The parallel with such an important, foundational, memory is very important. Ezra's prayer recorded in Nehemiah 9 specifically recalls Exodus 7:3-5, linking God's making a name for himself, *"as it is to this day"* (9:10), with the signs and wonders performed against Pharaoh and Egypt. This strengthens the view that there is a deliberate parallel between Nehemiah 6:15-16 and Exodus 7:3-5. Both are new beginnings. In both cases, God's salvific actions are the basis for covenant with him (Nehemiah 9:38; Exodus 19:4-5). In both cases, the history of God's actions has been carefully preserved (hence the emphasis on record-keeping in the book of Nehemiah), serving as a powerful memory inspiring obedience to God's commands among future generations of God's people.

The Egyptians are not the only nation besides Israel to whom God revealed himself through his actions. Isaiah 49:26 foretold that the restoration of Israel and the defeat of Israel's oppressors would lead *"all mankind"* to *"know that I, the LORD, am your Saviour, your Redeemer, the Mighty One of Jacob"* (NIV). *"They will know that I am the LORD"* is the dominant refrain of Ezekiel. God's actions will cause Israel to know that he is the LORD (many instances, for example, 5:13; 6:7; 13:9, 14; 16:62; 23:49; 33:29; 36:38; 37:6, 14). However, Ezekiel was also given a similar message to prophesy to Ammon (25:5, 7), Moab (25:11), the Philistines (25:17), Tyre (26:6), Sidon (28:22, 23), Egypt (29:6, 9, 16; 30:19, 26; 32:15), the allies of Egypt – including Cush, thought to have included the territory of South Sudan (30:8) and Edom (35:4, 9, 12, 15). Even creation itself will know the LORD through his actions (17:24; 36:11). Toward the end of the book, it is the nations in general (36:23, 36; 37:28; 38:23; 39:6, 7, 21, 23, 27) who will come to an understanding of God's holiness through his treatment of Israel. Clearly, God's action in human history is one of the primary ways in which he reveals himself. The prophet can help people to recognise his action by signposting it. God's supreme revelation in human history was in Jesus Christ, but he continues to reveal himself today through his intervention in history.

Nehemiah 6:15-16 represents a partial fulfilment of many of these prophecies. The nations around Israel saw what had happened and attributed it to God. Their respect for Israel and Israel's God increased.[28] As often happens when people become more aware of God's might and majesty, the nations recognised their own inadequacy. This happened to Peter, who came to an awareness of his own sin when he saw Jesus' power over nature (Luke 5:8).

Nehemiah saw the completion of the city walls. Some leaders see the Promised Land only in the distance, like Moses, without entering it (Deuteronomy 34:1-4). This was the case for Dr John Garang de Mabior, the First Vice-President of Sudan and President of the then Government of Southern Sudan, who led the SPLM/A for 21 years but died in August 2005 shortly after signing the Comprehensive Peace Agreement. Hebrews 11 gives a long list of those who *"though they were commended for their faith, did not receive what was promised"* (Hebrews 11:39). Not all of us will see the fruit of the good works God calls us to carry out (Ephesians 2:10). Nonetheless, all of us can learn from Nehemiah's faithful obedience to God's calling on his life, and his passion to complete it.

6:17-19 *Moreover in those days the nobles of Judah sent many letters to Tobiah, and Tobiah's letters came to them. For many in Judah were bound by oath to him, because he was the son-in-law of Shecaniah son of Arah: and his son Jehohanan had married the daughter of Meshullam son of Berechiah. Also they spoke of his good deeds in my presence, and reported my words to him. And Tobiah sent letters to intimidate me.*

Opposition persisted beyond the rebuilding of the walls. Tobiah was related by marriage to some of the rulers of the people of Judah. These links were embarrassing in themselves, but worse still, Tobiah exploited them by "intrigues, persuasive talk, leaks of information and threatening letters."[29] A lack of internal unity and political intrigues among the ruling class of the nation provided greater possibilities for external opponents to undermine the community than any threat they had been able to muster themselves.

South Sudan has many enemies who would like to see the new country fail. Enemies do not magically disappear on the assumption of statehood after two long civil wars. Just as Nehemiah did not underestimate the opposition he faced, South Sudan cannot be naïve about the threat it faces. Like Nehemiah, South Sudan faces a realistic threat of military incursions by its enemies. It must be prepared and take appropriate precautions.

Like Nehemiah, South Sudan's enemies attempt to smear its reputation so as to undermine its support from powerful international friends. South Sudan too must have a good communication strategy capable of rebutting the propaganda marshalled against it.

However, Nehemiah did not focus on his enemies. He kept a close eye on their movements and took action when he needed to, but his main focus was on the task of reconstruction, which he knew would provide security in itself. He did not allow threats to distract him from reconstruction. South Sudan can learn from Nehemiah in that respect too. We do not need to be afraid of the external threats our enemies muster against us. The reality is that just as they did for Nehemiah, internal disunity and political intrigues among the ruling class present greater dangers for South Sudan than external threats. Our enemies know how to exploit disunity between leaders and among the general population. Maintaining unity is therefore key. Nehemiah 5, to which we will shortly turn, offers some key lessons in how to maintain unity in the face of serious internal challenges.

Conclusion

Any attempt to make change is likely to meet opposition – especially when it challenges vested interests. When we participate in the work of God, we can expect even more opposition. Like Nehemiah, we will face obstacles and challenges in our ministries.

Rather than focus on the problem, Nehemiah focused on God and on completing the work God called him to. No problem is insurmountable. God is bigger than any challenge we might face. As we pray and read the Bible, he will give us wisdom through his Spirit to work through our problems.

Nehemiah 4 and 6 are very practical chapters. They show Nehemiah recognising and identifying problems quickly, and picking out the best option or combination of options for solving the problem. Nehemiah looked to see what resources—including human resources—were already available and used them to overcome obstacles to completion of the project, rather than designing solutions that relied on further support from the king. He recognised and harnessed the power of memory. And he prayed, not only in the lead-up to implementation of his project, but at all times.

We can learn from Nehemiah as individuals, but also as a nation. Many of the lessons for dealing with external opponents are particularly relevant for an underdeveloped nation recovering from years of war, with enemies on our doorstep and powerful but distant allies whose support is welcome but cannot be relied on. These lessons include the importance of national prayer, crediting God for our successes, keeping our focus on reconstruction, and reconciling divergent interests so our enemies cannot exploit disunity.

1   Packer, *A Passion for Faithfulness*, 99.
2   Evers, *Doing a Great Work*, 132.
3   Packer, *A Passion for Faithfulness*, 96.
4   Tollefson and Williamson, "Nehemiah as Cultural Revitalisation," 333.
5   Myers, *Ezra, Nehemiah*, 100.
6   Packer, *A Passion for Faithfulness*, 97.
7   Getz, "Nehemiah," 681.
8   Packer, *A Passion for Faithfulness*, 101.
9   Evers, *Doing a Great Work*, 128.
10 Ibid.
11 Getz, "Nehemiah," 682.
12 Packer, *A Passion for Faithfulness*, 103.
13 Williamson, *Ezra, Nehemiah*, 225.
14 Packer, *A Passion for Faithfulness*, 107.
15 Williamson, *Ezra, Nehemiah*, 226.
16 Kidner, *Ezra and Nehemiah*, 92–3.
17 Ibid., 93.
18 Weanzana, "Nehemiah," 548.
19 Ibid.
20 Williamson, *Ezra, Nehemiah*, 229.
21 Kidner, *Ezra and Nehemiah*, 98.
22 Ibid., 100.
23 Getz, "Nehemiah," 686.
24 Ibid.
25 Kidner, *Ezra and Nehemiah*, 100.
26 Evers, *Doing a Great Work*, 147–8.
27 The power of memory is a recurring theme in Walter Brueggemann's writings. See especially *Hopeful Imagination*, 101–2, 115, 124, 131–2.
28 Kidner, *Ezra and Nehemiah*, 101.
29 Ibid.

CHAPTER FIVE

Nehemiah faces internal problems

Nehemiah 5:1-5

Nehemiah 5:1-5 outlines the complaints brought to Nehemiah by disadvantaged members of the community. 5:6-13 details Nehemiah's response.

There is no consensus about the sequencing of this passage. Many commentators believe the events in Nehemiah 5:1-13 did not take place during the building of the wall, but at a later date. Throntveit believes that Nehemiah 5 was originally placed after Nehemiah 13, noting stylistic parallels between the two passages.[1] Grabbe appears to take the view that the events took place after the rebuilding of the wall but during Nehemiah's first term as governor. He argues that Nehemiah could not have brought Jews out of slavery (5:8) to foreigners in the short time it took to rebuild the wall.[2] However, Williamson reckons Nehemiah was referring to a redemption programme that had started before Nehemiah's arrival.[3] The objections that have been raised against the sequencing of this passage are circumstantial. No good reason has been provided to place Nehemiah 5 elsewhere in the story.

Nevertheless, it is clear that the passage is not placed in its present location purely for historical reasons. There are also theological factors to be considered. Sandwiched between Nehemiah 4 and 6, Nehemiah 5 shows that there were also internal threats, which were of more concern to Nehemiah than the external threats detailed in the preceding and following chapters. I showed in Chapter Three how Nehemiah did not allow external threats to distract from rebuilding the walls. He dealt with them as quickly as possible so that work could continue. Here, however, Nehemiah paused the work, and held a great assembly. He recognised that the threat from within was more dangerous because it undermined "the exiles' most precious asset, their unity."[4]

I have already shown how Nehemiah 3 highlights the importance of unity of intention. Nehemiah 5 shows Nehemiah taking every possible step to preserve unity. Unity was important for practical reasons. If Nehemiah had not acted, he might have lost many of his workers.[5] This would have delayed completion of the walls. Unity is also important in itself. Scripture tells us God delights in the unity of believers (Psalm 133:1). It is also a precondition for witnessing (John 17:23). We are bad witnesses when the Church is divided. If Nehemiah had not dealt with the threat to unity, and the community remained divided—and especially if this meant the project was not completed or took much longer to complete—the nations may not have seen God's hand in unfolding events.

Nehemiah 5 also gives clear lessons in how to preserve unity. True unity is not an imposed unity which masks inequality, or where some are first-class and others second-class citisens. That is the kind of unity which the South Sudanese rejected in January 2011. True unity is not achieved by sweeping division under the carpet. True unity exposes division and inequality so it can be dealt with. Nehemiah 5 is an important counter-balancing force to Nehemiah 3, which might otherwise suggest that "everything in the community was sweetness and light."[6]

South Sudan must not repeat the mistakes of the former Sudan by imposing a false unity which subsumes identities and masks inequalities. Allowing dissenting voices (especially the voices of the poor), including all communities, and respecting diversity are hallmarks of true unity. The National Programme for Healing, Peace and Reconciliation is an ideal opportunity for forging genuine unity by ensuring that all are included and all voices are heard.

Nehemiah 4-6 is an integrated unit. Nehemiah 4 presents a purely external threat. Nehemiah 5 presents internal threats. Nehemiah 6 begins with external threats and culminates in a combination of internal and external threat (Sanballat bribing Shemaiah to prophesy falsely to Nehemiah).[7] The three chapters are designed to climax at the end of Nehemiah 6, demonstrating that no threat could sabotage the work of reconstruction because the work was done with the help of God (6:16).

The location of Nehemiah 5 in the first half of the book also helps to connect the two parts of the book. It shows that the reconstruction of a covenantal community, characterised by a sense of solidarity and a commitment to God's law, was Nehemiah's priority from the beginning. He did not wait until the walls were rebuilt before starting to rebuild community. For us in South Sudan, the building of physical infrastructure cannot precede the healing of our communities, but must go alongside it. Material development alone will not solve our problems.

Although I reject Throntveit's assertion that Nehemiah 5 originally followed Nehemiah 13, his comments about the stylistic similarities between 5:1-19, 13:15-22 and 13:23-29 are helpful. He has shown that these three sections follow the same pattern:

1. Time reference: "In those days..." (15a, 23a)
2. Description of problem: "I saw..." (15a-16, 23a-24)
3. Rebuke: "I remonstrated/contended (both rib) with ...," making use of rhetorical questions and historical retrospects (17-18, 25-27)
4. Specific action (19-20, 28)
5. Threat (21, 29)
6. Statement of resolution (22a, 30-31a)
7. Remembrance formula: "Remember me..." (22b, 31b)

Nehemiah 5 foreshadows Nehemiah 13. It shows that the problems Nehemiah encountered on his return to Jerusalem were not new, but were a return to old ways. It emphasises the importance of social justice, one of the three key areas where God's people had failed, and the lack of which had helped bring about the exile. The need for social justice (a more equal society with less poverty and where the poor are fairly treated) is addressed in Ezra's prayer of confession, and in the new laws which the people subsequently committed themselves to. Nehemiah 5 prepares the reader for these events.

Isaiah 58 suggests that successful rebuilding is connected to the practice of social justice.[8] The rebuke "Look, you serve your own interest on your fast day, and oppress all your workers" (58:3b) is followed by the promise that "Your ancient ruins shall be rebuilt... If you refrain from trampling the sabbath; from pursuing your own interests on my holy day... not going your own ways, serving your own interests, or pursuing your own affairs;" (58:12-13). Isaiah 61:1-4 links the Day of Jubilee, a central part of the social justice provisions set out in the Mosaic law (Isaiah 61:2a, cf. Leviticus 25) with building up ancient ruins and repairing ruined cities (Isaiah 61:4).

Nehemiah 5 has much to teach us about resolving disputes, integrating the material, the social and the spiritual, and working for a more equal society. It is a crucial chapter which holds the whole book together. We ignore its message at our peril.

5:1 *Now there was a great outcry of the people and of their wives against their Jewish kin.*

It is likely that the issues identified in 5:2-5 had been problems for some time. The people raised them now in the hope that a new governor would be more willing than previous officials to address them. Nehemiah had quickly built a reputation as a man of action. Perhaps he would take some steps that others had not taken.

The wives of the people receive a special mention. Allen and Laniak follow Vogt in suggesting that a better translation would be "the people and especially their wives".[9] Some commentators have suggested that women were more aware of the problems, since they were at home during the crucial period of the harvest, whereas the men were building the wall.[10] There may be some truth in this. However, the impression given is of an unjust system which had been operating for some time. The work of rebuilding the walls was completed in 52 days. The builders must themselves have been aware of the problems.

In many communities within South Sudan, women play a traditional role as guardians of truth. Women have also played a crucial role in local peace processes. The successful Akobo conference in 1994 was used as a model for the celebrated Wunlit conference which reunited warring Dinka and Nuer tribes.[11] At Akobo,

> Women played a particularly effective witnessing role at the conference, acting as an informal "truth commission". Each a *maan naath* (mother of the nation), the Nuer women would shout down any man whose accounts contained falsehoods. The shame of the women's hoots drove a number of men to revise their testimony, to avoid the embarrassment of being tainted as liars.[12]

Women were also highly involved in mobilising for peace conferences, and held their own women's conferences as part of the people-to-people peacemaking process. We should not therefore be surprised to see that women played a prominent role in bringing to light the problems that plagued the people of Judah.

5:2 *For there were those who said, "With our sons and our daughters, we are many; we must get grain, so that we may eat and stay alive."*

There have been suggestions that there was not enough grain to eat because the people had left their day-to-day work to rebuild the walls. Kidner suggests that 5:2 should be interpreted as a complaint that "you can't eat walls."[13] The absence of men from their fields may have brought the problem to a head, but this has been overstated by many commentators. Fensham rightly says that the people "probably accepted the measures of Nehemiah as necessary" and points out that "their complaint was not levelled at Nehemiah".[14] The text itself gives clear reasons why there was not enough grain, including famine (5:3).

Nehemiah could easily have dismissed the complaint as the grumblings of lazy workers who wanted to leave their posts at the walls. Sometimes, even when we think a complaint is not justified, there may be underlying causes that need to be addressed. We need to pry deeper to find out the real problem, rather than sending the complainant away.

The complainants pointed out that they had large families and not enough food to feed them. Williamson writes that "Jews would never complain about the size of their families because children were regarded as a mark of God's blessing."[15] This is also the case in Africa. An old man I knew used to say he would continue to have children as long as he was able to. Then, at the beginning of every school term, he would beg for assistance to pay his children's school fees. Modern economic realities require us to use our God-given brains to limit the size of our families to what we can manage.

Some argue that South Sudan lost 2.2 million people during the war and that we need to replace them. They often quote the Bible: "be fruitful and multiply" (Genesis 1:28; 9:7; 35:11). I often respond by saying that God gave this command to humankind and that it was not to be fulfilled by a single individual. One person should not try to replace on his own the people who died during the war.

5:3 *There were also those who said, "We are having to pledge our fields, our vineyards, and our houses in order to get grain during the famine."*

Wealthier people in the community took advantage of conditions of famine to enrich themselves while leaving the poor even poorer. They lent money at exorbitant rates of interest[16] and took the houses and fields of the poor when they defaulted. They sold grain at high prices and bought land at low prices.

Technically, the system of pledges was permitted under the Mosaic law. The lenders may have claimed that they were not breaking the law and were just doing the best thing for their own families. However, the law also forbade people from taking advantage of the poor. Pledges were to be returned if keeping them would cause undue suffering (Deuteronomy 24:10-13; cf. Exodus 22:26). Legal rights were subject to the condition of love.[17] Chris Wright has written that biblical justice

> goes beyond a calculus of rights and deserts. Because it is fundamentally relational it always blends into *compassion* for those who are vulnerable. So, in biblical economics, wealth that God has enabled us to produce must always be held and used with a compassionate heart and hand. Compassion is, of course, a matter of the heart and emotions, but it is also a covenantal duty and can therefore be commanded. The important thing is not whether you *feel* compassion, but whether you *act* with compassion.[18]

The lack of love shown by the rich must have been a great source of disappointment to Nehemiah. No doubt this was part of Satan's attempt to discourage him. Behind unjust economic relations lies the greed of people. Behind greed lies the enemy.

Famines or poor harvests are common in South Sudan. If we are blessed and have more than others in our community, we must make sure we do not take advantage by selling to the poor at high prices, even if those high prices are the market rate. We must consider the matter from the perspective of the poor and not only what is best for our own families.

We also need to consider the background to this social conflict. As discussed under 1:2, the "elite of the land" (2 Kings 23:15) had been carried off into exile while the poorest had been left behind. It is likely that the poor took control of the land vacated by the rich. The rich used the conditions of famine to get back the land they considered theirs. They may have thought those who took their land were getting their just deserts. The poor, on the other hand, would have perceived the situation as "a simple case of class conflict in which wealthy landowners were exploiting deprived peasants."[19]

Nehemiah's family were part of the elite who had been carried off into exile. He was accustomed to mixing with the elite at the king's palace. We might assume his sympathies would lie with the rich: they did not. We might expect Nehemiah to find a compromise, or, as international mediators would call it, a 'win-win outcome': he did not. Nehemiah sided resolutely with the poor. The biblical text interprets the situation through the eyes of the poor, and does not take a balanced view.

We have a God who takes the side of the poor (1 Samuel 2:8; Luke 1:53; etc.). Nehemiah, despite sharing an economic and cultural background with the rich, exercised a preferential option for the poor. The liberation theologian Gustavo Gutierrez has written that our conversion to the Lord implies a conversion to the neighbour:

> To be converted is to commit oneself to the process of the liberation of the poor and oppressed, to commit oneself lucidly, realistically and concretely. It means to commit oneself not only generously, but also with an analysis of the situation and a strategy of action.[20]

This conversion is "not simply a matter of fulfilling a duty" but is

> a work of concrete, authentic love for the poor that is not possible apart from a certain integration into their world and apart from bonds of real friendship with those who suffer despoliation and injustice.[21]

For Nehemiah to be able to see the situation through the eyes of the poor, he had to live simply, have friendships with the poor and be integrated into their world. We shall see in Nehemiah 5:14-18 that this was indeed the case. The rich were not able to see the situation through the eyes of the poor until they had their eyes opened by Nehemiah. Their belief that the land belonged to them, and their greed, blinded them to the misery they were causing their brothers.

5:4 *And there were those who said, "We are having to borrow money on our fields and vineyards to pay the king's tax."*

Famine and exploitation by the rich were not the only causes of poverty. The people were also overburdened by high taxes.

Blenkinsopp has shown that the Babylonians and the Persians imposed taxes which increased with the passage of time to unmanageable levels, forcing farmers to produce surpluses. During a famine, this was obviously impossible, and farmers would be forced to seek loans from the wealthy, which they would often be unable to pay back. This only made it easier for the rich to exploit the poor. There was no way out of the situation. However hard the poor worked, they could not make enough to pay these taxes or repay their loans.

Howard-Brook suggests that it was the introduction of a money economy (in order to facilitate taxation) which "generated a scramble for advancement", adding that "The Persian system of 'royal grants' of property to favoured individuals re-created a highly stratified society. This in turn led to enormous anxiety and competition among people seeking access to privilege and favor of those 'above'".[22]

If the cause of the greed that threatened to divide the community was foreign, the solution must be to return to Israelite distinctiveness.[3] Here we see a conflict between different visions for organising land. One vision saw land as a commodity. The other saw it as a gift from God which could only be enjoyed under certain conditions, including love for the poor.

As the Government of the Republic of South Sudan makes moves to reduce its reliance on oil revenues by setting up a proper system of taxation, it is important to make sure that the system is fair and does not overburden those who live off the land at subsistence levels. In Western countries, it is often the case that the poor pay a higher percentage of their income in taxes, while the rich find ways of avoiding tax. We can show the way in setting up and implementing a fair system of taxation.

The emerging middle-class in South Sudan must also be careful not to be seduced by foreign standards of wealth. Coveting and attempting to mimic the lifestyles of consumers in the West will lead to a highly stratified society in which South Sudanese traditions and particularity will be threatened.

5:5 *"Now our flesh is the same as that of our kindred; our children are the same as their children; and yet we are forcing our sons and daughters to be slaves, and some of our daughters have been ravished; we are powerless, and our fields and vineyards now belong to others."*

The situation was so bad that the only way for the poor to pay their debts was to sell their children into slavery. This was a clear breach of the Mosaic law: *"If any of your fellow Israelites become poor and sell themselves to you, do not make them work as slaves. They are to be treated as hired workers or temporary residents among you; they are to work for you until the Year of Jubilee. Then they and their children are to be released, and they will go back to their own clans and to the property of their ancestors. Because the Israelites are my servants, whom I brought out of Egypt, they must not be sold as slaves. Do not rule over them ruthlessly, but fear your God."* (Leviticus 25:39-43).

Because God had delivered the Israelites from slavery, they were not to make each other slaves. Yet this was exactly what was happening. They had forgotten what God had done for them, and they had forgotten that they were one family.

The specific reference to daughters refers to the danger that a woman or girl taken into slavery would be taken "as wife for her new master or his son, a situation which could well be irreversible".[24] Whether forcibly married or not, there was a high likelihood that a woman or girl taken into slavery would be sexually abused.

Nehemiah 5:6-13

Because he identified with the poor, Nehemiah took their complaint seriously. He was angry at the injustice done to them, and took their side. He confronted the rich, but did it in a strategic way after thinking the matter over. He planned his intervention skilfully so that the solution he proposed was endorsed unanimously. By handling the matter in this way, he reconciled the community without compromising on justice.

Nehemiah's solution was inspired by scripture. Blenkinsopp describes his strategy as follows:

> The strategy, therefore, seems to have been to use the occasion of economic crisis to proclaim an emergency jubilee, somewhat comparable to the manumission of slaves by Zedekiah during the siege of Jerusalem (Jer. 34:8-22). Some interesting parallels with the stipulations for the jubilee year in the Holiness Code (Lev. 25) may be noted: the fear of God as the motivating force (v. 9; cf. Lev. 25:17, 36, 43); restitution of ancestral property (Lev. 25:27-28, 41); prohibition of reducing fellow Israelites to slavery (Lev. 25:39, 46) and of charging interest on loans to the poor (25:36).

The Day of Jubilee was supposed to be proclaimed in every fiftieth year. Land sold or forfeited as collateral on a loan was to be returned to the families who originally held it. Property was also to be returned. This meant that land was never sold permanently. It was, effectively, leased until the next day of Jubilee.

The Day of Jubilee was, as will be argued more closely in Chapter Eight of this book, closely connected to the principle of sabbath. Together, these laws prevented the gap between rich and poor from becoming too wide. They ensured that land was held by extended families/kinship networks and could not be transferred permanently. In theory, this meant that land ownership could not be concentrated, preventing the formation of a permanent underclass. However, the laws were rarely if ever implemented.

Land-grabbing is a serious problem in South Sudan and across Africa. It is a phenomenon that has greatly affected Juba, our capital. It is like a disease, which I call "grabiosis". It needs to be addressed urgently before it spreads throughout the country.

We need to make sure that land does not become a commodity to be speculated on by international financiers. Different models of land ownership, including community ownership, must be respected. We must not end up with a situation where families who have lived on the land for generations are dispossessed, and have nowhere of their own to live or cultivate, while land remains unused and unproductive.

5:6 *I was very angry when I heard their outcry and these complaints.*

Anger is legitimate, providing we are angry about the things that anger God. However, it must be expressed and used in the right way. Kidner cites Mark 3:5 and John 2:14 as times when Jesus was angry.[25] Nehemiah was not afraid of showing his emotions at the right time, as we saw in 2:1-3.

5:7 *After thinking it over, I brought charges against the nobles and the officials; I said to them, "You are all taking interest from your own people." And I called a great assembly to deal with them,*

Although Nehemiah got angry, he did not allow his anger to rule over him. He carefully thought things over, before making specific charges that he could substantiate. Then he called a great assembly. This would have necessitate a break from the work of rebuilding. Nonetheless, the threat to the community was so severe that a short break was necessary.

A representative assembly of the people is often the best way of dealing with divisions within a community or between neighbouring communities. It is inclusive and allows grievances to be aired publicly, so that each side understands the other's position and issues, and can empathise with them. The most successful people-to-people peace conferences in South Sudan have been conducted on this basis. Describing the use of Nilotic tradition in the Wunlit conference, John Ashworth and Maura Ryan write that

> peace can only be achieved when everyone knows fully what wrongs were committed. The two communities each have a chance to tell their story, to 'vomit out' all the suffering and bitterness. It is a painful time for all. There is also an opportunity for rebuttal, but often there is no rebuttal. Both sides acknowledge the truth of the accusations, but also recognise that they have both suffered in a similar way at the hands of the other. This leads to agreements including practical actions for peace, followed by the

signing of a covenant. Finally, the peace has to be taken home and acted upon.[26]

In the case of Nehemiah 5, the conflict was remarkably one-sided. This is rarely the case in ethnic conflicts. No rebuttal is recorded in the account of the assembly. If there was a rebuttal, it was unconvincing. The response of the nobles and officials suggests they had no legitimate defence and were forced to concede when confronted.

Plein has characterised the assembly as "a group protest that takes the form of a moral/theological appeal".[27] Part of the community-organising approach to grassroots politics involves arranging large public meetings where powerful people are shamed into agreeing to social and political change. It is possible to interpret Nehemiah 5:6-11 in this way. The need for an oath to be taken suggests that there was suspicion the nobles had not themselves experienced a "conversion to the neighbour"[28] but had simply succumbed to social pressure.

5:8 *and said to them, "As far as we were able, we have brought back our Jewish kindred who had been sold to other nations; but now you are selling your own kin, who must then be bought back by us!" They were silent, and could not find a word to say.*

Nehemiah is probably referring to a programme of redemption that had already begun, but which he had intensified. Williamson plausibly points that Nehemiah's logic in 5:8 is "far more effective if he is pointing to the self-contradictory nature of the Jews' actions"[29] than if the programme had been initiated by Nehemiah.

5:9 *So I said, "The thing that you are doing is not good. Should you not walk in the fear of our God, to prevent the taunts of the nations our enemies?..."*

McConville gives two ways of understanding Nehemiah's allusion to God's reputation. The first, that "if the exiles do not obey God, God will punish them, and that therefore he will be thought weak because of the reduced state of his people",[30] finds precedent in Moses' prayers in Exodus 32:11-12 and Numbers 14:13-16, and in God's words in Ezekiel 20:22. The "ancient mentality" that "a powerful nation must have a powerful god, and a weak nation a weak god"[31] is not so ancient in many parts of the world. It is legitimate to pray that Muslims in Sudan would see the success of Christians in South Sudan and attribute it to the power of Jesus' name. It is legitimate to pray that Muslims would not see the Government of Sudan's success in preventing resolution of the status of Abyei as a sign that God's favour is with them.

The second way of understanding the allusion to God's reputation, which McConville prefers, is that

> the character of the community reflects that of God. The brotherhood within Israel is meant to be a showpiece, a model of the potential human society. The nations should look at Israel and see a people harmonious, prosperous and content, and organised so as to be so rather than for the aggrandisement of the few.[32]

This understanding is more immediately relevant to the concerns expressed in Nehemiah 5:1-5. Throughout the first half of Nehemiah, we have seen the power of an obedient people's witness to God's power. In 6:16, the nations around were humbled because they recognised God's hand in the work of rebuilding. God's people are always witnesses to him. Sometimes we are good witnesses; sometimes we are bad witnesses. What we do affects what others think of our God. If we do not demonstrate God's love in the way we treat others, and especially the poor within our own communities, our (false) testimony is that our God is not powerful enough to transform society and social relationships.

In reality, McConville's two understandings are not mutually exclusive. The shame referred to in 1:3 and the taunts of Sanballat and Tobiah in 4:2-3 were still fresh in the nobles' minds. Lack of concern for the poor had been one of the leading causes of the exile. If they did not change, might not God abandon them to their enemies and to their shame again?

The reference to "the fear of our God" is almost certainly a reference to Leviticus 25. In this passage, fearing God is the opposite of lending money at interest or selling food at a profit (25:37) and it is the opposite of making a fellow Israelite work as a slave (25:43). The parallel is too striking to be a coincidence. The reference to Leviticus 25 prepares for the likelihood that Nehemiah will find the solution to the community's problems in God's word. In fact, he found the solution in the very same passage, Leviticus 25.

5:10-11 *"Moreover I and my brothers and my servants are lending them money and grain. Let us stop this taking of interest. Restore to them, this very day, their fields, their vineyards, their olive orchards, and their houses, and the interest on money, grain, wine, and oil that you have been exacting from them."*

As in 1:6, Nehemiah confessed his own guilt and the guilt of his family. As in 2:17, he identified with those he was asking to make a change, and set an example by being the first to take action. It is not a sign of weakness to admit when we are in the wrong and make a change.

Nehemiah had not been one of the worst offenders. We can tell this because of the switch from 'us' in "*Let us stop this taking of interest*" to 'you' in "*the interest on money, grain, wine, and oil that you have been exacting from them*".[33] As in 1:6, Nehemiah confessed his sin, even though his rebellion against God had not been as great as that of his fellow countrymen.

Nehemiah made two proposals. The first was effectively "an emergency jubilee".[34] The land and the houses that had been seised as collateral were to be returned unconditionally. Secondly, the interest that should not have been charged was to be returned. This solution was both novel and orthodox. It was novel in the sense that throughout Israel's history, the Day of Jubilee had rarely, if ever, been observed. It was orthodox in the sense that Nehemiah found his solution in scripture. He did not invent it out of thin air.

Nehemiah applied Leviticus 25 to his own context. The jubilee laws were not designed to be used as emergency measures. They were supposed to be observed regularly, every half-century. However, the crisis required an immediate response. The same passage was also the inspiration for the Jubilee 2000 campaign, which resulted in the cancellation of billions of dollars of unfair and unpayable international debt. Leviticus 25 was adapted to a 21st century context. The solutions to many of today's problems are to be found in scripture.

Some translations have 'percentage' or 'hundredth', e.g. "*Restore, I pray you, to them, even this day, their lands, their vineyards, their oliveyards, and their houses, also the hundredth part of the money, and of the corn, the wine, and the oil, that ye exact of them*" (KJV). This is unlikely to refer to an annual rate of 1% as this would be a low return. It is more likely to refer to a monthly rate, i.e. 12% per year.[35] Kidner offers another alternative.

> The demand in this half of the verse is for a refund either of interest charged on loans (cf. RSV), or (as I prefer) of the income derived by the creditors from the property they have taken in pledge (cf. NEB: 'Give back today to your debtors their fields and vineyards ..., as well as the income in money, and in corn...').[36]

Whatever the precise demand, restitution was costly. I am reminded of Zaccheus' voluntary commitment to give half of his possessions to the poor and to pay back four times the amount he had cheated from others (Luke 19:8). Israel's distinctiveness required "concrete, costly economic decisions."[37] Organising economic affairs according to the demands of the Torah must have seemed impractical in the context of the monetary economy introduced by the imperial power. Yet Nehemiah's instructions and example showed it was possible to live "without the abuses which they had come together to abolish."[38]

Today too, common sense suggests that we cannot live as the Bible commands. The example of the apostles, who *"had all things in common"* (Acts 2:45) and *"would sell their possessions and goods and distribute the proceeds to all, as any had need"* appears impractical in the context of global capitalism. Nehemiah 5 suggests that it is possible to find ways of applying biblical demands to our own situation, even during times of famine and when foreign powers have massive influence over our local economies.

5:12 *Then they said, "We will restore everything and demand nothing more from them. We will do as you say." And I called the priests, and made them take an oath to do as they had promised.*

The nobles and officials were shamed into compliance with Nehemiah's solution. Williamson gives two possible reasons why their word was not taken at face value and Nehemiah made them take an oath. Either "this was because they showed some reluctance or . . . Nehemiah wanted to impress the populace that the problem really had been dealt with so that they could now return without preoccupation to their work."[39]

5:13 *I also shook out the fold of my garment and said, "So may God shake out everyone from house and from property who does not perform this promise. Thus may they be shaken out and emptied." And all the assembly said "Amen," and praised the LORD. And the people did as they had promised.*

Nehemiah's shaking out of the fold of his garment is reminiscent of the prophetic actions of Isaiah (Isaiah 20:2-6), Ezekiel (Ezekiel 4:1-5:4; 24:1-27) and especially Jeremiah (Jeremiah 13:1-11; 16:1-9;19:1-15; 27:1-28:17; 31:1-25). Brown writes that the purpose of such acts "was not merely to illustrate truth and make the prophet's sayings more memorable. To the eastern mind the sign was inseparable from the event it portrayed. It almost initiated the action it described."[40]

The unity of the community was restored; the whole assembly gave its "Amen". Behind this unity lay mixed motives and reactions: the common people had been vindicated, but the nobles and officials had been shamed. Howard-Brook suggests that the elite agreed to Nehemiah's demand because his project had the support of the king. "Their long-term commitment to Persian largesse outweighed their interest in short-term exploitation of local workers."[41] I refer the reader back to my comment under 2:8b. God is capable of redeeming and working through our mixed motives.

The people also praised the Lord together. A response of praise suggests that we should not be too cynical about the motives of the officials in agreeing to Nehemiah's demands. At least for the time being, they found joy in the restoration of relationships rather than in profit. When we conduct and take part in local peace processes, restoration of relationships should be our ultimate goal. Acknowledgement of and compensation for past grievances can be a part of such processes, but it is not the end goal.

Nehemiah 5:14-19

Here we move from Nehemiah's emergency crisis response, to his regular and consistent practice over the whole of his first term as governor. The same principles that guided Nehemiah's response in 5:6-11 also informed his daily living. Some people are good in a crisis but struggle to live holy lives over a long period of time. Nehemiah had the character to live consistently. In 5:6-11, he placed severe demands on the nobles and officials. 5:14-19 shows that in his own life, he went over and beyond the demands he placed on others.

5:14a *Moreover from the time that I was appointed to be their governor in the land of Judah, from the twentieth year to the thirty-second year of King Artaxerxes,*

This is the first time that Nehemiah's appointment as governor is mentioned explicitly. Clines writes that "If he was not already officially governor when he left Susa, as some maintain, he was certainly appointed to the position during his first year in Jerusalem".[42] We cannot be certain exactly when Nehemiah was appointed governor. However, we should not assume that the failure to mention his position until now means that Nehemiah was not appointed governor on his departure from Susa. We saw the same pattern in Nehemiah 1, when Nehemiah did not mention his position as cupbearer until the story demanded it. It is entirely plausible that the belated reference to Nehemiah's position is due to his humility.

5:14b *neither I nor my brothers ate from the food allowance of the governor.*

Even though Nehemiah was legally entitled to the official food allowance, he refused it. The people were already overburdened with taxes. Nehemiah could not remove or reduce the king's tax, but by refusing the food allowance, he could reduce the local levy charged to the struggling people. Like Paul in 1 Corinthians 9:1-18, he gave up his rights for the good of others.

The decision to refuse the food allowance was a principled move, but it was also a smart political move. Nehemiah had enemies who would use any means to attack him. It was important for Nehemiah to ensure he was above reproach, especially as he took such a strong stance against corruption. Refusing the food allowance was a populist move that showed he was in touch with the people, doing what he could to lighten their load. Tollefson and Williamson suggest that this decision "helps to explain the support of the people and the effectiveness of the [building] project."[43] Leaders who wish to maintain public support during times of austerity would do well to follow Nehemiah's example and live simply.

5:15 *The former governors who were before me laid heavy burdens on the people, and took food and wine from them, besides forty shekels of silver. Even their servants lorded it over the people. But I did not do so, because of the fear of God.*

Some commentators have argued that the reference to *"former governors"* is a thinly veiled attack on Sanballat, since Judah and Jerusalem had previously been part of his territory.[44] The Samaritans would have heard that Nehemiah was refusing the food allowance and might have demanded Sanballat do likewise. It could even be that Nehemiah was deliberately fuelling internal rebellion against Sanballat in Samaria as a way of keeping him occupied there.

Nehemiah's primary reason for refusing the allowance was *"because of the fear of God"*, again harking back to Leviticus 25. Verse 19 shows that Nehemiah's actions were designed to win God's approval. Kidner suggests a second factor: "brotherly compassion",[45] an empathy with the people.

Throughout his first term as governor, Nehemiah evidenced the same ethics as he did in the early crisis of 5:1-13. His concern for social justice, emanating from a reverence for God and rooted in the demands of the Torah, was as strong in his twelfth year as in his first. His identification with the poor was not a tactic designed to win their support during the rebuilding project, but a way of life that continued long after the walls were completed.

5:16 *Indeed, I devoted myself to the work on this wall, and acquired no land; and all my servants were gathered there for the work.*

Nehemiah's single-minded devotion to the work God called him to do is evident again here. He was not distracted by the temptations of office. Where other kings used their power to centralise land, he respected the community land ownership system set out in the Torah. He used whatever he had at his disposal (including his personal servants) for the work of God.

5:17-9 *Moreover there were at my table one hundred fifty people, Jews and officials, besides those who came to us from the nations around us. Now that which was prepared for one day was one ox and six choice sheep; also fowls were prepared me, and every ten days skins of wine in abundance; yet with all this I did not demand the food allowance of the governor, because of the heavy burden of labour on the people. Remember for my good, O my God, all that I have done for this people.*

Nehemiah fed all the people who ate with him at his own expense. It has been estimated that the animals slaughtered would have fed up to 800 people daily. This suggests that *"those who came to us"* were greater in number than the leaders whom Nehemiah regularly entertained. Nehemiah's table was open to all: rich or poor, friend or stranger. No wonder Nehemiah asked God to remember his generosity.

Many of our leaders exercise hospitality on a continual basis. This applies to politicians as well as religious leaders. We need to appreciate them for this. However, the result is that their houses are full of relatives and friends who have come to stay. In urban centres, there are particular challenges accommodating and feeding so many guests. Often our leaders also have to provide transport money for them to return to their rural homes at the end of their visit.

Some of these visitors have genuine reasons for visiting. For example, they may be seeking medical treatment or have official business to attend to. Others simply wish to escape from the village. The expected cultural norm is to accept and host these people. If any leader was to send his relatives back, he would be the talk of the village. However, they would be more productive engaging in cultivation in rural areas.

Having to take care of so many people is not an easy task. Our leaders may be tempted to gain money through corrupt practices in order to avoid losing face by having to send relatives home. While this is not to excuse corruption, we need to be aware how it can be encouraged by some of our cultural practices.

I once visited a family in England who gave me the impression they were not happy that their 20-year-old child was still living with them. This surprised me. In England and other Western countries, a child is expected to fend for themselves after reaching a certain age, and especially after leaving university and getting a job. High house prices make this increasingly difficult. Many young people can not afford to buy or rent a house within a few years of leaving university. In our traditional African culture, a young adult can stay under the care of his or her parents for as long as necessary. We need to find the balance between these two cultural approaches.

Conclusion

Nehemiah treated internal threats to the unity of the nation even more seriously than external, armed threats. Nehemiah 5 cautions us to do likewise. It offers lessons in conflict resolution, offering hope that it is possible to reconcile divided communities without compromising on truth or justice. It demonstrates the importance of exercising a preferential option for the poor, and testifies that this is only possible when we identify with them and live out a consistent social ethic. It encourages us to look for solutions to modern problems in scripture. It warns us to reject the influence of the godless in the way we organise land ownership.

Nehemiah 5 prepares the reader for the events of chapters 8-10 and 13. At this stage Nehemiah relied "as did the prophets of old, on attempts to persuade the nobility to do justice".[46] However, Nehemiah knew that "social and ritual restructuring matters".[47] When the opportunity presented itself, he supported legal solutions to the same problem. Here an emergency jubilee was proclaimed. Emergency measures should not, however, be treated as long-term solutions. Later revisions to the law would integrate jubilee with other social justice requirements, in an attempt to ensure it was practised regularly according to an orderly implementation schedule.

The internal threat was the biggest test yet of Nehemiah's leadership. Williamson describes three leadership qualities showed by Nehemiah in 5:1-19.

First, he displays a disarming candor in admitting his own involvement, even if it was not particularly extensive. No one could accuse him of taking a superior or privileged attitude. Second, his proposals, though costly, were practical and simple. He left no room for casuistic maneuverings but confronted the wealthy with a direct challenge to charity and generosity. Finally, in the closing verses of the chapter, he showed how he was willing personally to take on a greater burden than that which he asked of others. It is a classic illustration of the obvious truth that leadership means going further than those one is leading.

There are many theological lessons to be drawn from Nehemiah 5. However, the most important and most urgent lesson is also the simplest. God's people cannot allow poverty, inequality and exploitation to continue. We have a responsibility to do something about them. Nehemiah's proposals were as practical as they were radical. It would be remiss of me to move on to Nehemiah 7 without first making practical proposals about the church's role in poverty alleviation.

Before speaking of poverty alleviation, we need to have some idea of what poverty actually is. We have seen that, in the Bible and especially in the Old Testament, those who are poor are primarily those who are vulnerable because they lack access to land. It will not be possible here to resolve the debate about how to characterise poverty, or whether it is a helpful term. Poverty can be understood as a lack of material goods or access to basic human needs, a state of vulnerability to crises, a lack of agency or incapacity to make personal choices, an inability to participate in decision-making, a system designed to keep people in their place, a social creation, marginalisation or exclusion, the manifestation of powers and principalities in the world, the reign of death, or the absence of love, shalom, well-being or good-relationships. All these characterisations are useful to some extent. I will not seek to come up with an all-encompassing definition here. It should, however, be clear that poverty is complex, multi-dimensional, and interlocking. It has material, physical, social, psychological and spiritual dimensions which often act to reinforce each other. It should not be understood in a purely material, or worse still, in a purely monetary sense.

Yet global institutions still understand poverty as primarily material. The World Bank definition, where households living on an income of less than $1.25 a day are identified as living in extreme poverty, is a case in point. It is estimated that nearly 1.3 billion people live on an income of $1.25 or less a day. 2.6 billion live on less than US $2 a day, "another common measurement of deep deprivation."[48] Poverty is defined as extreme, moderate, or relative (where household income level is below a given proportion of the national average).

Even when considering the material aspect of poverty, it is important to have wider definitions of wealth than monetary income alone. In many parts of South Sudan where money has not been the medium of transaction, there are households who own 100 heads of cattle. The head of this family might see himself as poor because he has been told by NGOs and UN agencies that he is living in extreme poverty. However, he has considerable resources at his disposal. Even if he simply converted his cattle into money, he could build a small house, send his children to school and buy a bicycle or a motorcycle for his transport. The focus on what households do not have, rather than what they do have, is dangerous. It encourages them to see themselves as trapped, dependent on others, and unable to take decisions to improve their own lives and communities.

In the early years following the Second World War, development was defined as economic growth and measured according to a country's Gross National Product. Secular agencies slowly realised what the Church had been saying for many years: that this approach is inadequate. From the 1970s, the emphasis shifted to "the reduction or elimination of unemployment, poverty and inequality."[49] If GNP is increasing, but unemployment, poverty or inequality are not reduced, it is not appropriate to speak of development having taken place. More recently, the Human Development Index and Multidimensional Poverty Index were developed to take account of a range of basic human needs. The Millennium Development Goals, adopted by all 191 members of the United Nations, also recognise the multi-dimensional nature of poverty. While the goals are unlikely to be met by 2015, they can be used as indicators for the performance of the Government of the Republic of South Sudan and global institutions. The 8 MDGs are:

1. Eradicate extreme poverty and hunger
2. Achieve universal primary education
3. Promote gender equality and empower women
4. Reduce child mortality
5. Improve maternal health
6. Combat HIV/AIDS, malaria and other diseases
7. Ensure environmental sustainability
8. Establish a global partnership for development [50]

Almost half of the population of Sub-Saharan Africa live on an average of below \$1.25 per day.[51] Material poverty is reinforced by the unequal distribution of wealth, resources, land, and poor economic and political policies. War and poverty are interlinked. Poverty fuels resentment, leading to conflict. War destroys families, livelihoods and properties, increasing the level of material poverty. Other factors include political instability, bad political and economic policies, the 'brain drain', and the concentration of economic development at the centre of nations and regions. Traditional religion keeps people in fear and encourages them to believe there is little they can do to alter their fate. The different aspects of poverty, and its causes, are deep-rooted and interlocking. Pro-poor policies need to be holistic, addressing different aspects of poverty (including spiritual aspects) simultaneously. They must address the root causes of poverty and not only its symptoms.

Global institutions, by their nature, are only able to measure poverty according to certain indicators (largely material) that can be compared like for like. The local church, also by its nature, has an ongoing presence at the grass roots. During the war, when NGOs left southern Sudan, the church remained. The church is able to find culturally appropriate ways of measuring poverty in every community where it is present. It will not ignore the spiritual dimensions of poverty. Part of the Church's role in poverty alleviation is getting alongside communities so they can decide for themselves what is important, who the poor within the community are, defining their needs and identifying the resources and skills they already have. The Church is in a better position than UN agencies or NGOs to make these kinds of judgments. The Church can help secular agencies to improve their understanding of poverty and its causes, including spiritual aspects.

The local church can also play a role as a provider of development assistance. Some professional aid providers appear to rejoice in the calamities that befall Africa. They move from place to place looking for the next calamity, so as to raise the needed funds and perpetuate their organisations. If there are no calamities, they speak of lack of funds. They use emotive pictures of suffering people to raise money. This gives people in the West a picture of Africans as victims who are unable to do things for themselves.

Some NGOs are created for purely selfish reasons. I heard a story circulating about a person who introduced himself as working for an NGO. When asked what his NGO does, he replied that his NGO was involved in anything that comes his way! The local church will continue to exist even if there are no calamities. Its motives are different from those of professional aid providers.

Aid is often criticised for making people dependent. It is true that poorly designed development assistance does create or perpetuate dependency. The 21 years of war in South Sudan left many people dependent on aid agencies for food and other basic needs. However, without this support the suffering of the South Sudanese people would have been much worse. Trade cannot lift our people out of poverty as we lack the infrastructure to transport goods. Our pastors encourage people to go back to their land and farm. However, the lack of all-weather roads connecting our country to Juba means there is little chance to market the food they produce.

We need to improve our infrastructure. In the meantime, aid should continue. However, it should be strategically targeted to support projects that enable people to come out of poverty. It should be disbursed through faith-based organisations (FBOs) where possible, in preference to NGOs or UN agencies. FBOs are truly local. We make faster decisions as we do not have long bureaucratic procedures, or an overseas headquarters which makes the decisions. Our presence within local areas means that we have a better understanding of local needs, and are able to "scratch where it is itching". We also better understand the dynamics within communities, because our members are part of those communities. This means that aid is more likely to be targeted to the people who need it the most, and less likely to be diverted. Churches also tend to have lower administrative costs than many NGOs, which are increasingly professionalised. Our church in Kajo-Keji was able to build one and a half schools for the same amount of money as secular NGOs spend on one equivalent school.

There is scope for NGOs and local churches to work together. Where this is the case, I prefer to call NGOs partners rather than donors. Partnership is an equal relation. Partners consult and respect each other. 'Donors' implies giving and receiving. Too often, donors demand accountability from those implementing their programmes without making themselves accountable to the recipients of assistance.

Churches should be careful what development projects they do and do not get involved with. Education is a field where the Church has traditionally been involved. Since 2005, with the support of our partners, the Diocese of Kajo-Keji has built ten primary schools and one secondary school. The Roman Catholic and Baptist churches have also established schools in Kajo-Keji.

Health is a trickier area. My own view is that churches should not run hospitals. This should be done by the government, the private sector, or a separate entity set up by the Church but independent from it. Churches should limit their role to basic health delivery services where there is no such service provided by the government. Several years ago, one of our overseas partners offered to help us establish a hospital. I politely declined the offer. Establishing a hospital would have entailed raising huge financial sums and employing massive numbers of people. The administrative burden on the church would have been huge. The church did not have the capacity, and it would have distracted from other activities. If the partner had offered to help us establish a health centre, I would have considered the offer more seriously. We have now partnered with two other organisations in a tripartite partnership to provide medical services. One of these partners has the requisite expertise in running hospitals.

Microfinance is one of the ways churches can help to lift people out of poverty. Churches are well-placed to identify people who might benefit from microfinance schemes. The Diocese of Kajo-Keji started a microfinance programme in April 1999 to 2011. Over 150 small groups of women have received loans ranging from $100 to $300. Many of these women have improved their livelihoods and are now able to send their children to school.

Some have argued that Christians should not be involved in development as we should focus on heavenly things. This false doctrine was taught for many years in the Anglican East African Revival Movement. A song encouraged believers to suffer silently so they would get their reward in heaven. My father discouraged the singing of this song, saying that it glorifies suffering and poverty and encourages people not to do anything about it. This teaching is not only unbiblical, but also oppressive and unfair.

I am a firm believer in a holistic approach to ministry. The gospel is good news for the whole person. We take our example from Jesus. Luke 4:18-19 contains what has been called the Nazareth Manifesto. Political parties use manifestoes to outline what they will do when they take power. Similarly, Jesus gave details of his life's ministry as he embarked on it. Luke 4:18-19 does not disassociate the spiritual from the physical. Neither should we, as Jesus' followers. The Nazareth manifesto also speaks of freeing prisoners from physical and spiritual oppression (4:18). Today, we should campaign for the release of those who are arrested unfairly, including those who are arrested for their faith. This is not 'playing politics'. Rather, it is part of our mission as Christians.

We cannot preach the good news to a hungry person and leave them to die from a lack of food. We encourage people to pray "Give us this day our daily bread" as part of the Lord's Prayer. In South Sudan, many families survive on one meal or less per day. When people pray this prayer, they mean it. In other parts of the world, this is not always the case. If we encourage people to pray this prayer, we must be willing to be part of God's answer to it.

The church in South Sudan has a role to play in the development of the nation. However, we must make sure that we are not merely "Christians doing development". Otherwise development will distract from evangelism. Christians should do development in a distinctive way and without dividing the material and the spiritual. We may need to say 'no' to partners who want us to implement programmes that do not fit our ethos, and especially those which will perpetuate poverty or make people dependent on aid. Like Nehemiah, we must support and advocate for policies that benefit the poor. Economic development can favour the rich but leave the poor worse off. We must do what we can to ensure that development benefits the poor.

1   Throntveit, *Ezra-Nehemiah*, 123.

2   Grabbe, *Ezra-Nehemiah*, 48.

3   Williamson, *Ezra, Nehemiah*, 239–40.

4   J G McConville, *Ezra, Nehemiah and Esther*, The Daily Study Bible (Edinburgh: The Saint Andrew press, 1985), 96.

5   Williamson, *Ezra, Nehemiah*, 235.

6   McConville, *Ezra, Nehemiah and Esther*, 96.

7   Grabbe, *Ezra-Nehemiah*, 48.

8   Howard-Brook, *Come Out My People!*, 266.

9   Allen and Laniak, *Ezra, Nehemiah, Esther*, 113.

10 Williamson, *Ezra, Nehemiah*, 236.

11 Mark Bradbury et al., *Local Peace Processes in Sudan: a Baseline Study* (London/ Nairobi: Rift Valley Institute, DFID, 2006), 38, http://citisenshift.org/sites/citisen. nfb.ca/files/Local_Peace_Processes_in_Sudan_May_2006.pdf.

12 Julia Aker Duany, "People-to-people Peacemaking: a Local Solution to Local Problems," in *Artisans of Peace: Grassroots Peacemaking Among Christian Communities*, ed. Mary Ann Cejka and Tomás Bamat (Maryknoll: Orbis Books, 2003), 217–8.

13 Kidner, *Ezra and Nehemiah*, 95.

14 F Charles Fensham, *The Book of Ezra, Nehemiah*, The New International Commentary on the Old Testament (Grand Rapids: Wm B Eerdmans Publishing Company, 1982), 191.

15 Williamson, *Ezra, Nehemiah*, 237.

16 Blenkinsopp, *Ezra-Nehemiah*, 257.

17 McConville, *Ezra, Nehemiah and Esther*, 98.

18 Christopher J H Wright, *Old Testament Ethics for the People of God* (Leicester: Inter-Varsity Press, 2004), 167.

19 Tollefson and Williamson, "Nehemiah as Cultural Revitalisation," 333.

20 Gustavo Gutierrez, *A Theology of Liberation*, trans. Sister Caridad Inda and John Eagleson (London: SCM Press Ltd, 1974), 205.

21 Gustavo Gutierrez, *We Drink from Our Own Wells: The Spiritual Journey of a People*, trans. Matthew J O'Connell (London: SCM Press Ltd, 2005), 104.

22 Howard-Brook, *Come Out My People!*, 246.

23 Walter Brueggemann, *Texts That Linger, Words That Explode: Listening to Prophetic Voices* (Minneapolis: Fortress Press, 2000), 69.

24 Blenkinsopp, *Ezra-Nehemiah*, 258–9.

25 Kidner, *Ezra and Nehemiah*, 95.

26 John Ashworth and Maura Ryan, "'One Nation from Every Tribe, Tongue, and People': The Church and Strategic Peacebuilding in South Sudan," *Journal of Catholic Social Thought* 10, no. 1 (2013): 56–7.

27 J David Pleins, *The Social Visions of the Hebrew Bible: a Theological Introduction* (Louisville: Westminster John Knox, 2000), 183.

28 Gutierrez, *A Theology of Liberation*, 205.

29 Williamson, *Ezra, Nehemiah*, 239.

30 McConville, *Ezra, Nehemiah and Esther*, 100.

31 Ibid.

32 Ibid.

33 Kidner, *Ezra and Nehemiah*, 97.

34 Blenkinsopp, *Ezra-Nehemiah*, 259.

35 Kidner, *Ezra and Nehemiah*, 97.

36 Ibid.

37 Brueggemann, *Texts That Linger, Words That Explode*, 69.

38 Blenkinsopp, *Ezra-Nehemiah*, 260.

39 Williamson, *Ezra, Nehemiah*, 241.

40 Brown, *The Message of Nehemiah*, 95.

41 Howard-Brook, *Come Out My People!*, 262.

42 Clines, *Ezra, Nehemiah, Esther*, 170.

43 Tollefson and Williamson, "Nehemiah as Cultural Revitalisation," 334.

44 Myers, *Ezra, Nehemiah*, 133.

45 Kidner, *Ezra and Nehemiah*, 98.

46 Pleins, *The Social Visions of the Hebrew Bible*, 185.

47 Ibid.

48 The World Bank Group, "Poverty Overview," *The World Bank: Working for a World*

Free of Poverty, 2013, http://www.worldbank.org/en/topic/poverty/overview.

49   Benaiah Yongo-Bure, *Economic Development of Southern Sudan* (Lanham: University Press of America, 2007), 2.

50   UN Department of Public Information, "Millennium Goals," *United Nations*, accessed September 9, 2013, www.un.org/millenniumgoals/.

51   The World Bank Group, "Poverty & Equity: Sub-Sarahan Africa," *The World Bank: Working for a World Free of Poverty*, 2013, http://povertydata.worldbank.org/poverty/region/SSA.

Chapter Six

Nehemiah the administrator
and reformer

Nehemiah 7:1-4

This section sets out the first actions Nehemiah took following the completion of the wall. It details the first appointments he made and the assignments he gave. Nehemiah went about these appointments in a businesslike and professional way, without ever losing sight of God's wider purposes for the city of Jerusalem.

7:1 *Now when the wall had been built and I had set up the doors, and the gatekeepers, the singers, and the Levites had been appointed,*

Nehemiah, acting as Governor of Judah, now appointed staff to take care of the affairs of the city. Security workers and worship leaders were his first appointments. This decision reflected Nehemiah's priorities. Opposition persisted and Nehemiah was realistic about the possibility of attack, especially while the city was still relatively unpopulated. Security workers were necessary to protect the work that had been done.

Nehemiah would no doubt be familiar with Psalm 127, a psalm of Solomon. Psalm 127:1a declares that *"Unless the Lord builds the house, the builders labour in vain"* (NIV). The work of building the walls of Jerusalem would have been futile if it had not been blessed of God. The next part of the verse was also relevant to the situation Nehemiah found himself in: *"Unless the Lord watches over the city, the guards stand watch in vain"* (NIV). Nehemiah appointed guards, but he well knew that restoration of the city walls was not God's ultimate purpose. The wider purpose was the restoration of relationship between God and his people. Without this, the guards would stand watch in vain.

The appointment of worship leaders related to Nehemiah's wider purpose. Jerusalem was to be a centre for worship for a covenantal community. Authentic worship was part of the Israelites' covenantal commitment. Before the exile, God's people had been criticised for assuming God's protection could be guaranteed by legalistic adherence to sacrificial rituals and empty platitudes (Jeremiah 7:4). God made it clear that worship at the temple was only pleasing to him if it was authentic and part of a consistent life-ethic (Jeremiah 7:5-15). The emphasis on joyous celebration in the later chapters of Nehemiah ensures that observance of God's commands does not become legalism. Nonetheless, sacrifice and sung worship were still required. True freedom from legalism means fulfilling God's commands joyously and out of love, rather than reluctantly and out of duty. It does not mean ignoring God's commands!

The priority given by Nehemiah to worship over administration challenges us to do likewise. We are never too busy to start the day in praise and we should not become so focused on our jobs or "doing things" that we do not meet together with God's people to worship him together.

7:2 *I gave my brother Hanani charge over Jerusalem, along with Hananiah the commander of the citadel, for he was a faithful man and feared God more than many.*

Once gatekeepers, singers and Levites had been appointed, Nehemiah placed two administrators under himself to deal with the day-to-day affairs of Jerusalem. As in Nehemiah 3, we see here a leader willing to delegate and give real responsibility to those under him. Nehemiah did not attempt to micro-manage everything from the centre, but allowed his officials to exercise meaningful powers using their own initiative. This required the appointment of trusted and qualified people of good character. Nehemiah made these appointments on a clear and transparent basis that no-one would be able to challenge.

Some commentators have suggested that Hanani and Hananiah were the same person.[1] The biblical text in its final form suggests otherwise, so I will treat them as two different people.

Hananiah was appointed as one of the administrators was because of his honest character and his reverence for God. Character is the most important requirement for a senior position. A person must be competent, but without integrity they may use their position for their own gain. Some of those people who feel they are entitled to a job because of their impressive qualifications, need to allow God to work on their character. The importance Nehemiah attached to the fear of God again shows his intention to build a covenantal community who kept God's commandments, not simply to put a functioning technocracy in place.

No such assurance is given of Hanani's character in this passage. All we are told here is that he was Nehemiah's brother. However, we should not assume that Nehemiah was practising nepotism. There is no need to outline Hanani's qualifications for the role, because we have already been introduced to him and seen his good character in action. Hanani was the one who brought a delegation to Susa to inform Nehemiah about the state of affairs in Jerusalem (1:2). In doing so, he had already displayed leadership qualities and a patriotic concern for the affairs of the nation.

This passage cannot, therefore, be used to justify nepotism. The saying "blood is thicker than water" is often used to excuse nepotism. According to this way of thinking, family members are more likely to be loyal and can therefore be trusted to carry out instructions. This way of thinking originates from a war mentality where people are suspicious of each other and do not know who they can trust. It is not appropriate for peacetime. Civil service positions and political appointments must be based on merit. Public appointments must be based on what you know (qualifications), not who you know (connections).

The Church needs to set an example. We must not place people on committees because they are related to us. Rather, we must select the right person for the right job. It is of paramount importance that all appointments in the church, public service and private sector are made on merit. We need a meritocracy, not an 'akwanocracy' (from the local Juba Arabic word for 'brother').

Nepotism is a serious disease in Africa. It increases the likelihood of abuse and mismanagement of resources (often referred to as corruption) because there is less accountability to those outside the family circle.

All organisations need to put in place mechanisms that encourage transparency and guard against the abuse and mismanagement of resources. This applies to NGOs and FBOs as well as to government. NGOs lobby for improved transparency and accountability in government, but they do not always realise how they are seen by local people. (Matthew 7:4). This is not necessarily because NGOs have mismanaged resources, but may arise because they do not always discuss their internal processes with or make financial information available to the people they serve.

One important mechanism all organisations should put in place is a proper recruitment process that is not based on hearsay or personal recommendations. I have had bad experiences when such mechanisms were not in place. When I became Bishop of Kajo-Keji diocese, the diocese did not have the funds to hire a driver at the market rate. One of our contacts recommended a neighbour who would do the job for less. On one of his first trips, he rolled the car. We ended up spending nearly $3,000 to have the vehicle repaired. I made it clear that from that time I needed a competent driver, even if his wages were more than we wanted to pay.

As part of a proper recruitment process, I instituted a panel to undertake all interviews for new staff and internal staff applying for new roles. This has helped us to ensure we get the best candidates. It also gives us credibility, demonstrating our fairness as an institution.

Proper recruitment processes require co-operation between employers. Sadly, it is rare for organisations to ask us for letters of reference for staff who have moved on from us. Sometimes staff have taken up new roles in other organisations without formally resigning from their current employer. Unless employers co-operate, we will end up with staff who move from place to place without following due process. People have the right to move from one employer to another, but this should be done according to set procedures. It is important that we give accurate letters of reference. This encourages staff to work hard and honestly as they know that if they do not, their bad deeds will follow them wherever they go.

Procedures are important, but ultimately it is fear of God that will stop a person from mismanaging resources. Nehemiah was right to put a premium on fear of God in his own recruitment process. Psalm 111:10 says that *"The fear of the Lord is the beginning of wisdom; all who follow his precepts have good understanding"* (NIV). Proverbs 1:7 tells us that *"The fear of the Lord is the beginning of knowledge, but fools despise wisdom and instruction"* (NIV). Similarly, Proverbs 9:10 says that *"The fear of the Lord is the beginning of wisdom, and knowledge of the Holy One is understanding"* (NIV). When Christian organisations appoint staff, fear of God is as important a qualification for those appointed to technical roles as it is for those appointed to teaching roles.

7:3 *And I said to them, "The gates of Jerusalem are not to be opened until the sun is hot; while the gatekeepers are still standing guard, let them shut and bar the doors. Appoint guards from among the inhabitants of Jerusalem, some at their watch posts, and others before their own houses."*

Nehemiah set out the role of the administrators very clearly. Their main function was to ensure peace and public safety. Gates had to be opened and shut at the right times. They were to maintain watch over the city and warn the city's inhabitants in case of any security breach.

When we give a person a role, it is important to describe exactly what is expected of them. (In Human Resource Management, this is referred to as a job description.) That way, everyone is clear what is expected. Misunderstandings will be avoided. Job descriptions can help to safeguard the rights of the worker. If an employer makes unreasonable demands that do not reflect the expectations of the worker, a job description can strengthen the position of the worker in refusing. Likewise, failure to fulfil duties set out in a job description is a proper basis for discipline. A job description helps ensure that discipline is appropriate and not arbitrary.

For example, it should be clear from the job description of a night watchman that he is expected to keep watch rather than sleeping at night. I am reminded of the story of the night watchman who told his employer of a dream he had. His employer was due to travel the same day. The guard dreamt that his boss would be involved in a bad accident. The owner of the house dismissed the guard, saying that he had accused himself of failing to do his duty, since one can only dream while sleeping!

Many people think that we should not use job descriptions or professional codes of conduct in the church. When I became Bishop, I found that some staff left their places of work at will, without informing anyone. Some had genuine reasons. They went to visit their families who were still living in refugee camps in Uganda. However, unexplained and unscheduled absences made it very difficult to plan or carry out work effectively.

I determined to resolve this issue without preventing staff from seeing their families. I told staff they should fill out forms whenever they took time off from work, and that the days they were away would be deducted from their annual leave. Each member of staff would be entitled to a set number of days annual leave. They would be free to do whatever they like with these days, including spending time on personal issues. The reaction to such a modest measure was perhaps surprising. One member of staff said that the diocese was not an NGO where people would need permission to take time off.

The reference to NGOs was a personal swipe at me. Before I became a bishop, I was chief executive of an NGO. The member of staff forgot that I was attached clergy during this time. I was not new to the Church and knew how things worked. I stood my ground and insisted on the procedure. The episode was a reminder that some people expect the Church to exhibit lower standards of professionalism than secular organisations. They seem to think that standards of professionalism are at odds with the nature of an organisation reliant on God and united in brotherly love. Nehemiah demonstrated that professional, strategic leadership was entirely consistent with dependence on God and strengthening fellowship. If we look carefully, we will see that the Bible is full of management concepts and practices which the church could benefit from.

7:4 *The city was wide and large, but the people within it were few and no houses had been built.*

This verse acts as a bridge between 7:1-3 and 7:5-73. It explains why Nehemiah decided extra measures were necessary to repopulate Jerusalem and why extra security measures were needed in the meantime.

Nehemiah 7:5-73

As in Nehemiah 3, I will make general comments on the significance of the list in this section, before making comments on individual verses. I will not make specific comments on every verse.

The list in 7:6-73 is essentially the same list found in Ezra 2. It includes all those who returned with Zerubbabel under Cyrus' decree. There are minor differences between the two lists, mainly in the numbers given. Kidner suggests that the occasional divergences could have arisen in the process of copying.[2]

There is a debate as who copied from who. The current consensus seems to be that "Ezra 2 is dependent on Neh 7".[3] While the debate is interesting, the more important issue is the reason for inclusion of the list at all.

Throntveit distinguishes between the purposes of the list in Nehemiah 7 and Ezra 2:

> Earlier in the narrative virtually the same list appeared at Ezra 2:1-70. There it functioned as a legitimation list furnished to Tattenai in connection with the temple investigations. Its purpose was to vouch for the authenticity of the members of the nascent Jewish community as against the Samaritans who were denied participation in the reconstruction of the temple (Ezra 4:1-3). Here, in what is probably the list's original setting (cf. Williamson, *Ezra, Nehemiah*, pp. 267f.), the list also functions as a legitimation list, though it serves a different purpose. In this setting, the list is used as a census list that provides the demographic data needed for the relocation of the population, a tithing of the people, to live in Jerusalem.[4]

Those who originally made the list could not have envisaged the use Nehemiah would put it to. Nehemiah used the list to assemble the people by their families, gathering them together to recommit themselves to God (9:38) and decide who among them would settle in Jerusalem (11:1). The list thus served an instrumental function as a census-list, calling people together.

The list also ensured that those selected to populate Jerusalem were taken from God's people. This was important in the light of continuing opposition. The requirement that the new residents be taken from the families of those who had returned under the first wave prevented foreign spies from joining their number. Neither of the functions outlined above could have been anticipated by those who originally made the list.

It is important that we too keep written records. It has been said that Africans are people of the spoken word and not of the written word. That is why many of us keep things in our memory. As more and more is written down, we must not lose the skill of story-telling or the habit of passing down wisdom from generation to generation. However, cultural difference is not an excuse for laziness. Information that should be written down includes:

Financial information: Keeping records of income and expenditure is important for both churches and individuals. When I worked for Scripture Union, the then Regional Secretary, Emmanuel Oladipo, used to tell us that "money without a piece of paper soon vanishes without any trace". An honest man will find that he ends up claiming less than he should if he does not keep records of his expenditure, to ensure he errs on the side of caution and does not take what he does not deserve.

Money can be the source of family quarrels. When money is short, a husband may accuse a wife of being extravagant (or vice-versa). Keeping a record of income and expenditure can help prevent unnecessary quarrels. Some people keep envelopes with labels indicating what each envelope is for. Labels could include feeding, transport, giving, rent, and school fees.

Registers: Lists of names occur in Nehemiah in chapters 3, 7, 8, 9, 10, 11 and 12. They were recorded for a variety of reasons. Relevant information for churches to keep includes the names of those who are baptised, confirmed, married and buried in the church, and regular counts of the numbers attending church services. At ECS Rumbek, South Sudan, the church includes God when they count those present! If they count 1,231, they will record the number present as 1,232. This is a good reminder of God's presence in our midst as we meet.

Minutes: It is important to make an accurate record of meetings held. It is not necessary to record every word spoken at a meeting. However, it is wise to write down all the important decisions agreed upon in meetings. Minutes should clearly indicate action points, who has agreed to carry out each action and by when. This is sometimes left off, and can lead to no action being taken until the next meeting!

It is also important that minutes are written up and circulated as soon as possible, ideally between 1 and 3 days after the meeting. This means that if the minute-taker made a mistake (or changed the content deliberately!), the meeting will still be fresh in the minds of those who attended, and the minutes can be amended as appropriate. This main purpose of minutes is to remind members what was agreed upon and what action each agreed to take before the next meeting. However, minutes can be invaluable in resolving disputes years later and for research purposes.

Church history: It is of paramount importance that church history is recorded so that it is not forgotten. This includes how the church was founded: the people who were involved, whether it was founded by nationals or missionaries from Europe, America or other parts of Africa, etc. Photos easily fade or become damaged, so should be scanned and kept electronically. Records should be kept of important events in the life of the church, including conferences, conventions and crusades. Briefer notes should be kept of regular services, including who preached and the topic they preached on.

By doing this we remember those who have given up their time and energy to God's service. We also keep records so that when we look back we will be able to see how God has been working in the lives of our congregations. All history is "His story" – God working through people to bring change to the world. The book of Nehemiah shows this clearly. It records the specific actions Nehemiah took, but credits God for their success, and locates them within an overall narrative showing how God was working in and through the nation. When we use church records to write up the history of our churches, we should do the same.

Memoirs/diaries: Even if we do not keep a diary systematically, it is good to keep records of significant events in our personal lives. These can then be used if we or others are writing books. They can also be helpful when telling our children and grandchildren their history.

After my predecessor, Bishop Manasseh Binyi Dawidi, died on 19th April 2013, we found a manuscript that he had written as an autobiography.

We were able to use this to put together a brief biography that was read during his funeral service. We then asked an editor to work on his draft so that it can be published. If it is published, he will continue to minister through the written word.

7:5 *Then my God put it into my mind to assemble the nobles and the officials and the people to be enrolled by genealogy. And I found the book of the genealogy of those who were the first to come back, and I found the following written in it:*

7:5 echoes 2:12. Other translations follow 2:12 in using "heart" instead of "mind" (DRC, ESV, KJV, NIV etc.). The difference between "heart" and "mind" is not significant here. God put in Nehemiah's heart the need to register the people in accordance with their genealogy. He did this before Nehemiah found the book of the genealogy, so that finding it would act as a confirmation. Often when God has put something in our heart to do, he will find a way of giving us an assurance that it is in accordance to his will.

Church leaders and other mature Christians can help to test our callings and look out for these signs. One of these signs is the receipt of peace which is beyond understanding (Philippians 4:7), especially when the particular calling is likely to make the person unpopular and it would not be normal to have a sense of peace about it.

If a child has a clear calling, his or her parents should not oppose this. I once heard a story about a father who wanted his son to be a doctor. The son did not want to be a doctor but, out of respect for his father, spent six years completing a medical course. When the six years were finished, he showed his father his medical degree. Then he branched off to do what was in his heart. The lesson for us parents is that we should not force our children to be what we ourselves wished to be.

7:7 *They came with Zerubbabel, Jeshua, Nehemiah, Azariah, Raamiah, Nahamani, Mordecai, Bilshan, Mispereth, Bigvai, Nehum, Baanah.*

This verse contains one of the differences between Nehemiah 7:6-73 and Ezra 2. Nehemiah's list gives the names of twelve leaders who accompanied the first wave of returned exiles back to Judah. Ezra's list gives only eleven. The number twelve is significant. It represents the twelve tribes of Israel, showing that those who returned were not a random selection of Israelites but representatives of the whole people of Israel. This is especially significant given the use of the list by Nehemiah. If the first returnees represented the whole people of Israel, so do their families. When the people confess their sins in 9:2, they act as representatives of the whole people. The covenant of 9:38 applies to all of Israel, even those who are still scattered in the diaspora. The worshipping community in Jerusalem acts on behalf of the whole people. Whatever the reason why Ezra names only eleven of the leaders who first came back to Judah, there are clear theological reasons for the inclusion of twelve names by Nehemiah.

7:68-9   *They had seven hundred thirty-six horse, two hundred forty-five mules, four hundred thirty-five camels, and six thousand seven hundred twenty donkeys.*

Nehemiah's enumeration includes a total of 8,136 animals. These were mainly donkeys. Getz calculates that there was "about one donkey for every seven people."[5] A report in 2013 indicated that South Sudan has over 30 million herds of cattle.[6] Assuming this is accurate, it means that with a population of 8 to 10 million, each person has on average 3 cows. We need to find way of using this resource effectively.

In Kajo-Keji, some people who have goats and cattle are not willing to sell them to raise money for school fees or medical expenses. As a church, we have tried to encourage people not to use animals for prestige and marriage only. After his son attended a church empowerment seminar, one of my retired clergy sold a number of cattle in order to build a small two bedroom house. If animals are not being used effectively, it may make sense to sell them and invest them in something useful. The money could be used for education, or for equipment that can be used to generate a regular income.

With appropriate infrastructure and facilities, the extent of livestock wealth in South Sudan suggests there is potential for a dairy industry. Local expertise about the kinds of cattle kept in South Sudan and how they respond to their environment would need to be combined with global expertise about crossbreeding techniques. Authorities would need to work together with communities to ensure reliable electricity supplies and road networks that allow distribution to take place. These issues are not easy to resolve. Nonetheless, we need to look for development solutions that utilise the resources we already have, not those we do not have. God has given us great livestock wealth. We must use what he has given us.

7:70-72   *Now some of the heads of ancestral houses contributed to the work. The governor gave to the treasury one thousand darics of gold, fifty basins, and*

five hundred thirty priestly robes. And some of the heads of ancestral houses gave into the building fund twenty thousand darics of gold and two thousand two hundred minas of silver. And what the rest of the people gave was twenty thousand darics of gold, two thousand minas of silver, and sixty-seven priestly robes.

The list in Nehemiah 7:6-73 again departs from that in Ezra 2. As elsewhere, the figures are slightly different. Perhaps more importantly, Nehemiah's list is more detailed. In Ezra 2, only the generosity of the heads of the families is recorded. Here, the amounts contributed by the governor, the heads of the families, and the people themselves are set out. Like the difference in 7:7, this is significant in the light of what will follow. One of the key reforms recorded in the later chapters of Nehemiah was a collective commitment to fund the continuing operations of the temple through giving (10:32-39). This would avoid a situation where the operations of the temple were reliant on support from political leaders or even foreign powers, who might try to use the temple to promote themselves rather than God. The inclusion of three different groups in the list of those who gave toward the earlier rebuilding of the temple provided a model and inspiration for giving. Everyone had a responsibility to give in proportion to how God had blessed them, whether they were political or administrative leaders, heads of families or ordinary people. The poor were expected to contribute, although those with wealth were expected to give more.

7:71-72 sets a model for our churches too. God provides for his churches through generous giving. We should not expect our churches to be funded by those overseas, who may have their own ideas about how the funds should be spent. Leaders should set an example by giving generously, as the governor of 7:70 did. Others should give in accordance with their wealth. No-one is exempted from the requirement to give, however poor. God may value and bless the cheerful gift of the poor more than the grudging duty done by the rich, even if the monetary value is lesser (Luke 21:1-4).

Conclusion

Nehemiah 7, located at the centre of the book of Nehemiah, plays an important role. It links the first half of the book, which focuses mainly on the reconstruction of the city walls, to the second half, which focuses on the reconstruction of a covenantal community. It shows why the repopulation of Jerusalem was necessary and how Nehemiah went about it. It also serves a theological purpose similar to that of Ezra 2, according to Throntveit.

> The placement of the list in Nehemiah 7 also evokes this sense of continuity, expanding it into the holy city itself. It is appropriate that the inhabitants of Jerusalem should be comprised of members of the community who had experienced God's grace in the second exodus of Ezra 1-6.[7]

This continuity is the basis from which the community will derive the authority to confess their sins and the sins of their ancestors, make a new covenant on behalf of all Israel, and live as the people of God.

The availability and use of historic records in Nehemiah 7 challenges us to think practically about what records we should keep and what use we put them to. The chapter also contains useful lessons on practical matters including employment practices, professionalism and giving.

1 Weanzana, "Nehemiah," 552.
2 Kidner, *Ezra and Nehemiah*, 103.
3 Williamson, *Ezra, Nehemiah*, 29.
4 Throntveit, *Ezra-Nehemiah*, 93.
5 Getz, "Nehemiah," 687.
6 Sudan Tribune, "South Sudan Leads World in Livestock Wealth," *Sudan Tribune*, January 25, 2013, http://www.sudantribune.com/spip.php?article45286.
7 Throntveit, *Ezra-Nehemiah*, 93.

CHAPTER SEVEN
The reading and impact of the word of God

NEHEMIAH 8 marks a turning point in the book of Nehemiah. The primary focus of the book is no longer on the physical reconstruction of the walls, but on a programme of spiritual reform. Nehemiah himself fades into the background and Ezra, the priest and scribe who dominates Ezra 7-10, takes centre-stage.

The shift is so marked that many scholars feel that chapters 8-10 are out of place. There is a debate as to whether the events in this section happened soon after the completion of the wall, as the sequencing suggests, or at another time. Some believe the section belongs after Ezra 8, or even Ezra 10.[1] I will not dwell on the arguments for or against these views, as they are beyond the scope of this book.

However, Nehemiah's lack of prominence is not necessarily evidence of textual rearrangement. It could simply reflect his humility.[2] I have already shown how physical and spiritual reconstruction go hand in hand in my treatment of Nehemiah 1-6. The shift of focus from physical to spiritual reconstruction in Nehemiah 8 is certainly noticeable. However, it can also be seen as a progression. A background theme in Nehemiah 1-6 now comes into the foreground.

Some of those who believe that Nehemiah is not chronologically ordered nonetheless argue that the placing of Nehemiah 8-10 in its current location is intentional and serves a structural purpose.[3]

Tollefson and Williamson have shown that from an anthropological perspective, the chronology makes sense in its current sequencing. Revitalisation movements often follow big projects like Nehemiah's building project. The radical changes described in Nehemiah 11-13 only make sense in the light of the kind of revitalisation described in Nehemiah 8-10. Furthermore, Nehemiah 1-6 receives theological significance "only in the light of the religious reordering of the community of faith in Nehemiah 8-10."[4] Nehemiah 8-10, different though it is to the rest of the book, makes sense both of what comes before and what comes after, and links them together.

As a section, Nehemiah 8-10 demonstrates the impact of the word of God on the people of Israel, and culminates in their response. The people are shown to have understood the word. In his prayer, Ezra recited the history of Israel's salvation, inspired by the biblical account he had read, in a way that demonstrated an awareness of the causes of the exile. The people responded to the reading of the word and to Ezra's prayer by making a new covenant, which included specific measures to avoid repeating the mistakes that had led to the exile.

Nehemiah 8:1-12

This section documents what appears to be the first public reading of scripture in many years. God had already been working in the lives of the people while they carried out his will by rebuilding the walls, evidenced by the people's desire to hear the word of God read, and their attentiveness while it was being read. Levites were on hand to ensure the people understood what they heard. The word had an immediate impact on those who heard and understood it.

I have already noted the importance of regular reading of the word for spiritual growth. As previously mentioned, prayer and Bible reading are the first two of Bill Bright's five principles for spiritual growth.[5] The link between Bible reading and spiritual growth is made in the Bible itself. Peter compared new believers to babies, saying that they should desire spiritual milk so that they can grow into salvation (1 Peter 2:2). A key source of spiritual milk is the word of God. The King James Version even translates "spiritual milk" in 1 Peter 2:2 as "milk of the word". The link is strengthened by a further reference to the word of God three verses later. Although it is the Holy Spirit who convicts man of sin, the Bible presents the living word of God (1 Peter 1:25) to the sinner and calls on him and her to repent and believe in Christ.

It is important to pray and read the Bible with other Christians, and not only on our own. Believers together are the body of Christ (1 Corinthians 12:27). Individual members of the body have different gifts, services, and activities allotted to them (1 Corinthians 12:4-6) by the Holy Spirit (1 Corinthians 12:11). We interpret scripture as a believing community. The different perspectives that members bring because of their different gifts and experiences help us to understand scripture in a more complete way and apply it properly. This book is itself the product of many years of discussion in pastors' seminars and leadership sessions within South Sudan, and dialogue with believers from different cultural traditions, especially in the US and the UK. Sometimes God will answer our prayers through another believer. If we believe this to be the case, we should test the answer against scripture. A genuine word from God will never contradict scripture.

8:1 *...all the people gathered together into the square before the Water Gate. They told the scribe Ezra to bring the book of the law of Moses, which the LORD had given to Israel.*

The importance of gathering together is easily missed. Fellowship with other believers is the third of Bill Bright's principles for spiritual growth.[6] The Christian must spend time in fellowship with other believers (Hebrews 10:25). Fellowship can be compared to wood or charcoal in a fire. More than one piece is needed for the fire to keep burning.

Other translations have "all the people gathered as one man" (ESV, KJV). This captures the single-mindedness of the people more clearly than the NRSV. This unity of purpose, seen clearly in Nehemiah 3, is reflected in their unanimous, single demand: for God's law to be read publicly so that all could hear it.

We too should be united on the importance of God's word in the life of the church. We may not agree on how to interpret every verse, but we should agree how crucial the Bible is. We must not allow differences over interpretation to damage the unity of the Church. The Church is a model for the world. By acting "as one man", while preserving their own identities, our denominations can show the way for our tribes to do likewise.

It is worth noting that it was "the people", rather than Nehemiah, who asked Ezra to bring the book of the law of Moses. We have already noted the shift from Nehemiah praying to "we" praying in Nehemiah 6. The desire to hear the word of God read is a further indication that God was working in the lives of the people, preparing them for revival.

Nehemiah himself fades into the background for a short time. There is no reference to him until 8:9. Weanzana argues that this reflects Nehemiah's humility.[7] He did not demand a central part in the reading of the law in recognition of his accomplishments. As a layman, he recognised Ezra's authority when it came to religious matters. We too must be humble and willing to fade into the background when appropriate.

8:2-3 *Accordingly, the priest Ezra brought the law before the assembly, both men and women and all who could hear with understanding. This was on the first day of the seventh month. He read from it facing the square before the Water Gate from early morning until midday, in the presence of the men and the women and those who could understand; and the ears of all the people were attentive to the book of the law.*

Ezra read the scriptures aloud for about five or six hours (*"from early morning until midday"*). Even more surprisingly, the congregation paid attention throughout! How many of us look at our watches when our Sunday services go on for more than two hours?! We should be hungry to hear scripture read aloud, as the people of Israel were on this occasion. It is good to devote time to the reading of God's word in our services. Reading scripture should not be rushed. Reading longer sections can help make sure we understand the Bible in context and do not misinterpret it.

In bringing the law before all those who could hear with understanding, Ezra showed willingness to put the word of God in the hands of the laity. He did not attempt to keep control over the scriptures in order to maintain his authority as the only one who could decide right and wrong. This insistence on opening up the scriptures and making them available to every believer was one of the main battles of the Reformation, and is also reflected in the Second Vatican Council.

8:4-5 *The scribe Ezra stood on a wooden platform that had been made for the purpose and beside him stood Mattithiah, Shema, Anaiah, Uriah, Hilkiah, and Maaseiah on his right hand; and Pedaiah, Mishael, Malchijah, Hashum, Hashbaddanah, Zechariah, and Meshullam on his left hand. And Ezra opened the book in the sight of all the people, for he was standing above all the people; and when he opened it, all the people stood up.*

Ezra made sure he could be seen by all the people. 8:5 makes it clear that the purpose of the platform was to enable Ezra to be seen. The platform was not to demonstrate Ezra's importance. It is important that those reading from and preaching on the word of God are visible. This will require different arrangements in different churches, depending on the size of the congregation and the seating arrangements.

8:6 *Then Ezra blessed the Lord, the great God, and all the people answered, "Amen, Amen," lifting up their hands. Then they bowed their heads and worshipped the Lord with their faces to the ground.*

The very fact of the people's response shows that Ezra was not only visible, but audible! When we pray in church, we should do so in an audible voice. There is a well-known and possibly apocryphal story about a woman who prayed inaudibly in church. Afterwards, a man complained that he could not hear her pray. The woman told him it did not matter, as she was not talking to him! While it is true that we pray to God and not to the people around us, it is important that others can hear so that they can be edified by our prayers and affirm them. If we are to say Amen (meaning, 'let it be so'), we should know what we are saying Amen to!

The word Amen used properly expresses agreement. In too many of our congregations, it is overused. I have heard preachers and others use 'Amen' or 'Praise the Lord' when they need time to think what to say next. Sometimes the words 'Praise the Lord' are used inappropriately, without regard to what is actually being said. A friend of mine heard a preacher tell a story about a man whose goats were eaten by a lion. He finished the tale by exclaiming 'Praise the Lord!', as if he was pleased the goats had been eaten. I hope that the owner of the goats was not in the congregation that day.

8:7-8 *Also Joshua, Bani, Sherebiah, Jamin, Akkub, Shabbethai, Hodiah, Maaseiah, Kelita, Azariah, Jozabad, Hanan, Pelaiah, the Levites, helped the people to understand the law, while the people remained in their paces. So they read from the book, from the law of God, with interpretation. They gave the sense, so that the people understood the reading.*

Ezra's openness is again evident. He allowed the Levites to interpret the law. He did not insist on being the only expositor. This is all the more remarkable when we consider that the Levites would have lacked experience in interpretation, given the widespread neglect of the word of God.

The Levites here played a similar role to those in our churches who lead mid-week Bible studies in small groups. The ministry of such people is vital. The word of God is not magic. In order to impact powerfully on the lives of those who receive it, it must be understood. Pastors have the responsibility to equip small group leaders with the tools to interpret the Bible properly, but must also display trust in them as they exercise their teaching ministry, even if they have little training.

8:9-12 *And Nehemiah, who was the governor, and Ezra the priest and scribe, and the Levites who taught the people said to all the people, "This day is holy to the LORD your God; do not mourn or weep." For all the people wept when they heard the words of the law. Then he said to them, "Go your way, eat the fat and drink sweet wine and send portions of them to those for whom nothing is prepared, for this day is holy to our LORD; and do not be grieved, for the joy of the LORD is your strength." So the Levites stilled all the people, saying, "Be quiet, for this day is holy; do not be grieved." And all the people went their way to eat and drink and to send portions and to make great rejoicing, because they had understood the words that were declared to them.*

When Nehemiah makes a reappearance, he does so acting in unity with Ezra and the Levites. It is significant that he is mentioned at this point. Previously, we have seen that Nehemiah was not too proud to weep at the appropriate time (1:4). The mention of Nehemiah's name makes it very clear that the people were told not to mourn because it was not the appropriate time to mourn, not because weeping is wrong in itself.

The people's reaction is understandable. When the law was read and explained to them, they realised how much of it they had disobeyed, and how seriously God took their disobedience. We should expect the word of God, when understood, to have an impact on those who receive it. It should provoke a strong reaction. It should stir a desire to be transformed. Our whole being, including our emotions, should respond to the reading of scripture.

There would come a time for mourning their sin; for confession; for crying out to God with a contrite heart (9:1-4). It is right to be grieved by the sin we have committed. If we are not, we have not begun to understand how our sin grieves our God. The famous Baptist preacher Charles Spurgeon, preaching on Zechariah 12:12-14, began by saying that "True repentance is always accompanied by sorrow."[8] He suggested that the combination of "The land shall mourn" with "each family by itself", shows that authentic mourning, even when it is national in character, is also individual. Nehemiah recognised his own part in the nation's sin when he confessed that "Both I and my family have sinned" in 1:6.

However, this was not the appropriate time for mourning. This was the Lord's holy day; a day for rejoicing. Again, I am reminded of Ecclesiastes 3:4. There is a time to mourn and a time to dance. This was a time for dancing. Rejoicing does not mean pretending we are happy when we have good reason to be unhappy. It means praising God in all circumstances (1 Thessalonians 5:16-18; Philippians 4:4), without pretending that everything is perfect. David worshipped God after his newborn son died (2 Samuel 12:20). He did not suddenly forget his grief. Rather, he chose to rejoice in the midst of his grief.

We can only gain the strength to rejoice in the midst of grief through God's Spirit. A friend of mine tells the story of a South Sudanese couple in Wau. They held a memorial service in 2010 for their young daughter who had died a year before. This is common practice in South Sudan. During the service, the couple praised and worshipped God with all of their hearts. The preacher read 2 Samuel 12:15-23 and pointed to the couple, saying that they had not suddenly forgotten their grief at losing their daughter; they could praise God because he gave them strength to do so, drawing alongside them in the midst of their suffering because he knew what it was to suffer himself. Asking others if they wanted to know that same God, who would draw alongside them in the midst of their suffering, a call was made and some of those present gave their lives to Christ. God used the example of that grieving couple, who rejoiced without pretending everything was perfect, to bring others to himself.

The emphasis on rejoicing ensures that religion is not reduced to careful observance of a list of commands. True religion is about relationship with God. It involves the whole person, including our emotions. The law was supposed to help people stay in relationship with God by showing them what he regarded as good and bad. If we think we are following God's commands but our hearts do not praise God, something is wrong. Fulfilling our part of God's covenant is not simply a list of do's and don't's. It includes rejoicing and weeping at the appropriate times.

Scripture is an indispensable tool, given to us by God, to help us grow in our relationship with him. It roots us and helps ensure we bear fruit at God's allotted time (Psalm 1:2-3). It is, however, a means rather than an end. It cannot replace our relationship with God and must not be idolised. The importance of a good knowledge of scripture should not be underestimated. However, it is not enough on its own.

Nehemiah 8:13-18

This passage reports back on a Bible study group meeting held the day after Ezra's public reading of scripture. Ezra took a back seat, facilitating the study without dictating to the group. The group discovered specific commands the people of Israel had not kept for hundreds of years, and set about resolving this. In doing so, they passed the first major test of obedience to God's commands since the completion of the walls.

The commandments they resolved to keep were highly relevant to their situation, suggesting the activity of God's Spirit in drawing their attention to a particular section of scripture that spoke into their context. The re-inaugurated rituals helped to meet the psychological needs of the community, and helped prepare them to stand firm against temptations they would soon face.

8:13 *On the second day the heads of ancestral houses of all the people, with the priests and the Levites, came together to the scribe Ezra in order to study the words of the law.*

A smaller group, made up of representatives of the people and religious officials, came back the next day to study the word further. They were hungry to study the scriptures in more detail. Somewhere, deep down, they realised that covenantal relationship with God required more than occasional doses of scripture on religious holidays. They needed to be rooted in the word of God. They needed to know it well. They needed to study it daily.

Ezra had fired the heads of ancestral houses, the priests and the Levites with a passion for the word of God. Good preaching should do this. It should not present the preacher as an expert who alone can interpret and apply the word. It should encourage those listening to explore the scriptures more deeply for themselves.

The presence of the heads of ancestral houses is further evidence that Ezra did not try to keep the scriptures in the hands of the religious establishment, but was determined to make them available to the laity and allow God to speak directly to them through his word.

8:14-16 *And they found it written in the law, which the LORD had commanded by Moses, that the people of Israel should live in booths during the festival of the seventh month, and that they should publish and proclaim in all their towns and in Jerusalem as follows, "Go out to the hills and bring branches of olive, wild olive, myrtle, palm, and other leafy trees to make booths, as it is written." So the people went out and brought them, and made booths for themselves, each on the roofs of their houses, and in their courts and in the courts of the house of God, and in the square at the Water Gate and in the square at the Gate of Ephraim.*

The passage the students found is almost certainly Leviticus 23:39-43 (although they may also have looked at Deuteronomy 16:13-15).[9] The passage refers to the festival of Sukkot, which God commanded the Israelites to keep as a way of reminding them of the time when they wandered in the desert for 40 years before entering the Promised Land. They used tents, or booths (*sukkot*) for temporary shelter as they moved from one place to another.

On one level, the decision to revive the festival of Sukkot and the practice of living in tents for seven days represented simple obedience to the commands the students found in scripture. It so happened that the time for the festival was approaching. Celebrating Sukkot in the way the scriptures set down was the first major test of whether the people had changed. If their grief at their sin (8:9) was genuine, it would result in a determination to live in a new way, in obedience to God's commands.

Obedience is the fifth and final principle of spiritual growth identified by Bill Bright,[10] and links the other four principles (prayer, Bible reading, fellowship and witnessing) together. The example of a bicycle wheel can be used to to demonstrate this. A bicycle wheel has a hub, spokes, and tube. The spokes represent the first four principles: prayer, study of the word, fellowship and witnessing. The tube represents obedience. The hub or centre of the wheel is Jesus Christ.

When all the parts of the wheel are sound, the bicycle will move without any problem. If any of the spokes is loose, it will affect the movement of the bicycle. If the hub has a problem with the bearings or has no grease, it can stop the bicycle from moving. If the pressure on the tube is low or there is a puncture, it will also stop the owner from using the bicycle.

Similarly, we can struggle along in our Christian lives if we are neglecting one of the first four principles. We will not move at all if we are not connected to Jesus Christ, or are not obedient to him. Obedience to God requires and facilitates each of the other principles of spiritual growth.

We have now seen all of Bright's five principles of spiritual growth evidenced in the book of Nehemiah. It is worth restating them:

- We must study God's word (Nehemiah 1:5-11; 6:11; 8:1-8, 13).
- We must pray (Nehemiah 1:4-11; 2:4; 4:4-5, 9 etc.).
- We must be in fellowship with other Christians (Nehemiah 8:1).
- We must witness for Christ (Nehemiah 2:18).
- We must obey God (Nehemiah 8:13-18).

For us to live fruitful Christian lives, we must grow in our faith by following these five principles of spiritual growth. This way, we will become increasingly mature in our faith. We need to remember that perfection cannot be attained while we are on this earth, but if we are growing, we will move from one level to another in our walk with God.

We grow in our spiritual lives by ensuring that we read the word of God regularly and pray at all times. By doing this we will improve our vertical relationship with God. We also need to work on our horizontal relationships with each other through fellowship and witnessing to our fellow human beings. Obedience to God requires and facilitates each of these elements of spiritual growth.

The people's simple obedience to what they found in scripture immediately strikes the reader. Yet there were also social and theological currents behind the decision to revive old practices. Often people find comfort and strength in reconnecting with their past during times of change. Old customs and traditions, including dance and folklore, are often revived during periods of flux. People feel the need to be rooted, and memory is a powerful force for achieving this. Tollefson and Williamson write that the feast "gave the people an alternative to their present existence and renewed a sense of continuity with the past."[11] Continuity in times of change is important in Nehemiah. We saw this in Nehemiah 7, in the use of the list of those who returned during Zerubbabel's time.

The festival of Sukkot itself seems particularly relevant to the situation the people of Israel found themselves in. I have already noted parallels between the Exodus and the events recorded in Nehemiah. Both were new beginnings. In both cases, God's salvific actions were the basis for covenant with him, and also served as a powerful witness to non-Israelites. God's actions ensured that Israel and its neighbours alike knew that *I am the LORD your God* (Exodus 7:3-5; cf Nehemiah 6:16). It is relevant then that Leviticus 23:42-3 commands Israelites to observe the festival of booths *so that your generations may know that I made the people of Israel live in booths when I brought them out of the land of Egypt: I am the LORD your God.* We need to keep repeating the story of God's actions in our community's history, using national days of celebration, symbols and any other means at hand to recall what God has done for us.

The Israelites had lived a precarious existence while in the wilderness. They had little in the way of security. They had to rely on God to provide food miraculously. They were not permitted to stockpile food, but had to wait for God to provide daily. By this experience, "Israel is shown that life-giving resources do not come from land but from Yahweh. Israel is not tied to, dependent upon, or subservient to the land. These resources are given to the landless by the Lord."[12]

Deuteronomy, presented as a reflection at the boundary of the Promised Land, used the memory of God's provision in the wilderness to guard against the coming temptations of land (Deuteronomy 8:19). The memory of God's provision in the wilderness was supposed to help the Israelites to remember that land was God's gift and should be enjoyed in accordance with his statutes. It was not a resource to be centralised, sold without restriction and plundered. It was not the means for Israel to control their own affairs without regard to God. The Torah included guidelines on land management "so that Israel will not forget whose land it is and how it was given."[13] If these guidelines were not respected, the land could be lost.

Before the rebuilding of the walls, the situation of the returned exiles was not dissimilar to that of the Israelites under Moses. They had little in the way of security. They lived in shame (1:3). They were vulnerable to famine (5:3). Now, the situation of the Israelites in Judah and Jerusalem was still precarious, but the completion of the city walls brought with it a new temptation. The risk was that the people would rely on the protection offered by walls and fortifications, or alliances with benevolent powers like the Persian king, rather than on God. The misuse of land by elites to secure their own position was a further temptation, as demonstrated in Nehemiah 5.

Obedience to the law was to be the primary means of avoiding these temptations. The guidelines it offered for land management would ensure that land was treated as a gift from God, not abused and lost as it was before. But part of the solution rested in a conscious remembering of God's provision and protection in history. When we remember what God has done for us in the past, our faith is strengthened and it is easier for us to believe he can protect and provide for us again. The odd sight of temporary shelters erected on top of rebuilt homes and in the shadow of newly-reconstructed city walls, reminded the Israelites that their security came from God and not from their own efforts.

What we believe about history affects how we act in the present. If we in South Sudan tell the story of our liberation without reference to God, we will start to believe that we can solve our own problems without taking them to him. Then we will wonder why we fail, and accuse God of abandoning us. Independence brings temptations. Inclusion in international institutions, the establishment of a diplomatic apparatus and the trappings of statehood encourage us to believe we can solve our problems and protect our nation through diplomatic manoeuvring. Isaiah 30:1-5 and 31:1-5 record God's reaction when Israel tried to do the same thing.

There is nothing wrong with having diplomats. It is important for South Sudan to do so. However, if we deviate from God's commands and rely on them alone, we will fail. If we allow the land of the poor to be plundered for natural resources, or bought and sold by speculators in order to buy friends in the international community who can protect us, we will fail.

Remembering how God was with us during times of war, when many of us were displaced and others went to the bush to fight, will help us avoid these temptations. We must remind each other how Christianity grew explosively during the second period of civil war, and how the church took a leading role in reconciliation efforts that were the basis for negotiating peace from a position of relative unity. We must remind each other how God worked through the church to strengthen those without hope. We must remind each other how some Christians stayed when many NGOs left South Sudan. We must recognise and celebrate God's actions in our history when we celebrate our national festivals. This includes 9th July (independence day) and 30th July (martyrs' day). Using national festivals to remind each other how God was with us during times of war is our equivalent of the Israelites putting up tents to remind each other how God was with them in the wilderness. It will give us the courage and faith to act justly in the knowledge that he is with us now, even when justice seems expensive or difficult, or others put pressure on us to act unjustly.

The 'they' of verse 14 may or may not include Ezra, but it certainly refers to those who had come to Ezra to study the scriptures. It was 'they' who found Leviticus 23 and realised how important it was for them. Ezra did not select it. Rather, when the heads of ancestral houses, the priests and the Levites studied the scriptures for themselves, God showed them what was relevant to their situation and how to apply it to their lives.

We can help people to understand the Bible, but we must allow them to interpret it for themselves, and trust God to speak to them through it. South Sudan needs help from outsiders in training our clergy and others who teach in our churches. During the war, many were appointed without any training, by necessity and through the laying on of hands. They need good biblical training. But those who help us must be careful not to impose their own interpretations on the people of South Sudan.

God has used his word to speak into situations in countries with cultures and needs very different from our own. He will use the scriptures to speak to South Sudanese in different ways appropriate to our own culture and history. Those who come alongside us need to be sensitive to this. Laying our own experiences in front of the biblical text, we will find in it things that Western friends (and even those from other parts of Africa) may not have discovered. If allowed to do this, we and our international brothers and sisters in Christ will be able to deepen and enrich each other's understanding of our God and his word.

8:17 *And all the assembly of those who had returned from the captivity made booths and lived in them; for from the days of Jeshua son of Nun to that day the people of Israel had not done so. And there was great rejoicing.*

The statement that *"the people of Israel had not done so"* does not necessarily mean that Sukkot had not been celebrated since the days of Joshua. The festival may have been kept in a tokenistic way without following all the prescriptions set out in the law. It is fairly clear, however, that the commandment to set up tents had not been kept all this time.

We cannot pick and choose which parts of the Christian faith we uphold. If the Israelites had done what God had commanded and set up tents every year, the memory of God's provision and protection may have inspired them to keep other commands they failed to keep. If we keep only the commands that feel right to us, we are likely to fall down in other areas of our lives too.

Previously, the people of Israel had wept when they should have been rejoicing (8:9). This time they got it right. They rejoiced at the appropriate time.

8:18 *And day by day, from the first day to the last day, he read from the book of the law of God. They kept the festival seven days; and on the eighth day there was a solemn assembly, according to the ordinance.*

It is difficult to underestimate the importance of reading God's word daily. Psalm 1:2 encourages us to go further, meditating on scripture "day and night". One of the choruses I sang as a youth puts it very simply:

> *Read your Bible, pray every day.*
> *Pray every day, pray every day.*
> *Read your Bible, pray every day if you want to grow.*
> *If you want to grow, if you want to grow.*
> *Read your Bible, pray every day if you want to grow.*
> *Don't read your Bible, forget to pray.*
> *Forget to pray, forget to pray.*
> *Don't read your Bible, forget to pray if you want to shrink.*

If you want to shrink, if you want to shrink.
Don't read your Bible, forget to pray if you want to shrink.[14]

The sense of 8:18 is that Ezra read the whole Torah (the first five books of the Bible) in their entirety. It is important that we teach the whole Bible in our churches. It is easy for preachers to keep returning to favourite parts of the Bible and give a partial picture of the whole counsel of God which reflects their own personality and preferences. One way to avoid this is to use a lectionary to select daily or weekly passages. However, even a lectionary is selective and does not cover the whole of scripture. Weekly Bible study groups may choose to go through books of the Bible systematically, while encouraging members to use a reading plan to read through the whole Bible in their daily devotions.

Conclusion

Nehemiah 8 demonstrates the importance of reading scripture. It has already been clear from Nehemiah's prayer in 1:5-11 and his rebuke to Shemaiah in 6:11 that Nehemiah himself was well-versed in scripture. In Nehemiah 8 we see the impact of the public reading of scripture on the gathered people. It had an immediate impact on the minds, hearts and actions of the people. They understood, wept, and changed their behaviour.

If only scripture had such a central part in all of our services! We should expect it to have the same impact today. We can also learn from Ezra's approach to teaching scripture. He preached the text as it was, trusted others to interpret it and allowed God to speak to people directly through it. He enthused the people with a passion for scripture, leading them to study it together in small groups outside of times of public worship.

The chapter is part of a unit comprising Nehemiah 8-10. Everything that happens in chapters 9 and 10 flows from the reading of scripture in Nehemiah 8. The process of reform was set in motion by the public reading of scripture.

---

1   Ibid., 94.
2   Weanzana, "Nehemiah," 553.
3   Throntveit, *Ezra-Nehemiah*, 96.
4   Tollefson and Williamson, "Nehemiah as Cultural Revitalisation," 336.
5   Bright, "Five Principles of Growth."
6   Ibid.

7   Weanzana, "Nehemiah," 553.

8   C H Spurgeon, "Apart" (Sermon, The Metropolitan Tabernacle, Newington, July 16, 1885), http://www.spurgeon.org/sermons/2510.htm.

9   Williamson, *Ezra, Nehemiah*, 294–5.

10   Bright, "Five Principles of Growth."

11   Tollefson and Williamson, "Nehemiah as Cultural Revitalisation," 337.

12   Brueggemann, *The Land*, 31.

13   Ibid., 61.

14   Unknown, "101 (English): Read Your Bible, Pray Every Day," in *Shukuru Yesu*, Third Edition (Juba: Scripture Union Sudan, 2000).

CHAPTER EIGHT
Retelling the story of Israel

Nehemiah 9:1-5

The sudden switch from celebration to grieving and the reference to separation from foreigners have caused consternation among a few scholars, who have been quick to suggest these features are evidence that Nehemiah 8-10 originally belonged elsewhere. Myers follows Rudolph in placing Nehemiah 9 after Ezra 10, on the assumption that the separation in Nehemiah 9:2 was the same separation described in Ezra 10.[1] However, we should not automatically assume that the reason for the separation from foreigners was the same as in Ezra 10 or Nehemiah 13. There is no reference to mixed marriages, the subject of the confession of Ezra 10, in 9:1-5, and the separation is from all foreigners, not foreign women as in Ezra 10.[2] The confession in 9:6-37 is much wider than the subject of mixed marriages alone. I have put forward another possible reason for the separation from foreigners below.

9:1 *Now on the twenty-fourth day of this month the people of Israel were assembled with fasting and in sackcloth, and with earth on their heads.*

Now that the festivities were done and the time for rejoicing was over, the people gathered together to confess their sins. They adopted the outward signs of mourning, wearing sackcloth and putting ashes or dust on their faces. Some communities in Africa grieve in the same way today.

9:2 *Then those of Israelite descent separated themselves from all foreigners, and stood and confessed their sins and the iniquities of their ancestors.*

The assembly represented the whole people of Israel by virtue of their connection to the first wave of returned exiles (7:5-73), who themselves represented every tribe (7:7) and had to prove their descent. The act of confession related to the Israelites' failure to keep their part of the covenant that God had made with them. Living out the covenant was their calling as a people. It was not appropriate for foreigners to join them in this act of confession[3] or the subsequent act of recommitment, as the covenant did not apply to them, and so they could not be guilty of failing to keep it.

We in South Sudan must take responsibility for our own failings. We cannot blame everything on former colonial powers, or on Sudan. The process of national reconciliation is an opportunity for us to mourn our sin and make acts of collective repentance as families, tribes, and as a nation. Some of these acts will relate to abuses our tribes have perpetrated against other tribes in South Sudan.

We may feel that we as individuals are less responsible than others in our tribes for abuses that took place during the war and which still continue in some places. We cannot absolve ourselves of responsibility. We are all culpable to some extent. Even if we did not carry out human rights abuses as individuals, we can facilitate the process of reconciliation by taking responsibility as a member of the families, tribes and kinship networks we are a part of.

Nehemiah was hardly among the worst offenders. He had done more to keep the covenant than most. Yet he took responsibility on himself for the sins of the nation (1:6) and acknowledged his own part in them. It is likely that the first wave of returned exiles and their descendants were among the most zealous of the Israelites. They had taken a risk in returning to Judah and Jerusalem when others remained in exile. Yet they took responsibility for the failure of the people to be zealous for God's law, and made a collective act of repentance.

The people followed Nehemiah's example (1:6) in confessing their sins and the sins of their ancestors. In doing so, they marked themselves out from their ancestors and showed their determination not to repeat their mistakes. Acknowledging the mistakes of the past opened up the possibility of living a new kind of life.

The importance placed on genealogy, and the honour given to ancestors who were the first to return to Judah and Jerusalem, shows that the people of Israel revered their ancestors. They were not ashamed of them. Many South Sudanese can recite their ancestors to the fifteenth generation. The people of Israel could go further. The genealogy in Matthew 1 suggests that the people of Israel, at the time of their confession in Nehemiah 9, could recite their ancestors to at least thirty generations.

Clearly, the people of Israel revered their ancestors. Yet it was not shameful for them to admit their ancestors' mistakes. The stories they repeated from generation to generation, and which are clearly recorded in the Bible, did not hide their ancestors' sins. The Bible is especially careful to record the sins of the Israelites' most illustrious ancestors. Abraham's failure to trust God to keep his promise that Sarah would bear a child, and his lack of courage when he pretended his wife was his sister, are prominent in the book of Genesis. 2 Samuel attests to David's adultery with Bathsheba and murder of her husband Uriah (2 Samuel 11:2-12:15). The text openly displays the full scorn of the prophet Nathan. (Interestingly, Nathan does not criticise Bathsheba, which has led to suggestions that David's offence was rape rather than adultery.) David was also responsible for the massacre of 70,000 of his own people (2 Samuel 24:15). David's sins were extremely serious, and God treated them as such. Yet David was regarded as Israel's greatest king, and Abraham as their common ancestor and a model of faith.

It is difficult for us to confess the sins of heroes of the liberation movement, or paramount chiefs, especially those of our own tribes. Yet the Bible shows us that it is possible to do so without bringing shame on them, and without honouring or revering them any less. Indeed, it is important that we do so as a precondition for living out our callings as individuals, families, tribes and nation.

9:3 *They stood up in their place and read from the book of the law of the LORD their God for a fourth part of the day, and for another fourth they made confession and worshipped the LORD their God.*

Again we see that the people did not rush away from God's presence. This was another long service, taking over six hours.

The people spent three hours reading from God's word and three hours praying. We are reminded that prayer and the reading of God's word have equal importance. Prayer and Bible reading are like the two legs of a human being. If one is not used properly, a person will limp and cover less ground. If one is missing he will struggle to walk at all. We need to spend time in prayer and read the Bible every day.

9:4-5 *Then Jeshua, Bani, Kadmiel, Shebaniah, Bunni, Sherebiah, Bani, and Chenani stood on the stairs of the Levites and cried out with a loud voice to the LORD their God. Then the Levites, Jeshua, Kadmiel, Bani, Hashabneiah, Sherebiah, Hodiah, Shebaniah, and Pethahiah, said, "Stand up and bless the LORD your God from everlasting to everlasting. Blessed be your glorious name, which is exalted above all blessing and praise.*

The actions of the Levites show that confession, in the truest sense of the word, involves acknowledging "God's glory and grace as well as man's ingratitude".[4] Confession is not a transaction. It is not a contract where we fulfil our responsibility by listing our sins, and God fulfils his by forgiving them. True sorrow over sin realises how God has blessed us and been gracious to us even when we have grieved him. It recognises something of the cost involved in taking away our sin and responds in praise.

Nehemiah 9:6-37

Ezra's prayer is one of the longest prayers in the Bible. Its influence has been widespread. Weanzana notes that some churches have incorporated it into their liturgy[5] and argues that "with their alternating sadness and joy, rejoicing and fasting (9:9, 17; 9:1-2)", Nehemiah 8 and 9 together "offer a model for the liturgy of the African church."[6]

The primary purpose of the prayer is confession, but it takes the form of a retelling of Israel's history, with special emphasis on the Exodus and wilderness period (cf. Psalm 106 for another example of this method).[7] Grabbe characterises the prayer as "a recital of past and present sins, interspersed with praise of God for his greatness and his mercies."[8]

Ezra follows the lead of the Levites in taking a wide view of confession that admits both human sin and God's gracious response (hence the praise Grabbe refers to). Some scholars even argue that Ezra's prayer has been mistakenly attributed, and 9:5b-37 is one prayer, offered by the Levites.[9] Others are more ambivalent.[10] Whether the prayer is attributed to Ezra or to the Levites does not change the theological significance of the prayer. Whoever prayed the prayer is clearly speaking on behalf of the whole community.

I shall assume that the prayer is Ezra's. While the theological significance of the passage is the same with or without the break in verse 6, when considered from an anthropological perspective, the break helps us to understand Nehemiah 8-10 as an integrated whole. The reading of the law leads into confession of past and present sins through the retelling of the events the community has just read about. This retelling was part of a series of events in Nehemiah 9 that motivated the community to make a new covenant with special measures to avoid repeating the sins of their ancestors.

Tollefson and Williamson show how tension builds throughout Nehemiah 9:

> In Nehemiah 9, three recognizable methods used for motivating group change are apparent; staging a public demonstration to rally the people (9.1-3), increasing the magnitude of cultural dissonance to an intolerable level (9.6-35), and rubbing raw public sores of discontent (9.36-37). First

there was a public demonstration led by a number of the Levites but involving the people as a whole. This was followed by a reading of the Law and a general confession of sins (9:1-5).

Secondly, a public prayer was used to increase the intensity of the cultural dissonance by drawing attention to the inconsistencies that existed between belief and circumstances (which in the theology of the prayer are linked with behaviour).[11]

Ezra capitalised on the actions of the Levites, elaborating on their prayer to expose the past and present sins of the community. In pinpointing the mistakes of the past, he enabled the community to turn their back on them, and to prepare to make a new commitment to live as God intended. Good leaders can see these moments when a community is hungry for change and lead them into it. Instead of whipping discontent into a destructive frenzy, they channel energies into constructive processes. They do not underplay the problems facing our communities (9:36-7) but they keep their focus on God (9:6 etc.) and facilitate peaceful change in united communities.

If, with Throntveit, we assume that 9:5b-37 is one prayer offered by the Levites, we may still gain an understanding of the theological significance of the prayer, but miss the social process unfolding through Nehemiah 9 and fail to learn from Ezra's example.

The special emphasis on the Exodus and wilderness period is not accidental. I have already noted that the events of Nehemiah can be depicted as a second exodus. The revival of Sukkot suggests that the people had this comparison in mind themselves. The way the text is presented (e.g. Nehemiah 6:16 and 9:10's conscious echo of Exodus 7:3-5) suggests that the events described in Nehemiah continued to be viewed through this lens.

Despite the successful rebuilding of the walls of Jerusalem, the people continued to live as subjects of a foreign power in their own land (9:36). They could not enjoy the fruits of the land (9:37). Other communities continued to press their claims to the land, and the process of repopulation was still at an early stage. Land was at the forefront of the people's consciousness. No wonder the people identified with their ancestors during the time of the Exodus — they wanted the same result! They hoped that they, like their ancestors, would be brought into the land (9:23), would possess the land (9:24a) and subdue the people of the land (9:24b).

Williamson's summary of Ezra's prayer suggests that each section is related to the theme of land:

6	Creation
7-8	Abraham
9-11	Exodus
12-21	Wilderness period
22-31	The land.[12]

Ezra's prayer picks up on the key concern of the people: possession and enjoyment of the land. It shows them what they need to do to achieve their aims: repent of the sins that led to them losing the land, and commit to living life in a new way. The prayer does the former together with them and leads them into the latter (9:38).

When we recite the histories of our communities, we tend to emphasise the aspects of the past that are most relevant to the present. Events that have some bearing on current circumstances are described in more detail. Where current political realities are contested, history is contested too. The basic facts of the story may be the same, but events which do not reflect well on the ancestors of particular individuals or tribes, or which do not serve the narrative being put forward by the one telling the history, are omitted. Conversely, other events viewed to be particularly instructive are emphasised with the intention, conscious or unconscious, of persuading others to make particular choices in the here and now.

So it is here. Ezra's prayer took the story the people have been listening to over a period of several days and condenses it, picking out the events that were most instructive. Where our histories tend to focus on the successes of our ancestors, Ezra's retelling is a litany of failure. By picking out the key failures of the community over several centuries, Ezra enabled them to see that their ancestors had failed in the same ways time and time again, and that they too were implicated in those failures. They needed to take radical action to break the cycle of failure.

As I comment on the prayer verse by verse, I will suggest reasons why Ezra highlighted particular events as he recited the community's history. The prayer often seems to pick up on events that seem marginal. It is my contention that Ezra picked up on these events deliberately to lead the people into understanding. Although influenced by the earlier reading of the word, Ezra's prayer is not a series of random recollections of scripture. There is a rationale behind the emphases laid.

9:6 *And Ezra said: "You are the LORD, you alone; you have made heaven, the heaven of heavens, with all their host, the earth and all that is on it, the seas and all that is in them. To all of them you give life, and the host of heaven worships you.*

I have already discussed in the section above why the NRSV's inclusion of *"And Ezra said"*, taken from the Septuagint (an early Greek translation of the Old Testament scriptures), is important.

The prayer begins with creation. In doing so, it concurs with the account of Israel's salvation history presented in scripture. It also recognises that salvation begins with God's initiative. It puts God at centre stage. Starting with creation is also of paramount significance to the theme of land. It recognises that God has given life to the land, and the land's purpose is to worship its Creator. It recognises that the earth and everything in it belongs to the Lord (Psalm 24:1). The land was a gift from God and did not belong to Israel by right or by its own merit. Even when given, the land remained God's. Israel were trustees and did not have the right to do whatever they wished with the land. The gift must be enjoyed under covenant. As Brueggemann writes, "Land... is in covenant with us but not totally at our disposal."[13]

This understanding is crucial in framing Ezra's prayer. Starting with Abraham would run the risk of territorialism, of prioritising Israel's rights to the land over God's universal purposes. Starting with creation starts with God's purposes and locates the gift of the land within those purposes.

Our understanding of land must also start with God's creation and ownership of it. He has apportioned land to us for particular purposes. We do not have a right to do with it whatever we wish, even if he has appointed us trustees of it (Leviticus 25:23). We must not mine its resources unsustainably, as "land has its own rights over us"[14] (Leviticus 26:34-35).

Many South Sudanese believe that God has given their land to them, as families, clans, tribes and nation. We must pray to God and discern his purposes for the land where he has placed us. Do we see land primarily as a resource to be managed and protected from others? Or is it a place to bring gifts to the Lord from (Isaiah 18:7) and to blow a trumpet and raise signals from (Isaiah 18:3) so that the nations around will know God and the good news of Jesus Christ? Do we believe that, like Israel, God has placed South Sudanese in a strategic location, to bring light to the nations around? If so, that will change the way we relate to land and the way we use it.

Ezra's prayer is saturated in scripture. An early indication of this is the reference to *"all their host"*, reflecting Genesis 2:1. We should not be surprised that the reading of the word in Nehemiah 8 influenced Ezra's prayer. As we read God's word more and more, we too will notice that our prayers reflect what we find there.

9:7 *You are the LORD, the God who chose Abram and brought him out of Ur of the Chaldeans and gave him the name Abraham;*

The phrase *"brought him out"* (cf. "brought you" in Genesis 15:7) implies deliverance[15] and connects Abraham, the Exodus, and the present situation of the returned exiles. I have already shown how the events of Nehemiah were understood by the returned exiles, and depicted by future generations, in terms of a second exodus.

As suggested above, the retelling of Israel's history focuses on events and is presented in terms which were particularly relevant to the gathered assembly. The specific reference to Ur strikes a parallel between Abraham and the returned exiles. "Abraham is called out of Ur of the Chaldeans, that is, Mesopotamia, to go on a journey of faith, the same journey on which the exiles in Babylon were summoned to venture."[16]

Kidner points out that "no other Old Testament passage after Genesis picks out for mention" the renaming of Abram (Genesis 17:4).[17] He is right to suggest that the reference "shows... the influence of the scripture reading of previous weeks".[18] However, he fails to draw any theological significance from the unique reference to this event.

The preceding verses help us to locate theological significance in 9:7. The God who created the whole world made Abraham the father of many nations, not the father of of the Jews alone. The universalising tendency of verses 6 and 7 guard against any racist interpretation of the subsequent separation from foreigners and the prohibition of mixed marriages. Neighbouring nations were not to be opposed on the grounds of ethnic background, as many had the same ancestor in Abraham. They were to be opposed and separated from on the basis of their opposition to God alone.

9:8 *and you found his heart faithful before you, and made with him a covenant to give to his descendants the land of the Canaanite, the Hittite, the Amorite, the Prizzite, the Jebusite, and the Girgashite; and you have fulfilled your promise, for you are righteous.*

The list of nations suggests the covenant referred to is the unconditional covenant of Genesis 15. Six of the ten nations listed in Genesis 15:19-21 are included here.[19] This emphasis on "the indefectible promise of the land"[20] is crucial. The people were not in a position to appeal to God for deliverance on the basis that they had fulfilled their part of the covenant. They could only appeal to God on the basis of his own righteousness, linked here to his faithful character. God keeps his promises even though human beings let him down: "because of God's 'righteousness,' they still dare to appeal to unfulfilled aspects of the original promise".[21]

9:9-10 *And you saw the distress of our ancestors in Egypt and heard their cry at the Red Sea. You performed signs and wonders against Pharaoh and all his servants and all the people of his land, for you knew that they acted insolently against our ancestors. You made a name for yourself, which remains to this day.*

The Exodus is the next significant event highlighted in Ezra's prayer. The Exodus was the founding event of the nation of Israel; the equivalent of South Sudan's referendum on independence. God is portrayed here as a God who responds to the distress of his people, acts in history to deliver them, and punishes those who act against those with whom he has made covenant. He does all this for the sake of his own name, so that others may come to know of him through what he has done.

The same pattern can be seen in Nehemiah. God saw the shame of the survivors (1:3). The gracious hand of God guaranteed the success of Nehemiah's endeavours (2:10, 18). God frustrated the plans of Nehemiah's enemies (4:15) in response to Nehemiah's plea for him to act against those who opposed him (4:4-5). He did all this for the sake of his own name, so that the nations would see that the work had been accomplished with the help of God, fear him and be humbled (6:16).

9:11 *And you divided the sea before them, so that they passed through the sea on dry land, but you threw their pursuers into the depths, like a stone into mighty waters.*

"Like a stone into mighty waters" deliberately echoes the song at the Red Sea (Exodus 15:5, 10).[22] This song emphasises God's might and his salvific actions. It is pure praise, based on a recital of God's achievements in Exodus 14.

Exodus 14 portrays the parting of the Red Sea as the final and determinative means by which God gained glory for himself and made his name known to the Egyptians (Exodus 14:17-18; Isaiah 63:12). The Egyptians recognised that the LORD was fighting for the Israelites (Exodus 14:25). Israel themselves saw what God had done and believed in him (Exodus 14:31).

Taken together, the first three sections of Ezra's prayer (verses 6, 7-8, and 9-11) focus on God's reputation and the character that reputation is based on. God is Creator; he is righteous and keeps his promises; he is Saviour and has "acted in concrete terms to bring his word to realisation."[23] Having established God's character, the prayer now moves into confession of past and present sins.

9:12 *Moreover, you led them by day with a pillar of cloud, and by night with a pillar of fire, to give them light on the way in which they should go.*

Williamson has identified a sequence of provision (12-15), rebellion (16-18) and God's continuing mercy (19-21) in the section of Ezra's prayer dealing with the Israelites in the wilderness.[24] Strict chronology has been sacrificed for the sake of this pattern. Provision includes guidance for the journey (12), good laws (13-14) material provision (15a) and renewal of the promise of land (15b).[25] Each of these gifts was refused by the Israelites in some way. They threatened to turn back to Egypt (Exodus 14:11-12; Numbers 14:2-4). They disobeyed the laws God gave them (Exodus 32:1-6). They grumbled about the food they were given (Numbers 11:4-6), and attempted to collect food for themselves rather than rely on God's continuing provision (Exodus 16:20). They refused to enter the promised land when they had the opportunity (Numbers 13:25 – 14:12).

9:13 *You came down also upon Mount Sinai, and spoke with them from heaven, and gave them right ordinances and true laws, good statues and commandments,*

"The giving of the law is accentuated",[26] yet the "Sinai event is not described as a covenant".[27] It has clearly been understood as a covenant elsewhere in Nehemiah (1:5-11). Fensham and Blenkinsopp agree that the reason it is not described as a covenant here is to emphasise the Abrahamic covenant, "because of its promissory character"[28] and in order to permit "a total concentration on the promise of land and nationhood."[29] Rather than appeal to the conditional covenant they had broken, the people appealed to the unconditional covenant which rested solely on the faithfulness of God.

By emphasising the giving of the law, the people were reminded that they had failed to keep it. Failure to keep God's commandments is one of the three repeated sins emphasised in Ezra's prayer. Each of these three areas also received special attention when a new covenant was made. In his retelling of the story of Israel, Ezra led the people in confessing specific sins so as to make a break with the past. Remembering the past is necessary if we are to break with it. Breaking with the past is necessary if we are to live in new ways. By highlighting the specific sins that led to loss of the land, Ezra strengthened the resolve of the people to live in new ways so they did not lose it again.

9:14 *and you made known your holy sabbath to them and gave them commandments and statues and a law through your servant Moses.*

Failure to keep the law emerges from Ezra's prayer as one of the chief causes of land loss. Sabbath, however, is named specifically. It is the "only legal prescription to be named".[30] All of the material included in this prayer is theologically significant. The specific inclusion of sabbath is therefore deliberate. This is confirmed by its importance in the covenant made in Nehemiah 10.

Sabbath was not merely a day to rest. It was an intrinsic part of the social justice measures set out in the law, along with the Day of Jubilee. Nehemiah 9:14 does not refer to the sabbath day, but rather to God's holy sabbath, i.e. the principle of sabbath/sabbath in general. This includes the sabbath year. Every seventh year, the land was to be allowed to rest (Leviticus 25:4). Nothing would be sown. Labourers and slaves would also rest. Families, slaves, bound labourers, livestock and wild animals alike would share in whatever the land yielded. This measure was, according to Chris Wright, "explicitly for the benefit of the poor".[31]

The concepts of sabbath and jubilee were closely related. Both are set out in Leviticus 25. The jubilee was to be held after every seven sabbath years. In Nehemiah 10:31b, the sabbath year and the exaction of debts are referred to in the same clause. If, as argued in Chapter Five of this book, Nehemiah proclaimed an emergency jubilee in 5:11, the book of Nehemiah has already spoken implicitly about the importance of sabbath.

Chris Wright argues that "sabbatical institutions" including "the seventh year fallow . . the release of pledges taken for debt (Deuteronomy 15:1-3) . . and the jubilee release of those whose land and labour were mortgaged to their creditors" were concerned especially with the "interests of . . those whose *only* asset was their labour"[32] (i.e. the poor). Sabbath and jubilee alike helped stop inequality from widening, provided for the needs of the poor, and guaranteed the rights of workers (including those who had sold themselves or their families into slavery).

Land needs rest and "has its own rights over us".[33] Land was itself a partner in a three-way covenant with God and with the people of Israel. God had responsibilities toward the land as well as his people. If the land was not given its rest, God would scatter the people and devastate the land (Leviticus 26:32-33). During its desolation, the land would enjoy the rest it did not have while the people were living on it (Leviticus 26:34-35). Leviticus 18:28 states boldly that if the Israelites defiled the land, it would vomit them out.

Sabbath, then, was an essential part of a functioning society. It was crucial for maintaining social justice and harmony, for protecting the environment and ensuring sustainability. Its importance was underlined by its inclusion as the fourth of the Ten Commandments. God took sabbath seriously, and continues to do so today. Keeping sabbath is about more than taking Sunday off work. It is also about the way we treat those who work for us, the way we treat the land, and the laws and economy of our nation.

The reference to sabbath was designed to remind the gathered assembly of their failure to implement social justice. They and their ancestors had oppressed the alien, the widow and the orphan (Jeremiah 7:6). The poor (which, in the Old Testament, generally refers to the landless),[34] had been marginalised. After the failure to keep God's commandments (in general), marginalisation is the second of Israel's repeated sins highlighted in Ezra's prayer.

9:15 *For their hunger you gave them bread from heaven, and for their thirst you brought water for them out of the rock, and you told them to go in to possess the land that you swore to give them.*

I have already discussed God's miraculous provision for the Israelites while they were in the wilderness, and its relevance to their stewardship of land at a time of new beginnings, under 8:14-16.

"The command to possess the land is given special prominence."[35] This again related to the specific circumstances of the day. Nehemiah 8-10 interrupts a process of repopulation, which begins in Nehemiah 7 with the enrolling of the people by genealogy (7:5) and continues in Nehemiah 11 with the casting of lots to decide which people would live in Jerusalem. The Israelites had refused to populate the promised land when they sided with the spies who said they would not be able to defeat the people of the land (Numbers 14:4). Consequently, God decreed that none of the people who refused to populate the land would ever enter it (Numbers 14:22-23).

Ezra's prayer equates the repopulation of Jerusalem with entry into the promised land. If the people had truly changed, they would not refuse to live in Jerusalem as their ancestors had. By highlighting the sin of their ancestors, Ezra showed the people what they must do next. Nehemiah 11:4 suggests Ezra was successful. All the people who entered Jerusalem did so voluntarily (11:2).

9:16-17 *But they and our ancestors acted presumptuously and stiffened their necks and did not obey your commandments; they refused to obey, and were not mindful of the wonders that you performed among them; but they stiffened their necks and determined to return to their slavery in Egypt. But you are a God ready to forgive, gracious and merciful, slow to anger and abounding in steadfast love, and you did not forsake them.*

The people's ancestors are here described in the same terms as the Egyptians. I have already shown how memory of God's actions is properly used as a basis for right conduct. When the Israelites did not remember ("were not mindful") of God's actions in history, the natural consequence was disobedience. The people preferred slavery in Egypt to freedom in the land.

9:18 *Even when they had cast an image of a calf for themselves and said, "This is your God who brought you up out of Egypt," and had committed great blasphemies,*

Fensham describes the making of the golden calf as the Israelites' "gravest sin".[36] Together with failing to obey God's Law (Jeremiah 7:9), and oppressing the alien, widow and orphan (Jeremiah 7:6), serving foreign gods (Jeremiah 7:18) came to be part of the dominant explanation for the exile. It is no coincidence that all three of these patterns of sin are given prominent place in this section. Israel had to change these behaviours if they were to enjoy God's gift of land without losing it again.

9:19-21 *you in your great mercies did not forsake them in the wilderness; the pillar of cloud that led them in the way did not leave them by day, nor the pillar of fire by night that gave them light on the way by which they should go. You gave your good spirit to instruct them, and did not withhold your manna from their mouths, and gave them water for their thirst. Forty years you sustained them in the wilderness so that they lacked nothing; their clothes did not wear out and their feet did not swell.*

God, in his grace, did not remove the provision he made for the Israelites.[37] The people were not faithful, but God was more than faithful.

9:22 *And you gave them kingdoms and peoples, and allotted to them every corner, so they took possession of the land of King Sihon of Heshbon and the land of King Og of Bashan.*

Williamson identifies the same sequence of provision, rebellion and continuing mercy in 9:22-31 as in 9:12-21.[38] However, the pattern repeats itself in a cyclical fashion to "see an intensification, if not of the people's rebellion (though vv 29-30 certainly contain the strongest statement in this regard), yet at least of the severity of God's judgment."[39]

Joshua does not receive a mention in the description of the conquest of the land.[40] As in 2:10, 2:18, 2:20, 4:20 and 6:16, God is recognised as the one who stands behind human actions and grants success. He alone is given credit.

It is striking that Ezra's prayer emphasises relatively minor victories rather than, for example, the more famous victories at Jericho (Joshua 6:20), Ai (Joshua 8:18ff) and over the armies of the five kings (Joshua 10:11). The two victories singled out took place before the Israelites crossed the Jordan and entered the promised land.

Fensham suggests that the mention of the two kings was conventional, "popular in the poetic description of Israelite history at a certain stage."[41] This is not a satisfying explanation. While poetry has clearly influenced the prayer, Fensham overestimates the extent to which it conforms to the poetic form. As Williamson has shown, "no exact parallels to this passage are to be found"[42] elsewhere in scripture. "Probably adapting material from a liturgy of public penance, our author has woven together several elements that were all associated with confession."[43]

The thesis that Ezra was following convention in including references to the two kings is undermined by the unusual material contained elsewhere in the prayer. Ezra was certainly not following convention when he made reference to Abram's change of name. It is not clear why he would suddenly do so here. In the context of the rest of the prayer, it is far more likely that the event was deliberately selected because it had theological significance for the gathered assembly.

Mendenhall has modified his earlier view of the conquest as a peasant revolt, but posits a gradual process where Israel grew numerically and geographically as people "converted" to Yahwism.[44] Israel was never an ethnically homogenous community (Exodus 12:38) but rather a self-selected community "composed of people who did not value power politics"[45] (cf. Judges 9:8-11, 14-15) and shared a voluntary acceptance of a covenant of obedience. 'Conquest' is Yahweh's routing of petty warlords who kept people in subjugation. Once liberated, the people became part of the tribes of Israel through a covenant.[46] While Mendenhall may overstate his proposition, his case is strongest when it comes to the kings Sihon and Og.[47]

If we see the defeat of these kings as the liberation of their people and the expansion of the people of Israel to include other ethnic groups who, by voluntarily participating in God's covenant, became part of the people of Israel before they entered the Promised Land, this sheds new light on their inclusion in Ezra's prayer. Like the reference to Abram's change of name, the reference qualifies the apparent antagonism to foreigners in Nehemiah 13. The problem with mixed marriage was not that the Israelites were marrying those who were not part of their own tribe. The reference to the two kings reminds Israel and us that it had been possible for people of other tribes to become part of Israel in the past. The problem was that they were marrying people who had not accepted God's covenant of obedience.

In remembering the decision of the village tribes of the Transjordan to accept God's covenant of obedience, Ezra highlighted the importance of covenant, and the failure of ethnic Israel to be obedient to it. In placing themselves under covenant, the Transjordan people had done what Israel, God's covenanted people, had failed to do. The reference to kings Sihon and Og points to the need for Israel to make a new covenant.

In remembering how God had liberated the Transjordan people from the oppressive kings Sihon and Og, Ezra reminded the returned exiles of their current subjugation (albeit under a more benevolent Persian regime) and warned them that living in freedom was not compatible with power politics. Nehemiah would later criticise King Solomon (13:26), the ultimate power politician. He bureaucratised and centralised land at the expense of the families who lived on it. He took advantage of the poor (landless), using them as forced labour for his own projects. He married women who were not under covenant and who led him astray, in order to cement alliances with foreign powers. A covenanted people should not control and manage land, or oppress their own people, as Solomon did. Before God would deliver them from Persian subjugation, Israel must commit to live in a different way.

9:23 *You multiplied their descendants like the stars of heaven, and brought them into the land that you had told their ancestors to enter and possess.*

God's righteous character as promise-keeper is stressed again here. He fulfilled both key aspects of the promise he had made to Abraham.

9:24-5 *So the descendants went in and possessed the land, and you subdued before them the inhabitants of the land, the Canaanites, and gave them into their hands, with their kings and the peoples of the land, to do with them as they pleased. And they captured fortress cities and a rich land, and took possession of houses filled with all sorts of goods, hewn cisterns, vineyards, olive orchard, and fruit trees in abundance; so they ate, and were filled and became fat, and delighted themselves in your great goodness.*

Unlike the Transjordan people, whose example the returned exiles must follow, the Canaanites are linked to those who have opposed the rebuilding work, with the phrases *"inhabitants of the land"* and *"peoples of the land"* (cf. Ezra 4:4).

The land is to be enjoyed as well as administered fairly and generously. Blenkinsopp points out that the descriptions of the various riches of the land are taken from Deuteronomy (3:5; 6:10; 6:11; 8:7-10; 32:13-14),[48] which the people had just heard read.

9:26 *Nevertheless they were disobedient and rebelled against you and cast your law behind their backs and killed your prophets, who had warned them in order to turn them back to you, and they committed great blasphemies.*

The section moves from provision to rebellion. In such a short summary, there are no specific sins listed. Nonetheless, the implication is that Israel has committed the same sins—disobedience to God's law, oppression of the poor, and idolatry—over and over again. There is a rough correspondence with the sins identified during the first sequence (9:12-21), listed here in the same order. The people's ancestors *"cast your law behind their backs"*, they *"killed your prophets"* with their social justice message,[49] and their repeated insistence that land must only be acquired in ways prescribed by the law, which guaranteed the rights of the marginalised,[50] and *"they committed great blasphemies"* (i.e., they worshipped idols).

9:27 *Therefore you gave them into the hands of their enemies, who made them suffer. Then in the time of their suffering they cried out to you and you heard*

*them from heaven, and according to your great mercies you gave them saviours
who saved them from the hands of their enemies.*

Suffering here is the consequence of rebellion. There are many causes of
suffering. Rebellion, i.e. deliberately cutting ourselves off from the bless-
ings of God, is one. The sequence is completed as the verse describes God's
continuing mercies in delivering the people.

9:28 *But after they had rest, they again did evil before you, and you abandoned
them to the hands of their enemies, so that they had dominion over them; yet
when they turned and cried to you, you heard from heaven, and many times you
rescued them according to your mercies.*

Now that the sequence has been established, it is summarised in a single
verse. God's provision is the same; the people's sins are the same; God's
continuing mercies are the same. The cycle repeats (*"many times"*) over and
over again. Having made it clear what the sins of the people were and what
they must now do to avoid falling back into the same errors, Ezra ramped
up the tension. The intention was to show that the cycle of "sin, decline,
appeal and rescue"[51] was so ingrained that radical action was needed to
break it.

Repeated sin becomes ingrained in our lives and difficult to break with.
It is better to deal with sin before it becomes a pattern and starts to feel
'normal'. If sin does become ingrained, confession to God, and to trusted
believers who can help to hold us accountable, is crucial. Then we need to
take practical measures to help us avoid falling back into old patterns of
behaviour. This was Ezra's prescription. He led the people in confessing
their sins to God and to each other. In the process, he made it clear that true
repentance meant making a concerted effort to live in new ways, pointing
toward the need to make a new covenant.

9:29-31 *And you warned them in order to turn them back to your law. Yet they
acted presumptuously and did not obey your commandments, but sinned against
your ordinances, by the observance of which a person shall live. They turned a
stubborn shoulder and stiffened their neck and would not obey. Many years you
were patient with them, and warned them by your spirit through your prophets;
yet they would not listen. Therefore you handed them over to the peoples of the
lands. Nevertheless, in your great mercies you did not make an end of them or
forsake them, for you are a gracious and merciful God.*

Williamson argues that the third cycle, detailed in 9:29-31, is incomplete.[52] There is no cry to help and no description of God's continuing and merciful provision (although the decision not to make an end of Israel is in itself described as one of God's mercies). This is because 9:30 brings the recital of history up to the exile, and history itself was incomplete. 9:32-37 constitute a cry for help on the assumption that God would continue to be faithful to his promises and would act mercifully as he had before.

9:32 *Now therefore, our God – the great and mighty and awesome God, keeping covenant and steadfast love – do not treat lightly all the hardship that has come upon us, upon our kings, our officials, our priests, our prophets, our ancestors, and all your people, since the time of the kings of Assyria until today.*

In the light of what has preceded this, it is clear that the covenant referred to is the Abrahamic covenant. The people have no right to appeal to the Sinai covenant as they and their ancestors had broken it consistently. The Abrahamic covenant, however, rested solely on God, who would never break covenant.

While it is acknowledged that the punishment of exile was deserved, the feeling is that the people had served their time (Isaiah 40:2). They had suffered long enough. 9:32 reminds me of David's cry in Psalm 13:1-2: *"How long O LORD? Will you forget me forever? How long will you hide your face from me? How long must I bear pain in my soul, and have sorrow in my heart all day long? How long shall my enemy be exalted over me?"* This is a legitimate prayer in times of suffering, even when some aspects of our suffering have been self-imposed.

9:33-5 *You have been just in all that has come upon us, for you have dealt faithfully and we have acted wickedly; our kings, our officials, our priests, and our ancestors have not kept your law or heeded the commandments and the warnings that you gave them. Even in their own kingdom, and in the great goodness you bestowed on them, and in the large and rich land that you set before them, they did not serve you and did not turn from their wicked works.*

The "present generation's solidarity with the sin of past generations"[53] is clear throughout Ezra s prayer. *"Our ancestors"* is used (9:9, 16) to stress the complicity of the current generation. In these verses, this complicity becomes more explicit. They are the collective equivalent of 1:6, when Nehemiah admits that *"I and my family have sinned"*. The dichotomy between *thou* and *they*[54] in the rest of the prayer switches to *you* and *we*.[55]

9:36-37 Here we are, slaves to this day – slaves in the land that you gave to our ancestors to enjoy its fruit and its good gifts. Its rich yield goes to the kings whom you have set over us because of our sins; they have power also over our bodies and over our livestock at their pleasure, and we are in great distress."

Tollefson and Williamson argue that Ezra's prayer "rubs raw specific social sores of discontent."[56]

"It reminds the people that their national life is in a state of economic bankruptcy, that they are slaves in their own land, and that their labour crops and cattle are being claimed in taxes by foreigners (9.36-37). Schaller (1972:89) observes that 'without discontent with the present situation there can be no planned, internally motivated and directed intentional change'. Change is threatening. Consequently, the leaders in the story prod the people to keep them moving toward their objective."[57]

By intensifying the contrast between the reality of God's promise and the reality of the current sorry state of affairs (described by Kidner as "the low ebb of God's people"),[58] Ezra gave the group the final push they needed to take action.

Satterthwaite and McConville suggest that these two verses display the most vehement opposition to Persian rule to be found in Ezra-Nehemiah. Previously,

"Persia has been cast in the role of benefactor, providing everything needed for the people of Judah to re-establish themselves in their homeland. Now the prayer sees the people as "slaves in the land that you gave to our ancestors", and laments that the land's wealth must go in tribute to an overlord (9:36-37)."[59]

The picture thus far in Nehemiah is not quite as uncritical as Satterthwaite and McConville make out. High levels of the king's tax was one of the complaints in Nehemiah 5 (v.4). Nonetheless, the opposition to foreign rule in 9:36-37 is striking. The phrase *"slaves in our own land"* will remind South Sudanese of the words of the late Dr John Garang, who asked if we wanted to be "second-class citisens in our own country". Just as in South Sudan, the Israelites did not have the freedom to invest their own resources while a foreign power ruled over the land.

9:38 *Because of all this we make a firm agreement in writing, and on that sealed document are inscribed the names of our officials, our Levites, and our priests.*

Ezra's prayer was a success. By the end of the prayer, the people understood where they and their ancestors had gone wrong. They had acknowledged responsibility for their present situation and confessed their sin to God and one another. They had appealed to God on the basis of his righteousness to deliver them. They were ready to take further action.

Conclusion

Nehemiah 9 is a testimony to the power of memory. I have already shown how important it is to identify God's actions and ensure that he receives the credit for deliverance when we tell our stories (individual and communal). Remembering what God has done helps us to trust him, as we remind ourselves that he is in control of history. It also guards us against the temptation to make our own history. Nehemiah 9 reinforces the importance given in the book of Nehemiah to how we tell our stories.

In Ezra's retelling of the story of Israel, the most important person is God. God was faithful and kept his promises even when the people of Israel did not. The people could appeal to him on the basis of his unconditional promises even though they had no right to appeal to him on the basis of their own actions. We do the same thing when we confess our sins, since scripture promises that "If we confess our sins, God is faithful and just and will forgive us our sins" (1 John 1:9, NIV).

Ezra retold his people's story in such a way that the people, in saying "Amen", acknowledged the goodness of God's actions and character, admitted that they deserved exile because of their rebellion against him, confessed specific repeated sins in their community's history and their own complicity in the sins of their ancestors, and were motivated to take practical measures to help them live in new ways. Just as everything that happened in Nehemiah 9 led on from the reading of scripture in Nehemiah 8, everything that happens in Nehemiah 10 leads on from Ezra's prayer of confession in Nehemiah 9.

Reading scripture is an important way of remembering what God has done. We also need to recite the stories of our own families, communities and nation as Ezra did. In our stories God must be the central character, just as he was in Ezra's prayer. We must confess the sins of our ancestors, since, because of our link to them, we can easily fall into the same patterns of sinful behaviour. We must acknowledge our complicity in these sins and break conclusively with them. We must recognise just how much God has done for us, but also recognise that the reason much of his promise is left unfulfilled and we do not enjoy our land in the way that he intends, is because of the legacy of our sins. This will help motivate us to take measures to ensure we live in new ways, in unity and peace with each other, respecting the land as God's gift and managing it according to biblical guidelines so it is available to the poor.

The National Programme for Healing, Peace and Reconciliation is an ideal opportunity to do this. Part of the vision set out by the committee for national reconciliation is to bring about a society that "clarifies and reconciles its divisive history to ensure the stories of all ethnic communities are represented."[60] By telling the stories of every section of our national community, and acknowledging the ways we have sinned against each other, we can forge a new, inclusive, national story in which the experiences of all peoples are recognised and God is acknowledged as the central actor. Having forged this story, we must retell it over and over again. Memorialisation: identifying and documenting sites of killing among various communities in order to "help communities develop and own a shared and reconciling narrative as basis for community healing and recovery",[61] is an important part of this process.

Our sins are not so different from the Israelites' sins. We have failed to keep God's commandments. Although God caused his church to grow during the time of war, it was also a lawless time when *the people did what was right in their own eyes*" (Judges 21:25). We have

> wounded ourselves through cattle stolen from each other, abducted children and women, land grabbed; we have killed and wounded one another and destroyed our own property. We have spawned a culture of violence, corruption, nepotism, and inequity.[62]

We are also in danger of following the example of our parent state, Sudan, in marginalising the peripheries. This is not exclusively the fault of the government. The concentration of NGOs in Juba is partly to blame. Nonetheless, the government must ensure that the vision of the SPLM, to "take the towns to the people" is fulfilled. Development must not be the preserve of Juba alone. Finally, our ancestors did not worship God, Father, Son and Holy Spirit, alone. Traditional religion is still prevalent in South Sudan and many, like the Israelites, think they can worship both God and clan spirits.

1   Myers, *Ezra, Nehemiah*, 165.
2   Blenkinsopp, *Ezra-Nehemiah*, 295.
3   Ibid., 296.
4   Kidner, *Ezra and Nehemiah*, 111.
5   Weanzana, "Nehemiah," 554.
6   Ibid., 555.
7   Fensham, *The Book of Ezra, Nehemiah*, 228.
8   Grabbe, *Ezra-Nehemiah*, 56.
9   Throntveit, *Ezra-Nehemiah*, 100, 102.
10 Kidner, *Ezra and Nehemiah*, 111.
11 Tollefson and Williamson, "Nehemiah as Cultural Revitalisation," 338.
12 Williamson, *Ezra, Nehemiah*, 305.
13 Brueggemann, *The Land*, 64.
14 Ibid.
15 Williamson, *Ezra, Nehemiah*, 312.
16 Blenkinsopp, *Ezra-Nehemiah*, 303.
17 Kidner, *Ezra and Nehemiah*, 111.
18 Ibid.
19 Fensham, *The Book of Ezra, Nehemiah*, 229.
20 Blenkinsopp, *Ezra-Nehemiah*, 303.
21 Williamson, *Ezra, Nehemiah*, 313.
22 Kidner, *Ezra and Nehemiah*, 112.
23 Williamson, *Ezra, Nehemiah*, 313.
24 Ibid., 313–4.
25 Ibid., 313.
26 Fensham, *The Book of Ezra, Nehemiah*, 229.
27 Blenkinsopp, *Ezra-Nehemiah*, 304.
28 Fensham, *The Book of Ezra, Nehemiah*, 229.
29 Blenkinsopp, *Ezra-Nehemiah*, 304.
30 Ibid.
31 Wright, *Old Testament Ethics for the People of God*, 159.
32 Ibid.
33 Brueggemann, *The Land*, 64.
34 Ibid., 65–6.
35 Blenkinsopp, *Ezra-Nehemiah*, 304.
36 Kidner, *Ezra and Nehemiah*, 112.
37 Williamson, *Ezra, Nehemiah*, 314.
38 Ibid., 314–6.
39 Ibid., 315.

40 Fensham, *The Book of Ezra, Nehemiah*, 231.

41 Ibid., 232.

42 Williamson, *Ezra, Nehemiah*, 306.

43 Ibid., 307.

44 George E Mendenhall, *Ancient Israel's Faith and History: An Introduction to the Bible in Context*, ed. Gary A Herion (Louisville: Westminster John Knox Press, 2001), 75–87.

45 Ibid., 78.

46 Ibid., 83.

47 Ibid., 81–3.

48 Blenkinsopp, *Ezra-Nehemiah*, 305.

49 Wright, *Old Testament Ethics for the People of God*, 159–60.

50 Brueggemann, *The Land*, 80.

51 Kidner, *Ezra and Nehemiah*, 112.

52 Williamson, *Ezra, Nehemiah*, 315–7.

53 Throntveit, *Ezra-Nehemiah*, 100.

54 Kidner, *Ezra and Nehemiah*, 112.

55 Weanzana, "Nehemiah," 555.

56 Tollefson and Williamson, "Nehemiah as Cultural Revitalisation," 338.

57 Ibid.

58 Kidner, *Ezra and Nehemiah*, 112.

59 Satterthwaite and McConville, *The Histories*, 252.

60 Deng Bul, "A Working Paper of the Committee for National Healing, Peace and Reconciliation," 6.

61 Ibid., 15.

62 Ibid., 5.

Chapter Nine
The making of a covenant

NEHEMIAH 9 CULMINATED in an important statement: "we are making a binding agreement" (NIV). In response to Ezra's prayer, chiefs, local government officials, religious leaders, opinion-shapers and ordinary people endorsed a written agreement. In this agreement, or covenant, the people promised to obey the Mosaic Law, and put additional specific obligations on themselves to avoid repeating the mistakes of the past.

The concept of covenant was not new. God made covenants with Noah, Abraham and Moses. Each of these covenants is described in the Pentateuch, the first five books of the Bible, which had been read in the preceding days and weeks. It is not surprising that when recommitting themselves, the people used the means God himself had established to institutionalise relationship with his people.

Covenants have been used throughout the history of the Church to make specific commitments to serve God in particular ways. Brown points out that "Wesley compiled a New Year Covenant Service for the Methodist people, which continues to be an important feature in the spiritual life of their churches".[1] The Anglican Communion began to draft an Anglican Covenant in March 2005, although there is no consensus on a final version at the time of writing.

The Lausanne Covenant is a good example of a cross-denominational covenant. It sets out its authors beliefs as to what mission involves in today's world, and commits the Church to specific kinds of action. Brown has described its value as follows:

> The Lausanne Covenant is a recent example of corporate commitment to evangelism and social action on the part of evangelical leaders form all over the world. The value of the covenant is that it saves our laudable desires from hovering in a pious void. Instead, we make firm decisions in God's presence to do his will over particular contemporary issues.[2]

Covenants must be taken seriously. When we agree to do something we must honour our word. This is true regardless of whether our agreement is written or verbal. Jesus told us to let our yes be yes, and our no, no (Matthew

5:37, cf. James 5:12). To break a covenant shows a lack of respect for the person or people we make a covenant with. It disrupts and makes it difficult to resume relationship with them.

South Sudanese should understand this better than anyone. Successive regimes in Khartoum made agreements with the South Sudanese that they did not keep. These included the Addis Ababa Agreement, signed in Ethiopia in 1972 and abrogated by President Gafaar Mohammed Nimeiri in 1983 when he divided Southern Sudan into three regions and imposed Sharia Law.

Abel Alier, a veteran South Sudanese politician, wrote a book called Southern Sudan: Too Many Agreements Dishonoured.[3] With this title, he neatly summed up the feelings of South Sudanese. In 1997, Dr Riek Machar entered into an agreement with the Government of Sudan, referred to as the Khartoum Peace Agreement. This agreement was never implemented. It was merely a means to exploit divisions between the liberation movement in South Sudan. Arop Madut-Arop subsequently wrote that the Khartoum Peace Agreement "validated and updated Abel Alier's Book".[4]

When the Comprehensive Peace Agreement (CPA) was drafted, South Sudanese leaders demanded all kinds of guarantees as they did not trust the intentions of the Government of Sudan. The international community, including the United States, Great Britain, EU countries, IGAD and the United Nations acted as guarantors and monitored the implementation of the CPA. The Sudan People's Liberation Army (SPLA) was not subsumed into the Sudanese Armed Forces but kept intact to act as an 'organic' guarantee.[5] South Sudanese had no trust in the Government of Sudan to implement agreements by its own volition.

The lack of respect that successive regimes in Sudan showed to the South Sudanese people, using agreements to manage and manipulate them but breaking those agreements whenever they were inconvenient to Sudan, persuaded many South Sudanese that true equality was not possible within a unified Sudan. Sudan's repeated failure to keep covenant was therefore a contributing factor to South Sudanese independence.

We must not be like the Government of Sudan, as individuals or as a nation. When we make an agreement, we must keep it. We should not rush into making promises, or we may overlook something that makes it difficult to honour our word. Once we make an agreement, we cannot break it simply because something has come up that we did not anticipate. Psalm 15 tells us that the righteous "stand by their oath even to their hurt" (v. 4b).

The Bible warns what happens when we rush into agreements. Judges 11:29-40 recounts the story of Jephthah. He was a warrior who made an agreement with God, promising that *"If you give the Ammonites into my hand, whatever comes out of the doors of my house to meet me, when I return victorious from the Ammonites, will be the LORD's, to be offered up by me as a burnt offering"* (Judges 11:30b-31). Jephthah fought the Ammonites and defeated them. When he returned to his home in Mizpah, the first person who came to meet him was his daughter. Because he had made his promise, he was bound to keep it. He killed her after allowing her two months to weep in the mountains. God did not lead Jephthah to make this particular agreement. He made it out of his own macho vanity.

We should not make pledges that we cannot meet. In my diocese, we were once raising funds for the purchase of motorbikes. For political reasons, one person pledged to buy one during a church service. Someone who knew him came to me after the service and told me not to believe or rely on this person's pledge until he fulfilled it. To date he has not fulfilled this pledge.

It is important to keep our commitments in small matters, as well as in large matters like peace agreements. When we say that we will visit a person, we must do it. If something urgent comes up, we should make an effort to reschedule the appointment. Sometimes it may be necessary to pass on something that seems more important in order to keep a commitment. By doing so we show that we value the person to whom we have made the commitment.

Many leaders are known for not keeping their appointments and not communicating with those affected when circumstances change. This is not a sign of their importance; it is a sign of discourtesy and untrustworthiness. Jesus made it clear that those who can be trusted with small things will be given more (Matthew 25:29). If these leaders cannot be trusted to keep an appointment, they should not be trusted with a portfolio or geographic area.

Nehemiah sets out the details of the covenant mentioned in 9:38 and the widespread support for it throughout the community. As with chapters 8 and 9, the origins and placement of this chapter are controversial. Some argue that Nehemiah 13 preceded this section. Some scholars even argue that the list in 10:1-28 is fabricated, cobbled together from other parts of Ezra and Nehemiah by an editor. Again, resolving this kind of debate is beyond the scope of this book.

Nehemiah 10:1-27

The purpose of the list in 10:1-27 is to demonstrate the consensus of support for the covenant within the community. The leaders who fixed their seals to the document represent the entire people.

10:1 *Upon the sealed document are the names of Nehemiah the governor, son of Hacaliah, and Zedekiah;*

The use of seals strengthens the argument that many of the names in the list to follow are family names and not names of individuals. It would also demonstrate to future generations that the agreement had not been tampered with.

Nehemiah is the first name in the list of signatories. Good leaders lead by example. In building the wall, Nehemiah showed he was ready to soil his hands in order to demonstrate what needed to be done. Once again, Nehemiah set a good example for the people here. Zedekiah was probably another civil official, possibly Nehemiah's secretary.[6]

10:2-8 *Seraiah, Azariah, Jeremiah, Pashhur, Amariah, Malchijah, Hattush, Shebaniah, Mulluch, Harim, Meremoth, Obadiah, Daniel, Ginnethon, Baruch, Medhullam, Abijah, Mijamin, Maaziah, Bilgai, Shemaiah; these are the priests.*

The names here are "virtually identical with the 22 said to have returned with Zerubbabel (12:1-7) and the 21 listed as heads of priestly phratries in the next generation (12:12-21)."[7] We must therefore assume that most or all of the names here are family names. Representatives of each family signed or sealed the document on behalf of the whole family. Kidner suggests that Ezra's name does not appear in the list because he was part of the house of Seraiah.[8] If Kidner is right, Ezra presumably used the family seal rather than his own name to endorse the document. However, others believe Azariah is a long form of Ezra.[9] Still others have suggested that Ezra's name was left out because, as author of the document, his endorsement was assumed.

10:9-13 *And the Levites: Jeshua son of Azaniah, Binnui of the sons of Henadad, Kadmiel; and their associates, Shebaniah, Hodiah, Kelita, Pelaiah, Hanan, Mica, Rehob, Hashabiah, Zaccur, Sherebiah, Shebaniah, Hodiah, Bani, Beninu.*

Kidner suggests plausibly that the names here represent a combination of family groups and individual names.[10] The first three names correspond with Nehemiah 12:8, Ezra 2:40 and 3:9. The other names seem to refer to a diverse group of individuals who had risen to prominence through a variety of means, and were obviously respected figures in the community who commanded personal followings due to their achievements. The inclusion of their names therefore demonstrated widespread support for the agreement. Even today, the names of respected figures are often displayed prominently in open letters to gain publicity and encourage readers to take the letters seriously.

If Kidner is correct about the identities of the men, what is striking is that they all rose to prominence by serving God, but in a variety of different ways. Kidner reckons six or seven (five according to Clines)[11] interpreted the law during the public reading (8:7).[12] Sherebiah was also one of those who bravely returned with Ezra before Nehemiah's arrival (Ezra 8:18). Hashabiah returned with him (Ezra 8:19) and was also one of those included in the roll-call of honour in Nehemiah 3. Here we have three distinct ways of serving God: as a faithful teacher of God's word, as a brave pioneer, and in practical service. Each, because they were doing God's work, contributed something that will last. None is given prominence above the other.

10:14-27 *The leaders of the people: Parosh, Pahath-moab, Elam, Zattu, Bani, Bunni, Azgad, Bebai, Adonijah, Bigvai, Adin, Ater, Hezekiah, Azzur, Hodiah, Hashum, Bezai, Hariph, Anathoth, Nebai, Magpiash, Medhullam, Hezir, Meshezabel, Zadok, Jaddua, Pelatiah, Hanan, Anaiah, Hoshea, Hananiah, Hasshub, Hollohesh, Pilha, Shobek, Rehum, Hashabnah, Maaseiah, Ahiah, Hanan, Anan, Malluch, Harim, and Baanah.*

Like the list of priests, most or all of these names appear to be family names. Around half are consistent with the lists in Ezra 2 and Nehemiah 7. Others are family names also given in Nehemiah 3. Others may represent families who arrived more recently, showing that the process of return was ongoing. It is not surprising that family names were used by the chiefs of the people. It is the same today in South Sudan. When an agreement is signed, the chiefs of local tribes will sign on behalf of their tribes. The returnees were representative of the whole people of Israel (7:7). The list of chiefs in 10:14-27 shows that the list of signatories to the new agreement represented the whole community in Judah and Jerusalem.

Local government officials, prominent figures in civil society and religious leaders sometimes counter-sign agreements made between chiefs of warring tribes, especially when the agreement is a major event and it is important to demonstrate buy-in from the whole community. This was the case with the agreement detailed in Nehemiah 10. The inclusion of

Nehemiah and Zedekiah (local government officials), priests (religious leaders), Levites (the equivalent of modern civil society, including learned laypeople and people who held no great position but whose achievements had earned them respect) and the heads of every major family/tribe/sub-tribe demonstrated the support of all types of leaders across the community. The author of the list has taken great care to demonstrate the breadth of buy-in from all sections of the community, lest anyone turn around at a later date and claim they had not supported it.

Nehemiah 10:28-39

This section sets out the stipulations of the new covenant. They include general and specific stipulations: a recommitment to existing laws and the establishment of new laws intended to help Israel keep the spirit, and not merely the letter, of the old laws. As I shall show, the specific stipulations relate to key areas where the people and their ancestors failed, and which were highlighted in Ezra's prayer.

10:28-9   The rest of the people, the priests, the Levites, the gatekeepers, the singers, the temple servants, and all who have separated themselves from the peoples of the lands to adhere to the law of God, their wives, their sons, their daughters, all who have knowledge and understanding join with their kin, their nobles, and enter into a curse and an oath to walk in God's law, which was given by Moses the servant of God, and to observe and do all the commandments of the LORD our Lord and his ordinances and his statutes.

The seals of such a vast array of leaders demonstrated the support of the whole community for the agreement. Nonetheless, the people were still invited to participate in the event, by entering into a voluntary curse and oath. This evokes memories of the South Sudanese referendum on independence. Independence was not achieved through the signatures of leaders on agreements alone, but through the voluntary participation of the whole people. The whole people can claim ownership over and participation in independence, just as the whole people of Israel could point to their involvement in covenantal renewal. I have already pointed out, while discussing the rebuilding of the walls, that participation in decision-making tends to increase motivation. In this instance it is likely that the people's involvement increased the likelihood of their fulfilling the new obligations.

The phrase *"all who have knowledge and understanding"* echoes 8:2, where the law was read before *"all who could hear with understanding"*. This suggests that all those who had been present at the reading of the law were also present here. The curse and the oath were not rash. Unlike Jephthah, the people knew exactly what they were committing themselves to. The similarity of the language also suggests the unity of chapters 8-10. They are an integrated unit within Nehemiah. The reading of the law leads into the prayer of confession, which culminates into the covenant specified in Nehemiah 10.

The major issue exposed and confessed in Ezra's prayer was the failure of the people and their ancestors to keep the Mosaic law. It is not surprising that this was the first issue addressed in the new covenant. The people committed to keeping the whole of the Mosaic law. Throntveit shows the influence of Ezra's prayer (which he believes was offered by the Levites) on the detail of the covenant:

> Neglect of the law, which had issued in the disastrous consequences brought before the people in the Levitical prayer of the previous chapter, is seen, at least for the moment, to be the primary problem the new community faced. From the small beginnings the reading of the law prompted in chapter 8, the reader senses the gratification that Ezra would have felt upon witnessing the hearty response of the community to the law rightly interpreted and rigorously applied.[13]

10:30 *We will not give our daughters to the peoples of the land or take their daughters for our sons;*

At first glance, it is curious that the prohibition on mixed marriages is so prominent in the new covenant. Mixed marriages were not mentioned in Ezra's prayer, which confessed the greatest of Israel's sins specifically. Why, then, is this issue seen to be so important?

The answer is to be found in Nehemiah 13:26. Nehemiah rebuked those who broke the promise made in 10:30: *"Did not King Solomon of Israel sin on account of such women?"* 1 Kings 11:1-8 shows how Solomon's marriages with foreign women caused him to sin. The marriages were not wrong because the women were foreign, but because these particular foreign women followed the traditional religions of their nations. Solomon began to follow other gods (1 Kings 11:4-5) and even appeased his wives by building places of worship for their gods (1 Kings 11:6-8).

Once we interpret the prohibition of mixed marriages as a means of preventing Israelites from following other gods, it becomes clear why it is included in the covenant stipulations. It is a response to Ezra's prayer. The prayer confessed the sin of idolatry, specifically in Nehemiah 9:18 and more obliquely in 9:26. In Ezra 9:12, the prohibition on mixed marriages is also presented as a consequence of the adoption of the traditional religions of the former peoples of the land by the Israelites. Such practices defiled the land. God purged the land, removing the Israelites from it in order to cleanse it.[14] If Israel wanted to keep the land this time, they must take measures to make sure they were not led into worship of other gods.

No doubt lust, self-indulgence and prestige were factors in Solomon's decision to marry so many women. However, many of the marriages would have been "political marriages", to "create a reliable network of alliances".[15] This network would improve his reputation with neighbouring countries, and make the prospect of war less likely.[16] Solomon had good reasons, therefore, for his marriages. They safeguarded the security of his country. But these reasons were not good enough to justify breaking God's commandments (Exodus 34:11-16). Solomon should have kept God's commands and trusted God for his security, rather than trying to make himself secure by getting into relationships that led him away from God.

In South Sudan, polygamy is still common. Some people justify such practices by arguing that they need many wives to bear children for themselves. Producing a large number of children increases a man's profile and reputation. Sons will be able to defend him if he is attacked. Polygamy makes sense from a security point of view. But it is also against God's word. We must not prize our security over following his commandments. Where the two are incompatible, we must follow God's commands and trust him for our security.

Williamson points out that

> marriage with foreigners in itself was not forbidden in the Mosaic law, and indeed not a few of the patriarchs and other heroes of the faith of Israel are said to have contracted such marriages (see, e.g., Gen 16:3; 41:45; Exod 2:21; Num 12:1; 2 Sam 3:3, etc.).[17]

Marriage with foreigners who had converted to Yahweh was not a problem. Hence, as Kidner points out, the "ready acceptance of Ruth".[18] God's law specifically warned against marriage with people from nations who opposed him (Exodus 34:11-16; Deuteronomy 7:1-4; 20:10-18). In this context, the use of the phrase *"peoples of the land"* is interesting. Ezra 4:4 suggests that this term usually refers to those who oppose God's purposes (in this context, those who spoke against or otherwise prevented the work of reconstruction).

The phrase "peoples of the land" was a "revision, or rather updating, of the law".[19] The list of nations whom the Israelites may not marry from (Exodus 34:11) included many nations "that had long since ceased to exist."[20] Clines points out that "a more literalistic interpretation of the Pentateuchal law would have allowed marriages with Ashdodites, Ammonites and Moabites—for they are not explicitly mentioned among the prohibited nations."[21] The new covenant restated the older law to recapture its original purpose, deemed to be "the call to purity of worship", or "rejection of foreign cults."[22] Throntveit relates this to Paul's "dichotomy between the letter and the spirit of the Law",[23] arguing that "Paul's hermeneutical principle of proposing adherence to the spirit of the law rather than the letter of the law is strongly foreshadowed in this chapter".[24]

This updating of the law represented an attempt to be faithful to the scriptures that Ezra and the people had read while applying them to their own context. This is something we must all do when we read the Bible. Indeed, this book is an attempt to be faithful to the book of Nehemiah while applying it to a South Sudanese context. We can learn from the exegetical methods and principles used in Ezra and Nehemiah and use them to guide our own interpretation of scripture.

Clines has written on the types of legal development that can be traced from Nehemiah 10 and the exegetical principles allowing these developments.[25] I will not reproduce his analysis in its entirety here, but my comments are based on his work. Readers looking for a more in-depth analysis are recommended to read his article.

There is nothing "radically new" in Nehemiah 10: every new law "has some connection with a Pentateuchal prescription."[26] When we interpret scripture, we should be careful of arriving at conclusions that God's Church has not previously reached. If something seems new, we should ask why God would wait until now, 2,000 years after he established his Church, to reveal it.

At the same time, scripture is "partially open: extension or reapplication is possible".[27] Our interpretation must never contradict the spirit of the law. However, we must be alive to the possibility that scripture will breathe different insights into different cultures at different times. If that was not true, there would be no point in this book. Enough commentaries have already been written on Nehemiah.

Clines writes that "Pentateuchal law requires ancillary law in order to be effective."[28] We must be careful not to stifle freedom by layering law upon law. We need not be fearful of failing to keep God's law, as we have his Holy Spirit to help us. However, there are some areas in which extra measures may be helpful to prevent us from breaking God's law. This is particularly the case in areas where we have repeatedly failed God. This was the case in Nehemiah 10. The community agreed to bind itself by new, additional rules to guard against falling into the sinful patterns of the past.

Clines' fourth and final exegetical principle is that "Pentateuchal law is regarded as essentially harmonious; apparent tensions tend to be solved by a principle of addition rather than by mediation or compromise."[29] Scripture does not contradict itself, but it does contain tensions. Our interpretation of one passage should not contradict another passage. We should not avoid some passages because we are uncomfortable with them and they challenge us. We cannot 'trump' one passage with another.

Clines also points out that where categories are redefined, this is "always in the direction of greater comprehensiveness".[30] In the case of mixed marriages, the catch-all "peoples of the land" is wider than the list of nations in Exodus 34:11. Jesus also redefined biblical commandments to give them a wider application. The law on divorce was made stricter (Matthew 5:31-32); restrictions on revenge were increased so that the wronged party must now turn the other cheek (Matthew 5:39) and murder and adultery were judged to be attitudes of the heart as well as actions (Matthew 5:21-30). We cannot be content with obeying a list of laws. Jesus demanded much more. He commanded us to *"Be perfect, therefore, as your heavenly Father is perfect"* (Matthew 5:48). This requires us to submit continually to God and let him transform us into the image of Christ (2 Corinthians 3:18).

In the case of mixed marriages, scripture itself gives us helpful clues in interpreting Nehemiah 10:30 for our own context. The New Testament commands us not to be yoked together with non-Christians (2 Corinthians 6:14). This is especially relevant for marriage. We share every aspect of life with our spouses. There is great potential for them to lead us astray. It is, therefore, a great risk to marry a non-Christian. The Israelites thought they could risk marrying foreign women who followed traditional religions, without being tempted to compromise their own religious beliefs. They were proved wrong. We should not be arrogant and assume that we are better than the Israelites and can stay faithful to God even if we marry a non-Christian. I have heard young people argue that if they marry a non-Christian, they will bring them to the Lord. However, there is no guarantee the non-Christian will become a believer after marriage.

2 Corinthians 6:14 is especially relevant to marriage, but it encompasses any kind of relationship with non-believers. We cannot and must not avoid non-Christians entirely. After all, we must witness to them. However, we should pick our closest friends carefully. Psalm 1 warns us not to *"follow the advice of the wicked"* or *"sit in the seat of scoffers"*. We need to be careful who and what we are influenced by. For example, watching television when we are tired, and less able to judge whether what we see is good or bad, may not be a good idea. It would be a mistake to go into business with someone who we suspect would act in corrupt ways.

10:31 *and if the peoples of the land bring in merchandise or any grain on the sabbath day to sell, we will not buy it from them on the sabbath or on a holy day; and we will forego the crops of the seventh year and the exaction of every debt.*

10:30 set the pattern for what would follow. Ezra's prayer made it clear that Israel had failed to keep sabbath, with its social justice requirements. It is evident from Nehemiah 5 that this failure persisted to the present day. Specific measures were needed to address this important issue. A general commitment to keep the law in its entirety was not sufficient to break habits that had become ingrained. Individual commitment to keeping God's law was necessary, but it was not enough on its own where the whole economic system was broken. Structural change was needed. That could only be achieved if the whole community agreed to order their affairs in new ways.

Israelites were prohibited from selling on the sabbath (cf. Amos 8:5). Clearly, this ruled out buying between Jews. However, if the seller was a non-Jew, a Jew could spend almost all the sabbath day shopping while remaining faithful to the letter of the law! The Pentateuch itself only specifically prohibits ploughing and harvesting (Exodus 34.21) and kindling a fire (Exodus 35.3). The reading of the law and Ezra's prayer of confession moved the people to a realisation that work reasonably understood included buying. As with the list of nations Israel was forbidden from marrying into, the law regarding sabbath was redefined "in the direction of greater comprehensiveness".[31] This protected unscrupulous households from getting round the law by giving their workers shopping duties on the sabbath. Workers were guaranteed a day off.

Williamson suggests that the sabbath year requirement, and the requirements to release Israelites who had become slaves and forgive debts every seven years (Exodus 21.2-6; Deuteronomy 15.1-8), were not observed simultaneously prior to the signing of the new covenant here.[32] Nehemiah 10:31 makes it clear that the two requirements were not alternatives. Both must be carried out. The reading of the law and Ezra's prayer of confession helped people to realise that both laws were an essential part of a just economic system. Both were about ensuring that vulnerable people were not oppressed and marginalised. If the poor (especially the alien, the orphan and the widow) were to be treated fairly, both laws must be fully implemented. Integrating them together helped to ensure this would actually happen.

10:32-3 *We also lay on ourselves the obligation to charge ourselves yearly one-third of a shekel for the service of the house of our God: for the rows of bread, the regular grain offering, the regular burnt offering, the sabbaths, the new moons, the appointed festivals, the sacred donations, and the sin offerings to make atonement for Israel, and for all the work of the house of our God.*

The finances necessary for carrying out the temple service could not be met from the occasional tax set out in Exodus 30.11-16. Yet it was not appropriate for the temple to be funded by those who might use it for their own glory. The assistance given by Darius and later by Artaxerxes could not be relied on. Foreign kings might put conditions on their support which would compromise the proper functioning of the temple service according to scriptural guidelines. Even the Israelite kings had faced the same temptations. Ahaz built his own altar and carried out sacrifices on it (2 Kings 16:10-13).

Protecting the temple service against the interference of foreign states, or even powerful Jews, meant putting in place a system that could fund temple services from the regular contributions of ordinary people. To do this, the people took the occasional tax set out in Exodus 30.11-16 and updated it, turning it into an annual levy.

Regular giving by ordinary Church members ensures the Church is not dependent on external sources who might try to use the Church to have its own way. The Church must preserve its independence from the government. It may sometimes need to speak out if it decides that the government is acting in ways contrary to God's will. This is more difficult if it is dependent on the government for funding. Similarly, it is difficult for the local church in South Sudan to be an independent voice if it is dependent on foreign funding. The South Sudanese church has a responsibility to seek God's will for the nation. Foreign partners may have good intentions, but they will have their own priorities and may not always agree with what the national church has discerned. This does not mean we should refuse gracious offers of support. However, like the Jews in Nehemiah 10:32-33, we should look to fund the regular operations of the Church from our own congregations as far as possible. This will require an increase in the general level of giving.

10:34 *We have also cast lots among the priests, the Levites, and the people, for the wood offering, to bring it into the house of our God, by ancestral houses, at appointed times, year by year, to burn on the altar of the LORD our God, as it is written in the law.*

Kidner suggests that the gathering of wood was not happening because "what is everybody's business is nobody's business".[33] A law was put in place allocating responsibility for the task, so that individuals could be held accountable if the work was not done. A rota was drawn up to ensure the burden was shared fairly.

10:35-7 *We obligate ourselves to bring the first fruits of our soil and the first fruits of all fruit of every tree, year by year, to the house of our LORD; also to bring to the house of our God, to the priests who minister in the house of our God, the firstborn of our sons and of our livestock, as it is written in the law, and the firstlings of our herds and of our flocks; and to bring the first of our dough, and our contributions, the fruit of every tree, the wine and the oil, to the priests, to the chambers of the house of our God; and to bring to the Levites the tithes from our soil, for it is the Levites who collect the tithes in all our rural towns.*

These verses describe and harmonise the various means by which the people should give to God's ministry, including the tithe.

Many churches in Africa have insufficient financial resources to undertake their ministries. This can be attributed to people failing to give according to biblical guidelines. It has been said that the health of a church is seen in two things: the way the members give, and the importance of the Bible in the life of the church and its members.

Many Christians make pledges in their baptism, or at their enrolment as members, to support the work of God. However, like the people in Nehemiah's time, they forget to give what they have pledged.

One way of ensuring that each of us implements the pledges we have made is to give the *first fruits* to God. We should not give whatever is left over after all our other expenses have been met. This suggests that God is an afterthought, and that we provide for him after we have provided for ourselves. The reality is that everything belongs to God, and he is the one who provides for all our needs. Giving first, and planning our budget around our offering, is one way of acknowledging that.

The New Testament reinforces this teaching. 2 Corinthians 9:7 encourages us to budget our offerings in advance. We must make this decision while we are still at home, not when we come under pressure to give during the service. This ensures we give for the right reasons – out of love, and to support God's work, not to avoid looking bad in front of other churchgoers.

People who give under pressure tend to find the smallest note (or even coin) they can. Someone once said that "The way some people give, you would think the church is coin-operated!" This is partly because of the way that many of us were brought up. We were given coins to put in the offering bag as children. What happens during childhood influences our giving habits later on in life. When this dawned on a clergy friend of mine, he stopped giving his children coins or small notes to put in the offering bag. If he does not have much money, he would rather give his children a larger note to put in the offering bag and put a smaller note or coin in himself.

In Nehemiah's time, the people agreed to give *both* the first of what they produced, and *also* to select the best, or *choice* part to offer.[34] Again, the passage in 2 Corinthians reinforces this. Giving is described as a form of sowing (2 Corinthians 9:6). We reap what we sow. When we sow sparingly we will reap sparingly, but when we sow bountifully, we will reap bountifully. The Greek word translated as 'bounty' is *eulogia*. It gives us the English word 'eulogy', used to describe a speech containing great praise, especially at a funeral. To the same extent that we are generous with our words when describing the deceased at funerals, we need to be generous in our giving to God.

The same passage encourages us to give cheerfully (2 Corinthians 9:7). It is not only what we give that matters. God is concerned about what is in our heart as we give. There is a popular preaching illustration, unattributed to my knowledge, that sums this up. It describes three types of givers—the stony giver, the spongy giver and the honeycomb.

The stony giver gives only under compulsion. A hammer must be used. When the hammer is applied, the stony giver yields small pieces. 'Hammers' could include threats not to baptise children or bury dead if the stony giver does not give. (I am not suggesting that any clergy should make these threats, only describing the kinds of measures needed to force a stony giver to give!) A stony giver gives tearfully, because of the hammering that occurs.

The spongy giver must be squeezed to get something out of them. The harder you squeeze the more you get. 'Squeezing' could include direct appeals, or sermons on giving. A spongy gives fearfully, as they are pressurised into giving.

The honeycomb giver is the ideal type of Christian giver. The honeycomb overflows with sweetness as you hold it. There is no need to use force to hammer or squeeze it. Honeycomb givers give because of the overflow of God's love within them. God himself is such a giver. He gave us his son out of his love (John 3:16, cf. Romans 5:8). He has placed the same love in our hearts through his Spirit (Romans 5:5). Our giving should reflect the generosity of our God.

When I visited Port Harcourt, Nigeria, in January 2012, I was amazed by the generosity of Nigerian Christians. At one of the church services I attended, people gave a thanksgiving offering, a tithe and a specific offering toward a church building project in addition to the usual Sunday offertory. This reminds me of the multiple offerings the people committed to make in Nehemiah 10:32-39. Two days prior to the service, I was asked to dedicate a brand-new vehicle for the parish. When I arrived, I found two vehicles given by different members of the parish for the use of their local church.

When I visited Cape Town, South Africa, in May 2013, people came forward during the service to give thanks to God for what he had done for them in the last week. At least 20 people came to share. As they did this, they gave a thanksgiving offering. The issues they thanked God for included good health, jobs and stable families. In one case, a lady gave thanks that she had been able to buy a vehicle. At the end of the service, I was asked to dedicate this vehicle to God. This is a good practice that should be encouraged in our churches. Upon my return from that visit, a local believer informed me that he had just bought a tractor and was going to bring it to Kajo-Keji. I encouraged him to have it dedicated in a thanksgiving service at his local church.

Here is a summary of the three types of givers:

Type of giver	Solution	Manner of giving
Stony	Hammer	Gives tearfully
Spongy	Squeezing	Gives fearfully
Honeycomb	Hold	Gives cheerfully

The logic of Nehemiah 10:35-7 is that God was the ultimate supplier of all that the people had. It was he who gave them the land and made it flourish. Giving the first and the best of all that the land produced demonstrated their reliance on God for provision. 2 Corinthians 10:8-11 makes the same point. God gives to us so that we too can give. This results in a harvest of righteousness. This is not a promise of wealth or the theology of prosperity. We do not give so that we can get for ourselves. Rather, when we show that we can be trusted to use what God has given us to his glory, we will be enriched so that we can give more.

John Wesley, the founder of Methodism, was a good example of this. It is said that when he earned £30 per week he lived on £28 and gave away £2. When his salary was doubled to £60, he continued to live on £28 and gave away the rest. As his income rose, his giving also rose. He continued to live on about £30 a week even when his income was £1,400. The rest was given away. He is reported to have said that if a man did not give all he could, he had more hope for Judas Iscariot than for that man!

Many of us do not want to allow God to control our money matters. Luther famously observed that there are three necessary conversions: the heart, mind and purse. We cannot claim to have surrendered our lives to God if we have not surrendered our money and other assets to him. We must give sacrificially so that we are always dependent on God.

Generous giving is for all believers and not only those who have been blessed with great incomes. Some rural areas do not have a functioning monetary economy. Where access to cash is limited, we should encourage believers to give tithes and other offerings in kind. This could include crops, chickens, goats and cattle. One of our clergy, Canon John Lomundu, once told me that in order to make sure he tithed his crop of sweet potatoes, he put a peg on every tenth heap as he harvested them. He then took them to church and offered them. His example is commendable and should be emulated. If it is not, churches in rural areas will not be adequately supported or self-sustaining.

All members of the Church have a responsibility to support it. We do this by giving ourselves, our talents, our time and our resources. If we do this, we will be good stewards of what God has given us. God himself is the greatest giver. Out of his love, he gave us his son Jesus Christ. We need to do the same. If we love God we will give to his work out of our love.

10:38 *And the priest, the descendant of Aaron, shall be with the Levites when the Levites receive the tithes; and the Levites shall bring up a tithe of the tithes to the house of our God, to the chambers of the storehouse.*

The Levites were to tithe the tithe. Some church leaders argue that they should not give money in church, as their service to God is already a form of giving in itself. This is not an excuse. Others serve God in a variety of ways and also give from their resources in church. Here we read that the Levites were asked to give. Church leaders must lead by example. This example must include the giving of tithes and offerings.

10:39 *For the people of Israel and the sons of Levi shall bring the contribution of grain, wine, and oil to the storerooms where the vessels of the sanctuary are, and where the priests that minister, and the gatekeepers and the singers are. We will not neglect the house of our God.*

Kidner points out that the commitment not to neglect the house of God "sums up not only the paragraph but much of the concern of the post-exilic prophets, Haggai, Zechariah and Malachi."[35] Malachi 3 is a favourite passage of preachers on the subject of the tithe. It shows the serious consequences of short-changing God by failing to offer the full tithe or giving something that is not our best.

Conclusion

Nehemiah 10 shows the influence of the reading of scripture and of Ezra's prayer. In this chapter, the people make a general commitment to obey God's law, and specific commitments in key areas where they and their ancestors had failed in the past. The prohibition of mixed marriages, and the arrangements for local upkeep of the temple, guarded against the dangers of being led astray by those who worshipped other gods. A re-ordered economy based on the spirit of the sabbath laws would better protect the poor.

The writer was keen to demonstrate the level of support for the covenant from all sections of the community. No-one could later claim that they had not obligated themselves to follow the new laws. The people's involvement in the covenant should also have motivated them to keep it.

Chapters 8–10 as a whole emphasise the sovereignty of God and the decisiveness of his action in history. The importance of the word of God as a testimony to that action is emphasised. When the community are rooted in the word of God, they are also better able to discern where they have gone wrong and the way forward, so that they can enjoy the land God has given them. They do this through testimony (retelling their story) and confession, which is the basis for new commitments. Although the land has been given to them, it still belongs to God. The people express their understanding of this by committing to give him the first and the best of what comes from the land.

The lessons for the Church should be obvious. Churches should centre all their church events and functions on the word of God. It should be preached as it is. Individuals and small groups should also be encouraged to study the Bible at other times. Charles Spurgeon is supposed to have said that "A Bible that's falling apart usually belongs to someone who isn't." Churches also need to facilitate confession and recommitment.

Sometimes collective confession of the sins of a community and commitment to new ways of behaviour will be necessary, so as to avoid the mistakes of the past. To facilitate this, it may first be necessary to forge a new community story that centres God and includes all sections of the community. The National Program for Healing, Peace and Reconciliation is, in part, an attempt to do this. If people are truly living for God, they will offer the first and the best of everything they have to God's work. Our churches will not be dependent on anyone else, and the poor will receive justice.

---

1   Brown, *The Message of Nehemiah*, 170.

2   Ibid.

3   Abel Alier, *Southern Sudan: Too Many Agreements Dishonoured* (Reading: Ithaca Press, 1992).

4   Arop Madut-Arop, *Sudan's Painful Road to Peace: a Full Story of the Founding and Development of SPLM/SPLA* (Charleston: BookSurge, 2006), 354.

5   Dr John Garang, quoted in ibid., 406.

6   Clines, *Ezra, Nehemiah, Esther*, 201.

7   Ibid.

8   Kidner, *Ezra and Nehemiah*, 114.

9   Clines, *Ezra, Nehemiah, Esther*, 202. Blenkinsopp, *Ezra-Nehemiah*, 312.

10   Kidner, *Ezra and Nehemiah*, 114.

11   Clines, *Ezra, Nehemiah, Esther*, 202.

12   Kidner, *Ezra and Nehemiah*, 114.

13   Throntveit, *Ezra-Nehemiah*, 109.

14   Brueggemann, *The Land*, 153.

15   Ibid., 77.

16 Ibid., 83.

17 Williamson, *Ezra, Nehemiah*, 130.

18 Kidner, *Ezra and Nehemiah*, 115.

19 David J A Clines, *On the Way to the Postmodern: Old Testament Essays, 1967-1998*, vol. 1, Journal for the Study of the Old Testament Supplement 292 (Sheffield: Sheffield Academic Press, 1998), 93.

20 Williamson, *Ezra, Nehemiah*, 334.

21 Clines, *On the Way to the Postmodern*, 1:93.

22 Ibid., 1:94.

23 Throntveit, *Ezra-Nehemiah*, 110.

24 Ibid.

25 Clines, *On the Way to the Postmodern*, 1:88–94, esp. 89–91.

26 Ibid., 1:90.

27 Ibid., 1:91.

28 Ibid.

29 Ibid.

30 Ibid., 1:90.

31 Ibid.

32 Williamson, *Ezra, Nehemiah*, 334.

33 Kidner, *Ezra and Nehemiah*, 116.

34 Williamson, *Ezra, Nehemiah*, 337–8.

35 Kidner, *Ezra and Nehemiah*, 116.

CHAPTER TEN
Jerusalem repopulated and the wall dedicated

Nehemiah 11:1-36

The wall of Jerusalem had been completed (Nehemiah 6:15), but there was a problem. Not many people lived in the newly fortified city of Jerusalem. Until recently it had been a city with a destroyed wall. Tollefson and Williamson write that

> The insecurity of the 'broken wall community' had contributed to low population density and to inadequate support for the temple. Broadly speaking, the leaders had been living in the city and the people in the countryside.[1]

This pattern of repopulation will be recognisable to many in South Sudan. In the case of Abyei, the first to repopulate the town in 2012 after it was destroyed in 2011 by the Sudanese Armed Forces were the Paramount Chief Kuol Deng, key elders, some former civil servants of Abyei Area Administration and poor families and widows, especially believers who understood return to be God's will. Others followed spontaneously over a period of time and began to rebuild homes and livelihoods.

Rebuilt walls and buildings would be lifeless and "nothing more than a liability"[2] without people living in the city. Inhabitants would develop Jerusalem further and provide it with protection. Williamson argues that the move to repopulate the city was "primarily for defensive purposes".[3] Some of the wording used in the list, including "valiant warriors" (11:6, 14), strengthens this case.[4]

The inclusion of the list in the book of Nehemiah "ties the community, newly reconstituted under Ezra's reforms in accordance with the law, to the land".[5] There can be no arguing, later on, that those living in Jerusalem had not placed themselves under the new stipulations outlined in Nehemiah 10. In fact, the act of repopulation was the first step in fulfilling the commitment not to neglect the house of God (10:39).

Throntveit notes that Nehemiah is not mentioned in Chapter 11 and suggests that the people themselves organised the process of return.[6] Williamson concurs, arguing that if Nehemiah had been involved, the arrangements would have been made on a more organised and less haphazard basis than casting lots.[7] Arguments from absence are not sufficient to assert with certainty that Nehemiah was not involved. Those who have witnessed the process of return, in Abyei or in other places in South Sudan, know that return is usually partly directed by community leaders and partly spontaneous. It is likely that more people returned once it became clear that conditions in the city were secure. 1 Chronicles 9, which mentions families not included in Nehemiah 11, suggests this was the case.

Nonetheless, it is fair to state, with Kidner, that the use of these lists (cf. Nehemiah 3; 7:6-73; 10:1-27; 11; 12:1-26), showing the involvement of large numbers of people in the implementation of God's purposes, stops history from being distorted by "concentration on outstanding people" (Zerubbabel, Ezra and Nehemiah) and redresses the balance somewhat.[8]

11:1-2 *Now the leaders of the people lived in Jerusalem; and the rest of the people cast lots to bring one out of ten to live in the holy city Jerusalem, while nine-tenths remained in the other towns. Ad the people blessed all those who willingly offered to live in Jerusalem.*

The people cast lots to decide who would live in the capital. A tithe of the people was made. One out of every ten relocated to Jerusalem. In tithing, and in casting lots, the people adapted forms that were specified in the stipulations they had just agreed to on giving (10:37) and gathering wood for the temple (10:34), demonstrating their commitment to the law.[9] Casting lots was seen to be a way of discerning God's will[10] (Proverbs 16:33; Joshua 14:2; 1 Samuel 14:41-2; Jonah 1:7), leaving the decision as to who would repopulate the city to him. By submitting to this process, everyone in the community showed their willingness, in theory, to relocate to Jerusalem.

Can we use the casting of lots as a way of discerning the will of God today? While the practice was common in Old Testament times, it is only used once in the New Testament. Matthias was chosen by lot as a replacement for Judas Iscariot (Acts 1:26). However, this was before the descent of the Holy Spirit. Evers writes that

> We are in a better position to discern the Lord's will than the people of
> God in Bible days. We now have the more widespread ministry of the

Holy Spirit plus the completed canon of Scripture. Therefore we are to direct our lives by the guidelines for godly living which God gives to us in his Word.[11]

11:25-35 *And as for the villages, with their fields, some of the people of Judah lived in Kiriath-arba and its villages, and in Dibon and its villages, and in Jekabzeel and its villages, and in Jeshua and in Moladah and Beth-pelet, in Hazar-shual, in Beersheba and its villages, in Ziklag, in Meconah and its villages, in En-rimon, in Zorah, in Jarmuth, Zanoah, Adullam, and their villages, Lachish and its fields, and Azekah and its villages. So they camped from Beer-sheba to the valley of Hinnom. The people of Benjamin also lived from Geba onward, at Michmash, Ajia, Bethel and its villages, Anathoth, Nob, Ananiah, Hazor, Ramah, Gitaim, Hadid, Zeboim, Neballat, Lod, and Ono, the valley of artisans.*

Williamson approves of von Rad's suggestion that the list of place-names in 11:25-35 was structured so as to remind the reader of Josiah's kingdom.[12] The list's concentration on the Judahites (vv.4-6), Benjaminites (vv.7-9) and Levites (vv.15-18) also recalls the kingdom of Judah as it was in Josiah's time. Of course, the places listed were still under Persian rule at the time of the resettlement. Presenting the list so as to recall past glories was a way of showing faith that God was already answering the appeal of 9:32-37 through the process of resettlement. God's people would not remain slaves in their own land forever. Readers will also recall that Josiah was the king who rediscovered the law and defiled altars built to other gods (2 Kings 22:8-23:25). 2 Kings 22:25 suggests he was the best king since David. In the value he placed on God's word, and his obedience to it, he was to some extent a model for the community.

Nehemiah 12:1-26

The first part of Nehemiah 12 is comprised of two lists. 12:1-11 lists the priests and Levites who accompanied Zerubbabel during the first wave of return. 12:12-26 lists the priests and Levites in Nehemiah's day, about a century later. By showing that the priests and Levites came from the same ancestral families, the author stressed continuity. Just as Nehemiah 11 ties the newly reconstituted community to the land, Nehemiah 12.1-26, "by recording the cultic personnel who have served the restoration community, links the contemporary cultic situation under Ezra and Nehemiah (Neh. 12:26) with the nascent situation that obtained at the time of Zerubbabel and Jeshua (Neh. 12:1)."[13] Ezra and Nehemiah may have reformed the

Jerusalem cult re-established by Zerubbabel, but they should not be seen as rivals. The same God worked through Zerubbabel and then through Ezra and Nehemiah. The relationship should be characterised in terms of progression, not competition.

Nehemiah 12:27-47

Finally, the time for dedicating the rebuilt walls of Jerusalem has arrived. The wall was finished some time ago (6:15). Why the delay? The intervening material, from Nehemiah 7 onwards, provides the answer. Rebuilt walls needed a repopulated city and a reconstituted people to dedicate them. Throntveit argues that

> Only now, after the covenant renewal that capped Ezra's task of reconstituting the people, and after the census and repopulating of the holy city, are the people (and the reader!) in a position to understand the full meaning and significance of the dedicatory service. This understanding of the service necessarily broadens its implications in that now it is to be seen as more than a dedication of just the walls. The temple, the city, and perhaps more significantly, the community that the walls circumscribe are also implicitly included.[14]

Grabbe notes the similarity between the dedication of the temple in Ezra 6.15-17 and the walls in Nehemiah 12.[15] He wonders why walls needed to be dedicated in the same way as the most holy of buildings, and concludes that repair of the wall was seen as a sacred task.[16] Whenever we carry out God's purposes as God's people, we are performing a sacred duty.

The dedication of the wall was an opportunity for the people to thank God for his faithfulness as they soldiered on, building the wall of Jerusalem in the face of many challenges. They needed to thank God for his provision to enable them to complete the work within a very short period of time. It was also a time to celebrate and rejoice over what God had done.

To dedicate means to devote or set something aside for holy use. Most churches encourage parents to dedicate their children to God or offer some prayers of thanksgiving when a baby is born. It is also good to dedicate whatever assets God gives us. In the last chapter, I discussed the dedication of vehicles to God. When we do this, it is not an opportunity to brag in front of other believers about our possessions. Rather, it is an acknowledgement that all things come from God, and a commitment to use the vehicle in ways that honour God and contribute to his purposes. There are secular equivalents of dedication, such as house-warming, the practice of throwing a party on the occupation of a new house.

12:27-29 *Now at the dedication of the wall of Jerusalem they sought out the Levites in all their places, to bring them to Jerusalem to celebrate the dedication with rejoicing, with thanksgivings and with signing, with cymbals, harps, and lyres. The companies of the singers gathered together from the circuit around Jerusalem and from the villages of the Netophathites; also from Beth-gilgal and from the region of Geba and Azmaveth; for the singers had built for themselves villages around Jerusalem.*

Nehemiah does not reappear until 12:31, when the first person narrative resumes. This is generally used as evidence that editorial work has been done to this section.[17]

There was a need to bring Levites from various towns to join those stationed in Jerusalem. This could have been due to a shortage of Levites in Jerusalem. The dedication ceremony was to be a time of singing and celebration.

12:30 *And the priests and the Levites purified themselves; and they purified the people and the gates and the wall.*

It is important to prepare ourselves for worship. We should not enter into the presence of God lightly. The priests and the Levites purified not only themselves, and the people, but the gates and the wall as well!

12:27-29 detail the practical preparations made for the dedication. 12:30 details the spiritual preparations. Both are important. Kidner points out that Jesus prepared himself in both these ways before his arrest and crucifixion:

> If the New Testament emphasises what is inward and spiritual worship, it has a place too for the natural means of encouraging and stirring us. Our Lord Jesus went to Gethsemane fortified not only by prayer but by the ceremonial meal and corporate singing, matters which engage not only the spirit but also the body and the senses.[18]

The ordering of 12:27-29 and 12:30, and indeed the ordering of the whole book of Nehemiah, with chapters 8-10 following the rebuilding of the walls and sandwiched by the enrolment of the people and the repopulation of Jerusalem, suggest that the physical is "a framework for the spiritual" and that the two cannot be separated but are "opposite faces of a single reality."[19]

12:31-39 *Then I brought the leaders of Judah up onto the wall, and appointed two great companies that gave thanks and went in procession. One went to the right on the wall to the Dung Gate; and after them went Hoshaiah and half the officials of Judah, and Azariah, Ezra, Meshullam, Judah, Benjamin, Shemaiah, and Jeremiah, and some of the young priests with trumpets: Zechariah son of Jonathan son of Shemaiah son of Mattaniah son of Micaiah son of Zaccur son of Asaph; and his kindred, Shemaiah, Azarel, Milalai, Gilalali, Maai, Nethanel, Judah, and Hanani, with the musical instruments of David the man of God; and the scribe Ezra went in front of them. At the Fountain Gate, in front of them, the went straight up by the stairs of the city of David, at the ascent of the wall, above the house of David, to the Water Gate on the east. The other company of those who gave thanks went to the left, and I followed them with half of the people on the wall, above the Tower of the Ovens, to the Broad Wall, and above the Gate of Ephraim, and by the Old Gate, and by the Fish Gate and the Tower of Hananel and the Tower of the Hundred, to the Sheep Gate; and they came to a halt at the Gate of the Guard.*

The narrative switches to the first person. We are back to Nehemiah's personal account. Kidner writes that Nehemiah's voice "was last heard directly at 7:5, where he introduced the list of the first homecomers; after that, the editor took up the narrative, speaking of Nehemiah in the third person (8:9; 10:1; 12:26)."[20]

Nehemiah brought the secular and religious leaders of Judah up on top of the wall. They marched in opposite directions, meeting at the temple for a service. Each group had a choir leading the procession. Each choir had priests blowing trumpets and Levites playing other musical instruments.

The act of marching on top of the wall was a swipe at Tobiah. Tobiah had mocked the builders, suggesting that the rebuilt walls could not bear the weight of a fox (4:3). By demonstrating that the walls could take the weight of an entire company, the people turned Tobiah's taunts back on his own head. Nehemiah's prayer (4:4) was partially answered. There is power in reclaiming an insult. When, in 2012, Sudan's President Bashir called protesters who called for his overthrow "elbow-lickers" (since licking your elbow is impossible), youth organisations named the next day of protest "elbow-licking Friday".[21] The term "Christian" was originally used as an insult.

Psalm 48 is often linked to this procession. It includes the exhortation to "Walk about Zion, go all around it, count its towers, consider well its ramparts; go through its citadels, that you may tell the next generation that this is God, our God forever and ever. He will be our guide forever" (Psalm 48:12-14). Williamson speculates that the Psalm may have been chanted as an accompaniment to the processions.[22] The Psalm reflects Nehemiah 6:16 in reporting the impact that the rebuilt walls had on the nations around (Psalm 48:4-7). The rebuilt walls testify to God's action and increase his reputation (Psalm 48:10). The importance of reciting the story of the events that have taken place, and acknowledging God's central role in them, is affirmed (Psalm 48:13b-14).

It is clear from the description of the procession that worship began before the temple service. Worshipping the Lord in spirit and in truth (John 4:24) requires the use of body, mind, heart and will. The physical and symbolic act of marching on top of the walls was part of Israel's act of worship.

Brown describes worship as "worth-ship", or acknowledging the worth of God.[23] He elaborates further:

> Worship is more than vocal and aural participation in a public service as we offer prayers, sing hymns and songs, hear readings, make offerings and listen to Christian preaching. It is the total submission of all that we have and are to everything we know of God.[24]

Sometimes in Africa, the spontaneous singing of choruses in church services is introduced as a 'time of praise and worship'. The implication is that the rest of the service is not praise or worship! The reality is that all aspects of our services are part of worship. Indeed, our whole lives should be worship.

Nehemiah involved many people in the procession. Again, we see his participatory style of leadership in evidence. We also see his humility. He did not take sole credit for the rebuilding of the walls. In the rebuilding of the walls, the whole community was involved, but the glory was given to God. It is the same here.

We too must involve as many people as possible in worship. Laity should be involved in leading services and even in preaching. When laity preach, it will often be necessary for a trained person to give them direction and guidance. In the Diocese of Kajo-Keji, I encourage preachers to use lectionary readings. This ensures that they do not concentrate on or preach from favourite passages or topics but use the whole Bible, and consequently preach the whole counsel of God.

Preachers with limited training may need additional guidance in how to use lectionary readings. Some preachers use all three lectionary readings. If the readings do not have a common thread or theme, they end up preaching two or three different sermons in one service. Taking care to coach preachers in how to use lectionary readings ensures that this problem is easily avoided.

12:43 *They offered great sacrifices that day and rejoiced, for God had made them rejoice with great joy; the women and children also rejoiced. The joy of Jerusalem was heard far away.*

In offering sacrifices, the people answered Sanballat's mocking question, *"Will they sacrifice?"* (4:2; see comment on 12:31-39 above).

In this verse, the word for 'joy' appears (in different forms) five times.[25] This rejoicing was heard far away, causing non-believers outside of Jerusalem to hear of God's glory (cf Psalm 48:10). Just as God had enabled the community to bring the rebuilding project to completion, it was God who made them rejoice. God is consistently portrayed as the initiator and origin of all good things in the book of Nehemiah.

The joy they felt at completing the building project can only be understood when we remember the context. Previous attempts to rebuild the walls had not reached the stage of completion. The walls had been lying in a state of ruin for many years. They stood as a testament to the people's weakness and had become a source of shame.

This scenario is familiar to many in South Sudan and other parts of Africa. Buildings lie in a permanent state of incompletion for years. Some are never finished and stand as a testament to bad planning and misappropriation of funds. They become a source of shame to the community.

When projects originate from God, involve the whole community and are led by men and women of Nehemiah's calibre, who plan effectively, they must succeed. Instead of ruins reminding us of years of war, and incomplete buildings testifying to bad planning and corruption, we will have rebuilt walls, testifying to God's action in the life of our communities. They will be a source of joy to us.

12:44 *On that day men were appointed over the chambers for the stores, the contributions, the first fruits, and the tithes, to gather into them the portions required by the law for the priests and for the Levites from the fields belonging to the towns; for Judah rejoiced over the priests and the Levites who ministered.*

The people gave willingly and cheerfully to support the priests and Levites. By doing so, they showed that they remembered the pledges they had made earlier (10:37-39).

12:45-46 *They performed the service of their God and the service of purification, as did the singers and the gatekeepers, according to the command of David and his son Solomon. For in the days of David and Asaph long ago there was a leader of the singers, and there were songs of praise and thanksgiving to God.*

The worshippers were keen to worship in the way prescribed by David and his son Solomon. They had set down a model for how worship should be conducted. There was some room for flexibility in worship (as demonstrated by the processions on top of the walls), as long as the worshippers remained faithful to the scriptural guidelines they had.

We also have guidelines on how worship should be carried out. Worshipping in spirit and truth means making sure God's word is the source of our worship. There is pressure for us to do things in modern, different ways. This is fine as long as the reading of the word of God remains a central part of our services. Church worship is not entertainment or "churchtainment". It is serious but joyous business. God must be the centre and the focus of our worship.

Ephesians 5:18-21 gives further guidelines for worship: ". . be filled with the Spirit, speaking to one another with psalms, hymns, and songs from the Spirit. Sing and make music from your heart to the Lord, always giving thanks to God the Father for everything, in the name of our Lord Jesus Christ" (NIV).

The size and type of church structure or sanctuary should not worry us. Whether we worship under a tree or in a grand cathedral is not important. What is important is that we worship God in spirit and in truth (John 4:24). If God has provided you with a church structure, thank him for it and worship him. If he has not provided you with such a structure, this should not stop you from worshipping him in spirit and in truth.

12:47 *In the days of Zerubbabel and in the days of Nehemiah all Israel gave the daily portions for the singers and the gatekeepers. The set apart that which was for the Levites; and the Levites set apart that which was for the descendants of Aaron.*

Brown has identified 6 characteristics of the people's giving, from 12:44-47:

> It was organised (*men were appointed*, 44), specific (*contributions, first-fruits and tithes*, 44); grateful (because the ministry of God's servants had brought them such delight: *for Judah was pleased with the ministering priests and Levites*, 44) obligatory (*all Israel contributed*, 47) regular

(*daily portions*, 47) and universal (everyone, including *the Levites* who were also to *set aside the portion* for the priests' support, *the descendants of Aaron*, 47).[26]

This is the ideal. However, as in many of our churches, the people started with the best of intentions, but did not keep it up. When Nehemiah left Jerusalem to return to Persia, things deteriorated badly.

Conclusion

The dedication of the walls is the high point in Ezra-Nehemiah. The two books climax at this point. A representative sample of the people have returned, the temple has been rebuilt, the walls rebuilt, the law placed at the centre of community life, communal confession made, reforms undertaken and Jerusalem repopulated. The community has both arrived and is "also just beginning to function as a complete restoration of the people of God."[27] The lists in Nehemiah 11 and the first part of Nehemiah 12 are designed to emphasise this by showing the continuity running through these processes. Each stage had been planned by God through faithful servants (Zerubbabel, Ezra, Nehemiah) who involved the whole community.

Nehemiah 11 and 12 together have been strategically placed

> to inform the reader that the work of the reformers has been successful. The temple has been rebuilt and is fully staffed with cultic personnel. Similarly, the walls have been rebuilt and the city is fully inhabited with people purified and covenantally bound together under the proclamation and exhortation of the Law.[28]

Nonetheless, the book does not end at its high point. Success is temporary. The biblical narrative demands a further chapter, which, as we shall see, shows that Israel was not capable of keeping the law, even with the extra safeguards they had put in place.

Before we turn to Nehemiah 13, it is worth reflecting on the parallels between the dedication of the city walls and the dedications of churches today. As Bishop of the Diocese of Kajo-Keji I have taken part in the dedication of a number of churches. As a new bishop, it fell to me to dedicate 39 churches built as a collaborative venture between Samaritan's Purse (SP) and Diocese of Kajo-Keji. SP also built churches for the Sudan Pentecostal Churches (SPC).

The whole process was collaborative. Volunteers from the church community helped clear the land, gathered sand and crushed the stones needed for the foundation. With technical assistance from SP, they worked on the concrete blocks. The SP team then set the concrete blocks and metal beams in place. When a church was completed, hundreds of people gathered for a dedication celebration that often lasted the whole day. The church service and speeches lasted around four hours and were usually followed by a meal. Most churches would slaughter a bull or bulls for all those who attended the services.

The fortieth church that Samaritan's Purse helped build for us was our cathedral. When I was elected as a Bishop in March 2007, we did not have a cathedral per se. The cathedral was in a small grass-thatched church which could not accommodate all the people who came for my enthronement service in June 2007.

As in Nehemiah 3, the whole community was involved in building the new cathedral. SP helped build the roof and the frames. Christians of all ages and backgrounds raised money, food items, goats, chickens and bulls. An elderly man called Modi walked several kilometres to gather stones. In spite of his age and frailty he wanted to make his contribution towards the construction of God's house. A young girl called Sylvian Poni, then 12, gave a chicken as a contribution towards construction costs. Two retired church leaders, my predecessor Bishop Manasseh Binyi Dawidi and Rev Canon Natana Duku, gave a bull each. Holy Trinity church in Aylesbury, England gave a percentage of the funds received for renovation of their own church. The Governor of Central Equatoria State, Major General Clement Wani Konga gave a generous amount on behalf of the Government of Central Equatoria State and also made a generous personal contribution. He encouraged his ministers to follow suit.

Our Archbishop, Daniel Deng Bul, dedicated the cathedral. As in Nehemiah 12, representatives of those who had been involved in construction attended, including Samaritan's Purse, SOMA, Holy Trinity Church Aylesbury, and the State Governor. Nicholas Ramsden, the Archbishop's International Co-ordinator, summed up the dedication as follows:

> The Episcopal Church of the Sudan (ECS) Diocese of Kajo-Keji was singing and dancing in celebration of their new cathedral, Emmanuel, on Palm Sunday this year. Approximately 2000 members of the Kajo-Keji

community, including government officials, turned out to participate in what proved to be a very lively event. The six-hour service was a scene of laughter, joy and praise to God for the beautiful cathedral the community are now able to enjoy.[29]

A more detailed description of the service followed:

The service began promptly at 8.45am with short prayers for the pastors and blessing of the oil and water, which would be used for anointing the cathedral. Leading the procession around the cathedral was a youth choir, with the bishops and the clergy in the middle and the Mothers' Union and other laity bringing up the rear. They then marched slowly into the cathedral once the Archbishop had ceremonially knocked on the main door and the jubilation and ululating continued. After many songs, the consecration of the various parts of, and articles within, the cathedral, dancing and more ululating, the Archbishop stood to give a brief message. "We must give thanks to God for this cathedral," he began. "This cathedral will be of use to future generations." To him, the cathedral would serve as a place of resolving issues, and receiving blessing and healing. "The building of the temple is a sign of peace and stability," a meaningful statement for the community of Kajo-Keji who had scores of churches destroyed during the war. He urged the community, and the politicians to keep the peace that they have. "We don't need to take our people back to war. We reject any politician who wants to be violent or tribalistic." In conclusion he praised the bishop and the people of Kajo-Keji for the good work they were doing and encouraged them to complete the finishing touches to the construction.

After the sermon, the Eucharist was conducted. With the large number of congregants, Holy Communion took about 30 minutes and it was very clear with the queues going out of the building how important the celebration of Holy Communion on such as occasion was to the people of Kajo-Keji.[30]

It is clear from this report that there are many similarities between the dedication of Emmanuel Cathedral and the dedication of the city walls in Nehemiah 12. Both events included celebration and thanksgiving. Both were characterised by joy. Both included ceremonial processions! Both communities had seen places of worship destroyed in the past. In both cases, the completed building work acted as a symbol which took away the shame of the community and offered new hope for the future.

Coventry Cathedral is another building that stands as a symbol of peace and hope in a former war zone. In February 2013, I participated at a "Faith in Conflict" conference held at Coventry. A new cathedral, consecrated in 1962, stands alongside the ruined structure of the old, bombed in 1940 during the Second World War. When I arrived, I was struck by the ruins. They reminded me of the many destroyed houses and churches in South Sudan during the civil war, and of the scene that must have confronted Nehemiah as he toured the ruined city walls of Jerusalem (Nehemiah 2:13-15).

The response to the bombing by the Provost of the day, Dick Howard, was amazing. Rather than urging retaliation, he sent forth a message of peace, forgiveness and reconciliation. The Provost had the words 'Father Forgive' inscribed on the wall behind the altar of the ruined building. These words echo Jesus' own words on the cross (Luke 23:24). However, the word "them" is missing. The Provost explained that only Jesus could say "Father, forgive them", as he did not need to be forgiven himself, because he had never sinned. For everyone else, "Father, forgive us" is more appropriate. This understanding echoes Nehemiah 1:6, in which Nehemiah acknowledged that he could not ask for forgiveness for others only, as he too had sinned. "Father, forgive" is the refrain of the Coventry Litany of Reconciliation, reproduced here in full:

> *All have sinned and fallen short of the glory of God.*
> The hatred which divides nation from nation, race from race, class from class,
> *Father Forgive.*
> The covetous desires of people and nations to possess what is not their own,
> *Father Forgive.*
> The greed which exploits the work of human hands and lays waste the earth,
> *Father Forgive.*
> Our envy of the welfare and happiness of others,
> *Father Forgive.*
> Our indifference to the plight of the imprisoned, the homeless, the refugee,
> *Father Forgive.*
> The lust which dishonours the bodies of men, women and children,

Father Forgive.
The pride which leads us to trust in ourselves and not in God,
Father Forgive.
Be kind to one another, tender-hearted, forgiving one another,
as God in Christ forgave you.[31]

The new cathedral stands alongside the ruins of the old cathedral as a reminder of God's power at work in his world to reconcile and renew. The same can be said of Emmanuel Cathedral, and the Jerusalem city walls on the occasion of their dedication in Nehemiah 12.

1 Tollefson and Williamson, "Nehemiah as Cultural Revitalisation," 340.
2 Williamson, *Ezra, Nehemiah*, 354.
3 Ibid.
4 Ibid., 347.
5 Throntveit, *Ezra-Nehemiah*, 112.
6 Ibid.
7 Williamson, *Ezra, Nehemiah*, 345.
8 Kidner, *Ezra and Nehemiah*, 121.
9 Tollefson and Williamson, "Nehemiah as Cultural Revitalisation," 340.
10 Throntveit, *Ezra-Nehemiah*, 112–3.
11 Evers, *Doing a Great Work*, 185.
12 Williamson, *Ezra, Nehemiah*, 350.
13 Throntveit, *Ezra-Nehemiah*, 112.
14 Ibid., 117.
15 Grabbe, *Ezra-Nehemiah*, 63.
16 Ibid.
17 Williamson, *Ezra, Nehemiah*, 369–70.
18 Kidner, *Ezra and Nehemiah*, 126.
19 Williamson, *Ezra, Nehemiah*, 377.
20 Kidner, *Ezra and Nehemiah*, 125.
21 James Copnall, "Sudan 'Elbow-lickers' Are Turning Omar Al Bashir's Jibe Against Him: Khartoum Protests Against the Fuel Subsidy Cuts Now Target Panicky Military Regime That Has Begun Arresting Activists," *The Guardian*, June 28, 2012, http://www.theguardian.com/world/2012/jun/28/sudan-protests-elbow-lickers-bashir
22 Williamson, *Ezra, Nehemiah*, 374.
23 Brown, *The Message of Nehemiah*, 205.
24 Ibid.

25 Williamson, *Ezra, Nehemiah*, 376.
26 Brown, *The Message of Nehemiah*, 217.
27 Throntveit, *Ezra-Nehemiah*, 118.
28 Ibid., 113.
29 Nicholas Ramsden, "The Dedication of Emmanuel Cathedral 17th April 2011," 2011, http://www.kajokeji.anglican.org/index.php?PageID=cathedralddctnrpt
30 Ibid.
31 Canon Joseph Poole, "Coventry Litany of Reconciliation," 1958, http://www.coventrycathedral.org.uk/about-us/our-reconciliation-ministry/coventry-litany-of-reconciliation.php

CHAPTER ELEVEN

Nehemiah's return

Nehemiah 13:1-31

The phrases *"On that day"* (13:1) and *"Now before this"* (13:4) have been interpreted in various ways to justify placing the events of Nehemiah 13 during his first term as governor, even prior to the covenant signing in Nehemiah 10. The dating of this passage is controversial and there is no consensus on exactly when these events took place. Some scholars believe that Nehemiah did not return for a second term as governor.

The passage itself clearly states that after Nehemiah finished his first term as governor (cf. 5:14), some time passed before he returned. The events of Nehemiah 13 suggest that local officials in Jerusalem were behaving in ways that they knew Nehemiah would not approve of. They were not expecting him to return. Clearly, enough time had passed that any objections that appealed to Nehemiah's words and actions could be dealt with by the claim that the situation had changed and Nehemiah's prescriptions were no longer relevant. The events of Nehemiah 13 make most sense when we accept the text's claim that Nehemiah returned after spending a good deal of time back in Persia. We should not make too much of ambiguous phrases like "On that day" or "before this" to justify extensive resequencing that contradicts the claims of the text.

It is clear that Nehemiah's authority was respected on his return. Nehemiah 13 does not specifically state that Nehemiah served a second term as governor. It is possible that he commanded authority and respect because of his past achievements and position. However, if the king sent Nehemiah to Judah as governor the first time he allowed him to leave the palace, and still employed Nehemiah (as is evident from Nehemiah's need to ask the king for permission to go back in 13:6), it is plausible that he sent Nehemiah as governor again.

I mention these issues so that readers are not surprised when they come across different views on the text. However, there is little value in getting bogged down in these matters. The text itself is clear. I will take its claims at face value. Nehemiah 13 describes events that occurred when Nehemiah returned after spending a good deal of time in Persia. He probably returned as governor and served a second term.

Many things had gone wrong while Nehemiah was away. In part, this was Nehemiah's fault. He had not devoted enough time to training potential successors while he was himself in office. He had not left in place a competent and trustworthy team who could continue his work after he left his post. Adequate mechanisms for monitoring and evaluation had not been set up. When Nehemiah left, the "elite began to compete for the wealth created under his leadership."[1]

Nehemiah had excellent leadership skills. However, he was not perfect. Like every leader, there were areas where he needed to improve. Each one of us must acknowledge that there are areas where we can improve. In Africa, and in the South Sudanese church in particular, we have the same weaknesses as Nehemiah. Often, the leadership is so keen to demonstrate authority that junior staff are not allowed to make decisions. When they eventually become leaders, they do not have the experience they need. Sometimes this is a way that existing leaders use to hold on to power! If we do not plan succession properly, we will find like Nehemiah that much of our work is undone quickly.

13:1-3 *On that day they read from the book of Moses in the hearing of the people; and in it was found written that no Ammonite or Moabite should ever enter the assembly of God, because they did not meet the Israelites with bread and water, but hired Balaam against them to curse them – yet our God turned the curse into a blessing. When the people heard the law, they separated from Israel all those of foreign descent.*

Yet again the reading of scripture provided the stimulus for change. It had an immediate impact. It also prepared the people for the actions Nehemiah would take against Tobiah.

The passage read must have included Deuteronomy 23:3-5, reproduced here almost word for word. The Balaam incident is recounted in more detail in Numbers 22. It is notable that the Ammonites and Moabites are referred to specifically, in contrast to the more general term "peoples of the land" used to prohibit mixed marriages in 10:30. This reinforces Williamson's point that the separation referred to in 13:1 is not to do with marriages, but concerns who was allowed to enter the assembly of God (13:2) and who was not.[2]

At first glance, it may seem harsh to single out the Ammonites and Moabites because of the actions of their ancestors centuries earlier. However, long before the Moabites schemed against Israel, God had made a promise to the father of the Jewish people, Abraham, that "I will bless those who bless you, and the one who curses you I will curse; and in you all the families of the earth shall be blessed." (Genesis 12:3). God always fulfils his promises, as Ezra's prayer in Nehemiah 9 makes clear. When the Moabites hired Balaam to curse the Israelites, God was bound to curse them. However, the acceptance of Ruth the Moabitess makes it clear that individuals could escape this curse by converting to Yahweh.

The inclusion of the Ammonites (as per Deuteronomy 23:3-5) is important as Tobiah was an Ammonite. It strengthened the case against him being allowed a room inside the temple.

13:4-9 *Now before this, the priest Eliashib, who was appointed over the chambers of the house of our God, and who was related to Tobiah, prepared for Tobiah a large room where they had previously put the grain offering, the frankincense, the vessels, and the tithes of grain, wine, and oil, which were given by commandment to the Levites, singers, and gatekeepers, and the contributions for the priests. While this was taking place I was not in Jerusalem, for in the thirty-second year of King Artaxerxes of Babylon I went to the king. After some time I asked leave of the king and returned to Jerusalem. I then discovered the wrong that Eliashib had done on behalf of Tobiah, preparing a room for him in the courts of the house of God. And I was very angry, and I threw all the household furniture of Tobiah out of the room. Then I gave orders and the cleansed the chambers, and I brought back the vessels of the house of God, with the grain offering and the frankincense.*

Nehemiah was shocked to find that Tobiah, who had opposed the building of the wall, had been given a room in the temple by Eliashib, the priest. (This Eliashib may not be the same priest as in 3:1. Children were often named after their grandfathers.)

Tobiah was related to the chief priest. It is possible that nepotism was being practised. He had an extensive series of contacts. It is also possible that the high priest did not want to alienate an important figure with links to the ruling regime. Whatever the reason for this deal, Tobiah was now "at the nerve-centre of Jerusalem, ideally placed for influence and intrigue".[3]

Nehemiah was jealous for God's holiness and furious at the misuse of God's house. His actions in throwing out Tobiah's furniture foreshadow Jesus' actions in turning over the moneylenders' tables. Tobiah only occupied one room, but the offence was so serious that all the chambers had to be purified.[4]

13:10-13 *I also found out that the portions of the Levites had not been given to them; so that the Levites and the singers, who had conducted the service, had gone back to their fields. So I remonstrated with the officials and said, "Why is the house of God forsaken?" And I gathered them together and set them in their stations. Then all Judah brought the tithe of the grain, wine, and oil into the storehouses. And I appointed as treasurers over the storehouses the priest Shelemiah, the scribe Zadok, and Pedaiah of the Levites, and as their assistant Hanan son of Zaccur son of Mattaniah, for they were considered faithful; and their duty was to distribute to their associates.*

Nehemiah found that the people were not fulfilling the pledges they had made (10:35-39). As a consequence, the temple staff were not supported. Each one of them was busy in the fields to ensure that they had food for themselves (13:10). The people had neglected the house of their God (cf. 10:29).

Nehemiah remonstrated with the officials (13:10), rather than with the people. This suggests that the problem was not only a lack of motivation on the part of the people. There may also have been corruption. Nehemiah's response was to ensure the system that had been set up was working, and to improve accountability. Under the previous arrangement, the Levites collected the tithe under the oversight of a priest. The tithes were then taken to the storehouse. Nehemiah now improved the system of oversight, appointing qualified men who had the confidence of the people as treasurers with the responsibility of distributing funds to their colleagues. As in 7:2, faithfulness was the key decision in making appointments. Qualifications are important but it is fear of God that will stop the deliberate mismanagement of resources.

Where adequate systems for the collection and disbursal of church funds are not in place, some people are reluctant to give. It is important to be transparent and open about how much is collected and how it is used. Often when churches are more transparent and especially where the needs of the church are articulated clearly in advance, people are more willing to give.

However, the failure of some churches to report back properly is not an excuse for disobeying God's commands. If funds are not being utilised well, church members have the right to raise the issue. Nonetheless, their responsibility to support God's work continues. Ultimately, leaders who misuse funds collected by the church will be accountable to God.

Williamson highlights the likelihood that "the people's failure to give tithes to the Levites and the fact that Eliashib had a siseable spare room to put at Tobiah's disposal are closely connected."[5] Sin in one area of our lives is likely to lead to sin in other areas unless properly dealt with.

13:14 *Remember me, O my God, concerning this, and do not wipe out my good deeds that I have done for the house of my God and for his people.*

Nehemiah used the word "remember" frequently in his prayers. In 1:8 it is part of an appeal to God to keep his covenant and bring his people back to the land. In 5:19 it is used to seek God's blessing. In 6:14 remembering is presented as part of doing justice. It ensures that sin is not ignored and has consequences. In Nehemiah 13, remembering is used primarily to seek God's blessing, as in 5:19. *"Do not wipe out my good deeds"* has an immediate dimension. Nehemiah wanted his reforms to last longer than the previous reforms had. It also has an eternal dimension. Good deeds built on the foundation that God has laid will be revealed by fire. If they survive, the builder will receive a reward (1 Corinthians 3:10-15).

God's remembering "always implies His intervention, not merely His recollection or recognition."[6] In Genesis 8:1, God's action to cause the waters of the flood to subside is linked to his remembering of Noah. God's deliverance of Lot in Genesis 19:29 is because he "remembered Abraham". God opened Rachel's womb when he remembered her (Genesis 30:22). The deliverance of the Israelites from slavery is repeatedly described as God remembering his covenant (Exodus 2:24; 6:5 Psalm 105:42). A man as well-versed in scripture as Nehemiah was surely aware of this tradition. When Nehemiah asked God to remember him, he was asking God to act on his behalf.

Remembering God is a basis for action (fighting for kin, sons, daughters, wives and homes) in Nehemiah 4:14. It also serves as a basis for confession (9:2, 6-37), recommitment (9:38; 10:28-39), and as a way of guarding against temptation. Remembering is not a passive thing. As we have seen, the way we remember things influences the way we act in the future. Remembrance is always linked to action.

13:15 *In those days I saw in Judah people treading wine presses on the sabbath, and bringing in heaps of grain and loading them on donkeys; and also wine, grapes, figs, and all kinds of burdens, which they brought into Jerusalem on the sabbath day; and I warned them at that time against selling food.*

Again we see that the people were not fulfilling the covenant they had made in Nehemiah 10. Buying and selling was taking place on the sabbath day. Although the text does not clearly say whether the people Nehemiah warned were Jews or Gentiles, the implication is that they were Jews. This is strengthened by the contrast with Tyrians in the next verse.

Clines argues that whereas the previous abuses could be attributed mainly to particular individuals and to officials, "the guilt of sabbath-breaking, however, lay more squarely on the common people."[7] Clines overstates his point. The people, as well as officials, were to blame for the failure to observe the tithe. Nehemiah 13, taken as a whole, shows clearly that the whole of the community had failed to keep the covenant detailed in Nehemiah 10. This included ordinary people, but special responsibility was placed on civic and religious leaders. The New Testament also teaches that Christian leaders will be "judged with greater strictness" (James 3:1). If leaders will be judged more strictly, good character is especially important in leaders.

The reference to the carrying of burdens evokes Jeremiah 17:21. The reference to ancestors and to exile in 13:18 suggests that the comparison was intended. Nehemiah warned the people as soon as he saw what was happening. When they did not respond, he took further action.

13:16-18 *Tyrians also, who lived in the city, brought in fish and all kinds of merchandise and sold them on the sabbath to the people of Judah, and in Jerusalem. Then I remonstrated with the nobles of Judah and said to them, "What is this evil thing that you are doing, profaning the sabbath day? Did not your ancestors acts in this way, and did not God bring all this disaster on us and on this city? Yet you bring more wrath on Israel by profaning the sabbath.*

Nehemiah remonstrated with the nobles (see above). They may not have been guilty of the specific offence of buying or selling on the sabbath. However, they were aware of what was taking place and had failed to take action to prevent it. It is possible that they were benefiting indirectly from the practice.

Nehemiah reminded the nobles that the failure to observe sabbath had been a leading cause of the destruction of Jerusalem and the exile. Evidently, Ezra's version of history (9:6-31) was now accepted and could be appealed to as a basis for corrective action. This underscores the importance of how we tell our story as a national community. When things go wrong, it can be used as a basis for correction and restoration, but only if it has been firmly established in the national consciousness.

13:19-22 *When it began to be dark at the gates of Jerusalem before the sabbath, I commanded that the doors should be shut and gave orders that they should not be opened until after the sabbath. And I set some of my servants over the gates, to prevent any burden from being brought in on the sabbath day. Then the merchants and sellers of all kinds of merchandise spent the night outside Jerusalem once or twice. But I warned them and said to them, "Why do you spend the night in front of the wall? If you do so again, I will lay hands on you." From that time on they did not come on the sabbath. And I commanded the Levites that they should purify themselves and come and guard the gates, to keep the sabbath day holy. Remember this also in my favour, O my God, and spare me according to the greatness of your steadfast love.*

When warnings were not heeded, Nehemiah took action. When a few persistent troublemakers continued to rebel, Nehemiah threatened to use force. It should be noted that force was only threatened as a last resort, after all other available means had been tried. Even then, it was only to be used by legitimate authorities to enforce a law that had been agreed by all the people.

Guarding the gates was seen as a holy task. Reliable Levites were chosen for the purpose. Nehemiah selected the right people for the right job. Staff recruitment was one of his strengths.

13:23-29 *In those days also I saw Jews who had married women of Ashdod, Ammon, and Moab; and half of their children spoke the language of Ashdod, and they could not speak the language of Judah, but spoke the language of various peoples. And I contended with them and cursed them and beat some of them and pulled out their hair; and I made them take an oath in the name of God, saying, "You shall not give your daughters to their sons, or take their daughters for your sons or for yourselves. Did not King Solomon of Israel sin on account of such women? Among the many nations there was no king like him, and he was beloved by his God, and God made him king over all Israel; nevertheless, foreign women made even him to sin. Shall we then listen to you and do all this great evil and act treacherously against our God by marrying foreign women?" And one of the sons of Jehoiada, son of the high priest Eliashib, was the son-in-law* *of Sanballat the Horonite; I chased him away from me. Remember them, O my God, because they have defiled the priesthood, the covenant of the priests and the Levites.*

Many men had broken the commitment the community had made, not to intermarry with non-believers (10:30). Nehemiah 13 shows that the people had broken each of the general and specific commitments they made in Nehemiah 10. They had forgotten God's law (13:1-9, cf. 10:28-29), they had not given what they had pledged to give (13:10-14, cf. 10:32-39), they had neglected the sabbath (13:15-22, cf 10:31) and they had married non-believers (13:23-29, cf. 10:30).

Nehemiah did not hide his anger. His extreme reaction recalls Ezra's response to a similar scenario (Ezra 9:3). The reference to Solomon shows why Nehemiah was so angry. If foreign women could lead God's appointed king into idolatry, it was arrogant for others to imagine they would not be vulnerable. (The modern-day equivalent of the prohibition of mixed marriages is the New Testament command not to be yoked together with non-believers. For a fuller discussion, see my comment above under 10:30.)

The children of those men who married Ashdodites spoke the language of Ashdod. The Hebrew language was the language of scripture.[8] Children who did not speak the language would find it hard to practise their religion. They were more likely to follow other religions. This underlines the importance of having scriptures available in the languages that people speak. It is another good reason why believers should marry other believers. Where both parents are not committed to bringing their child up in a Christian environment and witnessing to him or her, the child is more likely to follow other ways. This is especially the case when the believing parent has less contact with the child than the non-believing parent (for example, in cultures where the child spends a number of years with maternal kin).

Marriage restrictions were stricter for priests than for other Jews (cf. James 3:1). The Mosaic law specifically stipulated that they must marry one of their own kin (Leviticus 21:13-25; Ezekiel 44:22). The discovery that one of the grandsons of the current high priest Eliashib had married a daughter of Nehemiah's opponent Sanballat was therefore of special concern. This unnamed grandson had defiled the priesthood and was driven out of Jerusalem.

Nehemiah could have used the divorce procedure set up by Ezra (Ezra 10:10-44). He chose not to, preferring to contain the problem by taking steps to ensure further illicit marriages were not contracted. Kidner suggests that this was in part because Nehemiah had seen the effects of the break-up of families when Ezra had forced Jews to divorce their foreign wives and send away their children.[9]

The Church in South Sudan faces a similar issue today in deciding how to deal with polygamy, the custom of having more than one wife at the same time. (Polyandry, the custom of a woman having more than one husband at the same time, is rarely practised in South Sudan. In the West, many people practice "serial polygamy", the habit of marrying a wife, divorcing her and marrying another.)

In the past, some churches asked polygamists to choose one of their wives and send away the rest. The result was a number of divorced and unsupported women with fatherless children. A more practical approach is not to allow polygamists to take any positions of responsibility. Some churches are more lenient to those who became polygamists before they were baptised. Some churches accept polygamists as full members of the church with the right to partake in Holy Communion; others do not allow them to partake of the Lord's Supper. Most churches agree that polygamists should not be given leadership positions in the church (1 Timothy 3:2, 12; Titus 1:6).

Apologists for polygamy often argue that the Old Testament endorses polygamy, since great men such as David and Solomon were polygamists. While the Bible is full of examples of polygamous men, it also exposes the problems polygamy caused them. Jacob was unable to love Leah as he loved Rachel (Genesis 29:30-31). There was much jealousy between the two wives (Genesis 30:1). Solomon was led away from God and into idolatry by his many wives (2 Kings 11:1-8).

It has been argued that polygamy is the original cause of the present-day Middle East conflict. Sarai, later Sarah, was without children and past childbearing age. She suggested to Abraham that he should build a family through her Egyptian maid, Hagar (Genesis 16:2). When Hagar was pregnant, she began to despise Sarai (v.4). She then bore Ishmael. Later, Sarah became pregnant and bore a son, Isaac. Ishmael and Hagar were sent away (21:9). This marked the beginning of conflict between the descendants of Sarah and Hagar.

Polygamy is still widespread in South Sudan. It is seen by some as a way of taking care of orphans and widows. Wives are inherited from family members who have died. Others argue that polygamy is necessary because the war has left us with many more women than men. Most African governments do not have extensive social security schemes. While we need to preach against polygamy and show how the Bible opposes it, we also need to make sure that orphans and widows are taken better care of, so that polygamy is not perceived to be the only option.

It may be the case that urbanisation and economic hardship will discourage polygamy. It is hard to maintain more than one family in a town setting. Contact with other cultures will also have an influence. Many western countries have laws against polygamy. A person can be convicted for bigamy, the crime of marrying when you are still legally married to someone else. There have been allegations that polygamous men declare their second spouses as 'sisters' when processing settlement to the West.

In the new post–conflict dispensation, there is the opportunity to do things differently. Women and children deserve to be part of a stable family and to experience the love and care of a husband and father who is not shared with others. God's original intention was for one man to be married to one woman. This is what I call 'marriagocracy': one wife, one husband, as opposed to democracy: one man, one vote. Monogamous marriages provide for more meaningful relationships than being 'one of many', a concept that speaks more of property than relationships.

13:30-31 *Thus I cleansed them from everything foreign, and I established the duties of the priests and Levites, each in his work; and I provided for the wood offering, at appointed times, and for the first fruits. Remember me, O my God, for good.*

Weanzana compares Nehemiah's plea in 13:31b: *"Remember me, O my God, for good"* to Paul's remarks in 2 Timothy 4:7-8: *"I have fought the good fight, I have finished the race, I have kept the faith. From now on there is reserved for me the crown of righteousness, which the Lord, the righteous judge, will give me on that day, and not only to me but also to all who have longed for his appearing."* Nehemiah, like Paul, seeks God's blessing because he "has fulfilled the mission he was sent to achieve."[10]

It is interesting that Nehemiah's own summary of his actions does not include rebuilding the walls, which most would see as his crowning achievement. Rather, his most important work was "the making of his people."[11] The rebuilding of the walls and the repopulation of Jerusalem were important aspects of this work that cannot be disentangled from the legal and spiritual dimensions of reconstruction emphasised in chapters 8-10 and 13. Nonetheless, it is these latter dimensions that Nehemiah clearly regarded as most important. Obedience to God's law set out in scripture was his priority.

Conclusion

The book of Nehemiah begins and ends with highly personal accounts from Nehemiah himself, including some of his most intimate prayers. Book-ending Nehemiah in this way ensures that the reader understands his central role throughout the book. Nehemiah 13 makes sure the reader appreciates Nehemiah's personal contribution to the cultic reforms rather than assuming his role was marginal from Nehemiah 7 onwards. While the book is not simply a leadership manual, we are intended to learn from Nehemiah as an individual. We learn just how much can be achieved when an individual submits totally to God and sacrifices whatever they have, to live out God's calling on their life.

As seen in the last chapter, the climax to the book is found in Nehemiah 12. Nehemiah 13 is something of an anti-climax. It is theologically important for precisely this reason. The high point of Nehemiah 12 is not the end of the story. Cultic reforms alone could not secure obedient relationship. In his discussion of 13:22, Clines suggests that the attempt to legislate faithfulness by devising laws that would prevent Israel from falling into old habits (what Brueggemann calls "the extremity of carefulness"[12]) contained within it the seeds of Pharisaism:

> Nehemiah's measure is an excellent example of the Jewish tendency to make "a hedge about the Torah": lest the sabbath law of burden-carrying should be broken, with fearful consequences (v.18), he removes as far as possible any opportunity for breaking the law. But to forcibly prevent one's fellows from disobeying God's law is not usually the best way of encouraging their willing obedience...[13]

A crudely legalistic reading of Nehemiah should be resisted. The importance of weeping and rejoicing at appropriate times is emphasised throughout the book. The book itself points to the inadequacy of cultic reform when it is not accompanied by transformation of the heart and daily submission to God's will. Nehemiah 13 testifies that "spiritual growth is generally better gauged by the quality of what passes as normal than by the fleeting moments of particular uplift."[14]

1   Mugambi, "Africa and the Old Testament," 20.
2   Williamson, *Ezra, Nehemiah*, 385–6.
3   Kidner, *Ezra and Nehemiah*, 129.
4   Williamson, *Ezra, Nehemiah*, 387.
5   Ibid.
6   Kidner, *Ezra and Nehemiah*, 130.
7   Clines, *Ezra, Nehemiah, Esther*, 242.
8   Williamson, *Ezra, Nehemiah*, 397.
9   Kidner, *Ezra and Nehemiah*, 131–2.
10 Weanzana, "Nehemiah," 558.
11 Kidner, *Ezra and Nehemiah*, 133.
12 Brueggemann, *The Land*, 151.
13 Clines, *Ezra, Nehemiah, Esther*, 245.
14 Williamson, *Ezra, Nehemiah*, 389.

CHAPTER TWELVE

Church and state

ASTUTE READERS will have noticed that I have not yet addressed one of the key issues that arises from the text. This is the thorny issue of the separation of state and religion. Nehemiah was a state official who was also a believer. He was engaged in physical development, and political and spiritual reform. Nehemiah 5 and 13 show that political and spiritual reform were not divided. He also worked very closely with Ezra, a priest.

This is a difficult matter. We all see how much division party politics has brought in Africa. Christians have hated and even killed each other. During the 2010 elections in the then Sudan, the Episcopal Church of the Sudan decided not to side with one political party against another. This is because if you do so as a church or a church leader, you divide the people. In one case one of the candidates came to me to complain that one of my clergy had joined his opponent's campaign committee. I had to issue a directive that no pastor was to openly canvass support for electoral candidates.

Recently, parts of the Church in South Sudan called on the government to review the policy of separation of Church and state.[1] The SPLM called for a secular state during the war because Khartoum wanted to make Sharia law the basis for all legislation in the whole country. The policy recognises that religious identity cannot be imposed by the state.

The policy is good, but more clarity is needed in how to interpret it. It should not be understood to mean that religion has no role in public life. Some government leaders and bureaucrats ask religious leaders to keep away from politics. What they actually mean is "do not criticise us". They find the Church useful when they have a message to be passed to the people (for example, public health campaigns). Nehemiah's economic and political reforms in Nehemiah 5, clearly based on scripture, and the role of confession leading to the new covenant stipulations in Nehemiah 9-10, testify that religion has a role in public life. If we withdraw from it we will regret it. Churches in the West find that, having withdrawn from public life, they now face obstacles and criticism when they try to re-engage.

Henry Okullu has written that

the *separation* is institutional only, but at a different, deeper level, the two are bound together in the realm of ethics by owing their origin to God. Both are established for the service of God and persons. The recognition of the separation of Church and state at the institutional level must be seasoned by an equally vigorous recognition of the integrated view of life at a deeper level.[2]

Equally, we should not try to prevent government officials from praying or seeking God's will as they carry out their jobs. Nehemiah prayed together with the people at important functions and at key times during the rebuilding project (Nehemiah 4:9). In Eastern Africa, God is mentioned in most national anthems. The South Sudanese national anthem begins with the words "Oh God, we praise and glorify you for your grace on South Sudan." The Kenyan anthem begins "Oh God of all creation". In Uganda, it is "Oh Uganda may God uphold you". It is right to acknowledge God's sovereignty in this way. The separation of religion and state does not mean our officials should be prevented from praying or from pursuing God's truth as outlined in his word in our public life.

On the opposite side, some have suggested that the salaries of senior Church leaders should be paid for by the state. I have gone on record to say that I oppose such a move. It would compromise the independence and integrity of bishops and other Church leaders. The Church must not be dependent on the state. This would compromise the Church in its prophetic role.

The Church should act as a watchdog for society. Some African leaders have encouraged the Church to play this role. Henry Okullu quotes Julius Nyerere as saying

> Everything which prevents a person from living in dignity and decency must therefore be under attack from the Church and its workers.[3]

before going on to outline the Church's prophetic role in more detail:

> . . the duty rests squarely on the Church leadership who must not only publicly denounce evil in society but also enable individual Christians to fulfil their prophetic role in society . . When a road is to be built, a churchman may be consulted on technical details only if he is a qualified engineer. But it does not follow that he abdicates his responsibility to demand that no bribery is involved in the appointment of the contractor and that the bridges on that road are safe for motorists. Churchmen may not have

the expertise to reform an economic system. But they have the duty to say that a system which leave the majority of our people poor and jobless and without proper housing is immoral and unjust, and should be corrected by the appropriate specialists. Our prophetic role requires us to ask moral questions concerned with national projects and demand answers from political leaders.[4]

Packer argues that "Nehemiah is our model here, a very relevant model for our time."[5] We have an obligation to stand against those who "oppose obedience to God's truth"[6] including, if need be, politicians and public officials.

This includes standing against individual politicians who are corrupt. In 2009, Roman Catholic bishops attending their month-long Synod in Rome issued a blunt ultimatum to corrupt Catholic political leaders in Africa. Their message was: repent or leave public office. The bishops said Africa needs "saintly politicians who will clean the continent of corruption".[7]

Although Nehemiah was a believer involved in public life, his actions suggest he would have approved of the policy of separation of Church and state. He did not attempt to muscle in on the reading and interpretation of scripture. He allowed Ezra to lead proceedings at religious gatherings. He was angered by Tobiah's use of the temple for political and commercial purposes, and threw him and his possessions out. Even though Nehemiah was a public official with links to the king, he had harsh words for religious leaders who cosied up to governors who opposed God's work, and abdicated their prophetic role.

The most important thing is that there is no state religion. The retired Anglican Archbishop of Kenya, the Most Rev Dr David Gitari, put it well when he said that the relationship between the Church and the state should be like the relationship between human beings and fire. If we are too close it is too hot. If we are too far away, it is too cold.

Okullu sums up the meaning of the separation of Church and state as follows:

In practical terms, separation for the Church means guaranteed freedom from interference with doctrine or ritual. State officials cannot and should not exert pressure on the appointment of church leaders, and politicians cannot intrude on the inner life of the Church. Secondly, such freedom means that the Church can and should have its own financial resources and is free to determine the use of those resources. Thirdly, each national church must be free to have contacts with other churches. The international nature of the Church is essential for its world mission, and must be recognised and maintained, although each church has a responsibility to relate and be relevant to its own particular culture and political situation.[8]

Church and state in South Sudan

The Sudanese Church played a significant role during the war. John Ashworth affirms that the Church was "the only institution that remained on the ground with the people."[9] It provided basic services like health and education, and was involved in conflict resolution and international advocacy. This gave the Church "a remarkable degree of credibility and moral authority".[10]

The Church's attitude toward the de facto authorities varied in different areas. In areas controlled by the Government of Sudan, the Sudan Council of Churches and some of its member churches resisted the Sudanese state's policies. In areas controlled by the SPLM/A, the New Sudan Council of Churches and its member churches initially supported the liberation struggle. A now infamous public letter in 1993, To Our Flock, charged that "some of our liberators have become oppressors". At a later stage the position shifted to "critical and constructive collaboration".

The Church collaborated with the Southern Sudanese government during the CPA interim period. Churches used their pulpits to encourage people to take part in the 2008 census, the 2010 elections and the 2011 referendum, and explained how to participate. The Church was careful to retain its impartiality and did not tell Christians how to vote in the elections or referendum.

In 2009, a government minister in the then Government of Southern Sudan asked churches to assist the government in preaching a message of peace and in holding reconciliation initiatives to build unity in the lead-up to the referendum. The reconciliation initiatives organised by the Church during the war were the most successful held by any group. The secular Rift Valley Institute (RVI) has admitted that the Church had greater success than secular organisations who tried to copy her model, arguing that secular organisations

> were less concerned to explore the spiritual dimension in reconciliation, and arguably and for better or worse, were less closely tied to existing institutions in the field. It is doubtful if any of them could have orchestrated an event with the impact of the Wunlit conference.[11]

In reconciling warring ethnic groups within South Sudan, they paved the way for factions of the SPLM/A to reconcile, a necessary precondition for the successful negotiations that produced the CPA and ended the war. The RVI also admits in the same report that "the Wunlit conference, the maintenance of the Wunlit agreement and the subsequent local peace initiatives owe much to the relationship forged between the SPLM/A and the churches after 1997."[12]

After independence, there was an expectation the Church would play a public role in the new nation by leading reconciliation initiatives. In early 2012 Salva Kiir, the President of South Sudan, asked the ECS Archbishop, the Most Rev. Dr Daniel Deng Bul, to chair the government's Jonglei peace committee. In May 2012, fourteen bishops representing the Catholic and Episcopal Churches of South Sudan, led by the Catholic Archbishop Paulino Lukudu Loro and the ECS Archbishop Daniel Deng Bul, met in Yei to pray and reflect together on the responsibilities, and the role they can play in bringing peace and understanding between Sudan and South Sudan. At this meeting, the bishops released a Message of Peace. This included the following words, which summarise the Message well.

We dream of two nations which are democratic and free, where people of all religions, all ethnic groups, all cultures and all languages enjoy equal human rights based on citisenship. We dream of two nations at peace with each other, cooperating to make the best use of their God-given resources, promoting free interaction between their citisens, living side by side in solidarity and mutual respect, celebrating their shared history and forgiving any wrongs they may have done to each other. We dream of people no longer traumatised, of children who can go to school, of mothers who can attend clinics, of an end to poverty and malnutrition, and of Christians and Muslims who can attend church or mosque freely without fear. Enough is enough. There should be no more war between Sudan and South Sudan![13]

The Church should continue to play this role. The Church's mission is reconciliation (2 Corinthians 5:18-20; Ephesians 2:15-18). However, it is important that its role in public life is not limited to reconciliation initiatives alone.

During the war, the Church was involved in public service delivery, reconciliation, advocacy and information dissemination. It co-operated with the *de facto* state in the liberated areas, but also criticised where necessary. The

Church played a significant role in public life while retaining its independence and institutional separation from the state. This should continue in peacetime.

1   Sudan Tribune, "South Sudan Church Calls to Review Separation of Religion and State," *Sudan Tribune*, February 6, 2013, http://www.sudantribune.com/spip.php?article45420

2   J Henry Okullu, *Church and State in Nation Building and Human Development* (Nairobi: Uzima Press Ltd, 1987), 63.

3   Ibid., 19.

4   Ibid., 19–20.

5   Packer, *A Passion for Faithfulness*, 98.

6   Ibid.

7   CBC News, "Catholic Bishops Slam Corrupt African Leaders," *CBC News*, October 23, 2009, http://www.cbc.ca/news/world/story/2009/10/23/catholic-bishops-africa-corrupt.html

8   Okullu, *Church and State*, 64.

9   Ashworth and Ryan, "'One Nation from Every Tribe, Tongue, and People': The Church and Strategic Peacebuilding in South Sudan," 47.

10 Ibid.

11 Bradbury et al., *Local Peace Processes in Sudan*, 31.

12 Ibid., 36.

13 Message of Peace from the Episcopal and Catholic Bishops of South Sudan meeting in Yei, 9th -11th May 2012: 'We Have a Dream of Peace Justice and Freedom', May 11, 2012, para. 25, http://blog.caritas.org/2012/05/14/a-dream-of-peace-justce-and-freedom-for-south-sudan/

Conclusion

Learning from Nehemiah's example

Nehemiah was a successful leader. He was a man of action who mobilised a community paralysed by shame to complete a national reconstruction project of significant proportions. While in political office he restructured the national economy so that the poor would receive justice, building solidarity between all sections of society. He worked with religious leaders to rebuild a covenantal community, rooted in and obedient to the word of God. Nehemiah was concerned with physical, social and spiritual dimensions of community life and achieved some measure of success in each of these areas.

I have presented some of Nehemiah's key characteristics, so that they may be used by preachers wishing to highlight some of the lessons learned from this book to their congregations.

Nehemiah was:

- *Patriotic.* Although Nehemiah had a good job serving in the king's palace, he was moved by the situation in Jerusalem and left his comfortable lifestyle to help rebuild his nation.

- *Prayerful.* He spent months in prayer seeking God's will. He prayed continually, offering 'arrow' prayers while he took action. He prayed in private and he led the community in praying. He prayed for God's will to be done.

- A *planner.* He worked out what resources he would need to rebuild the walls before presenting his idea to the king. He approached his boss at the right time and in the right way. He researched and followed protocol. He thought about the obstacles that opponents would put in his path and incorporated measures to deal with them into his plan.

- *Patient.* The period of preparation was longer than the time it took to implement his project!

- Someone who *persevered* in the face of external threats and internal challenges. He took external threats seriously, but did not allow them to distract him or the community from the task of reconstruction. When the threat became physical, he took defensive action to prevent attack, while continuing with the work. He did not give up even when his own life was threatened. He took threats to internal unity even more seriously than external threats and dealt with the underlying causes comprehensively, even though doing so meant a temporary halt to the work.

- A *participatory* leader. He listened to others, especially to the poor. He delegated authority and involved others in decision-making. He made use of people according to the gifts God had given them. As a consequence, the work was characterised by a unity of intention and the people felt ownership over the project.

- Actively involved in alleviating *poverty*. He did not side with those of his own privileged background, but took the side of the poor. He recognised that poverty was partly the result of unjust structures and took action to change them, rather than solving the problem temporarily with handouts. He identified with the poor and lived out a consistent social ethic.

Covenant

Although we can learn a lot from Nehemiah, the most important character in the book of Nehemiah is God. God is shown to be reliable. He keeps covenant. Remembering what he has done by reading and obeying his word, by giving personal testimony and reciting their collective story helps his people to keep covenant. Special measures can also be helpful where patterns of sinful behaviour have become ingrained. However, Nehemiah 13 shows that extra regulations on their own are not sufficient. After a time, God's people broke covenant again. Inward transformation was necessary.

The book of Nehemiah makes it clear that God was behind Nehemiah's success. He laid a burden in Nehemiah's heart to rebuild the walls. The walls were completed with his help. The nations around Jerusalem and Judah were humbled because they recognised God's hand in the unfolding events. Nehemiah should strengthen our faith that God has a plan for our lives, our cities and nations, and an overall salvation plan. We are supposed to understand that God had a plan for bringing inward transformation. The prophets foretold this plan in part, but it was revealed fully in Jesus Christ. God brings transformation by writing his law on our hearts through his Spirit, who helps us to keep the new covenant sealed with Christ's blood.

Land

Keeping covenant is linked to enjoyment of God's gift of land. Land is not ours to do as we wish. It can only be enjoyed in certain ways. We must take care of the land, allowing it rest at appropriate times. We should not plunder it. Our use of the land should be sustainable. Land should be organised according to biblical guidelines. The poor must have access to the land to cultivate. Land is not for speculation and should not be centralised. There is a role for community ownership of land organised through extended family networks. We have to think carefully about what this means in the modern world. However, it is clear that we are not permitted to seise land or dispossess the poor based on historic claims. Solidarity and social justice must be prioritised in arrangements for managing and distributing land. All land remains God's and it is the responsibility of the community to use it according to his purposes.

Construction and reconstruction

In the introduction to this book, I quoted Mugambi's definition of reconstruction:

> Reconstruction is done when an existing complex becomes dysfunctional, for whatever reason, and the user still requires using it. New specification may be made in the new designs, while some aspects of the old complex are retained in the new.[1]

We have seen that in Nehemiah, physical reconstruction is linked to social and spiritual reconstruction. The old complex (law) is retained in the new design, but new specifications are made in Nehemiah 10 to apply the law to the postexilic situation. Our designs for our nation must be based on God's blueprint. We must not reject the old complex in our fascination with the new.

The book of Nehemiah shows the importance of memory as a basis for keeping covenant. The process of reconciliation is an opportunity to forge an inclusive national story with God at its centre. We must listen to all communities and especially to the marginalised in constructing this story. We must document the process carefully. Having done so, it will serve as an aid to remember how God has delivered us. We must locate our particular story in the universal story of salvation set out in the Bible. This requires a good understanding of scripture. Finally, we must retell our story so it becomes embedded in the collective consciousness of the nation and is repeated to future generations.

Reconciliation is part of the social and spiritual reconstruction of our nation. It should not be separated from physical reconstruction, but fully integrated with it. Nehemiah mobilised a traumatised community to participate in God's work of reconstruction. May God do the same through us.

---

1   Mugambi, *From Liberation to Reconstruction*, 12.

Bibliography

Alier, Abel. *Southern Sudan: Too Many Agreements Dishonoured*. Reading: Ithaca Press, 1992.

Allen, Leslie C, and Timothy Laniak. *Ezra, Nehemiah, Esther*. New International Biblical Commentary 9. Carlisle: Hendrickson Publishers; Paternoster Press, 2003.

Ashworth, John, and Maura Ryan. "'One Nation from Every Tribe, Tongue, and People': The Church and Strategic Peacebuilding in South Sudan." *Journal of Catholic Social Thought* 10, no. 1 (2013): 47–67.

Blenkinsopp, Joseph. *Ezra-Nehemiah*. Old Testament Library. London: SCM Press Ltd, 1989.

———. "The Bible, Archaeology and Politics; or The Empty Land Revisited." *Journal for the Study of the Old Testament* 27, no. 2 (December 2002).

Bradbury, Mark, John Ryle, Michael Medley, and Kwesi Sansculotte-Greenidge. *Local Peace Processes in Sudan: A Baseline Study*. London/Nairobi: Rift Valley Institute, DFID, 2006. http://citisenshift.org/sites/citisen.nfb.ca/files/Local_Peace_Processes_in_Sudan_May_2006.pdf.

Bright, Bill. "Five Principles of Growth." *Cru (Campus Crusade for Christ)*, August 9, 2013. http://www.cru.org/training-and-growth/classics/10-basic-steps/1-the-christian-adventure/03-five-principles-of-growth.htm.

Brown, Raymond. *The Message of Nehemiah: God's Servant in a Time of Change*. The Bible Speaks Today. Leicester: Inter-Varsity Press, 1998.

Brueggemann, Walter. *Hopeful Imagination: Prophetic Voices in Exile*. London: SCM Press Ltd, 1992.

———. *Texts That Linger, Words That Explode: Listening to Prophetic Voices*. Minneapolis: Fortress Press, 2000.

———. *The Land: Place as Gift, Promise, and Challenge in Biblical Faith*. Overtures to Biblical Theology 1. Philadelphia: Fortress Press, 1977.

CBC News. "Catholic Bishops Slam Corrupt African Leaders." *CBC News*, October 23, 2009. http://www.cbc.ca/news/world/story/2009/10/23/catholic-bishops-africa-corrupt.html.

Childs, Brevard S. *Introduction to the Old Testament as Scripture*. London: SCM Press Ltd, 1979.

Clines, David J A. *Ezra, Nehemiah, Esther*. The New Century Bible Commentary. Grand Rapids; Basingstoke: Wm B Eerdmans Publishing Company; Marshall Morgan and Scott, 1984.

————. *On the Way to the Postmodern: Old Testament Essays, 1967-1998*. Vol. 1. Journal for the Study of the Old Testament Supplement 292. Sheffield: Sheffield Academic Press, 1998.

Copnall, James. "Sudan 'Elbow-Lickers' Are Turning Omar Al Bashir's Jibe against Him: Khartoum Protests against the Fuel Subsidy Cuts Now Target Panicky Military Regime That Has Begun Arresting Activists." *The Guardian*, June 28, 2012. http://www.theguardian.com/world/2012/jun/28/sudan-protests-elbow-lickers-bashir.

Deng Bul, Daniel. *A Working Paper of the Committee for National Healing, Peace and Reconciliation: Comprehensive Strategic Dimensions for Healing, Peace and Reconciliation for All South Sudanese: The Way Forward*, July 2013.

Department of Public Information, UN. "Millennium Goals." *United Nations*, September 9, 2013. www.un.org/millenniumgoals/.

Duany, Julia Aker. "People-to-People Peacemaking: A Local Solution to Local Problems." In *Artisans of Peace: Grassroots Peacemaking among Christian Communities*, edited by Mary Ann Cejka and Tomás Bamat. Maryknoll: Orbis Books, 2003.

Evers, Stan K. *Doing a Great Work: Ezra and Nehemiah Simply Explained*. Darlington: Evangelical Press, 1996.

Fensham, F. Charles. *The Book of Ezra, Nehemiah*. The New International Commentary on the Old Testament. Grand Rapids: Wm B Eerdmans Publishing Company, 1982.

Getz, Gene M. "Nehemiah." In *The Bible Knowledge Commentary: An Exposition of the Scriptures*, edited by John F Walvoord and Roy B Zuck. Wheaton: Victor Books, 1985.

Government of the Republic of South Sudan. "State Symbols." *Government of the Republic of South Sudan*, July 12, 2011. http://www.goss-online.org/magnoliaPublic/en/about/symbols.html.

Grabbe, Lester L. *Ezra-Nehemiah*. Old Testament Readings. London: Routledge, 1998.

Gutiérrez, Gustavo. *A Theology of Liberation*. Translated by Sister Caridad Inda and John Eagleson. London: SCM Press Ltd, 1974.

———. *We Drink from Our Own Wells: The Spiritual Journey of a People*. Translated by Matthew J O'Connell. London: SCM Press Ltd, 2005.

Howard-Brook, Wes. *"Come out My People!": God's Call out of Empire in the Bible and beyond*. Maryknoll: Orbis Books, 2010.

Hybels, Bill, and Mark Mittelberg. *Becoming a Contagious Christian*. Grand Rapids: Zondervan, 1994.

Johnson, Douglas H. *The Root Causes of Sudan's Civil Wars*. African Issues. Oxford: James Currey, 2003.

Kidner, Derek. *Ezra and Nehemiah: An Introduction and Commentary*. Tyndale Old Testament Commentaries. Leicester: Inter-Varsity Press, 1979.

Klein, Ralph W. "Nehemiah." In *Harper's Bible Commentary*, edited by James Luther Mays. San Francisco: HarperCollins Publishers Limited, 1988.

Luck, G. Coleman. *Ezra and Nehemiah*. Chicago: Moody Press, 1961.

Madut-Arop, Arop. *Sudan's Painful Road to Peace: A Full Story of the Founding and Development of SPLM/SPLA*. Charleston: BookSurge, 2006.

McConville, J G. *Ezra, Nehemiah and Esther*. The Daily Study Bible. Edinburgh: Saint Andrew Press, 1985.

Mendenhall, George E. *Ancient Israel's Faith and History: An Introduction to the Bible in Context*. Edited by Gary A Herion. Louisville: Westminster John Knox Press, 2001.

Mugambi, Jesse. "Africa and the Old Testament." In *Interpreting the Old Testament in Africa: Papers from the International Symposium on Africa and the Old Testament in Nairobi, October 1999*, edited by Mary N. Getui, Knut Holter, and Victor Zinkuratire. Vol. 2. Bible and Theology in Africa. New York: Peter Lang Publishing, 2001.

———. *From Liberation to Reconstruction: African Christian Theology after the Cold War*. Nairobi: East African Educational Publishers, 1995.

Myers, Jacob M. *Ezra, Nehemiah*. The Anchor Bible 14. Garden City: Doubleday, 1965.

Okullu, J Henry. *Church and State in Nation Building and Human Development*. Nairobi: Uzima Press Ltd, 1987.

Packer, J I. *A Passion for Faithfulness: Wisdom from the Book of Nehemiah*. London: Hodder & Stoughton Ltd, 1995.

Pleins, J David. *The Social Visions of the Hebrew Bible: A Theological Introduction.* Louisville: Westminster John Knox, 2000.

Poole, Canon Joseph. "Coventry Litany of Reconciliation." 1958. http://www. coventrycathedral.org.uk/about-us/our-reconciliation-ministry/coventry-litany-of-reconciliation.php.

Ramsden, Nicholas. "The Dedication of Emmanuel Cathedral 17th April 2011." 2011. http://www.kajokeji.anglican.org/index.php?PageID=cathedralddct nrpt.

Satterthwaite, Philip, and Gordon McConville. *The Histories.* Exploring the Old Testament 2. London: SPCK, 2007.

Spurgeon, C H. "Apart." Sermon, The Metropolitan Tabernacle, Newington, July 16, 1885. http://www.spurgeon.org/sermons/2510.htm.

Sudan Tribune. "South Sudan Church Calls to Review Separation of Religion and State." *Sudan Tribune*, February 6, 2013. http://www.sudantribune. com/spip.php?article45420.

———. "South Sudan Leads World in Livestock Wealth." *Sudan Tribune*, January 25, 2013. http://www.sudantribune.com/spip.php?article45286.

The Bishops of the Catholic Church and the Episcopal Church of Sudan. "Message of Peace from the Episcopal and Catholic Bishops of South Sudan Meeting in Yei, 9th-11th May 2012: 'We Have a Dream of Peace Justice and Freedom,'" May 11, 2012.

Throntveit, Mark A. *Ezra-Nehemiah.* Interpretation, a Bible Commentary for Teaching and Preaching. Louisville: John Knox Press, 1992.

Todaro, Michael P., and Stephen C Smith. *Economic Development.* 8th edition. Addison-Wesley Series in Economics. Boston: Addison Wesley, 2003.

Tollefson, Kenneth D., and Hugh G M Williamson. "Nehemiah as Cultural Revitalisation: An Anthropological Perspective." In *The Historical Books*, edited by J. Cheryl Exum. The Biblical Seminar 40. Sheffield: Sheffield Academic Press, 1997.

UNHCR. "Convention and Protocol Relating to the Status of Refugees." UNHCR communications and public information service, December 2010. http://www.unhcr.org/3b66c2aa10.html.

Unknown. "101 (English): Read Your Bible, Pray Every Day." In *Shukuru Yesu.* Third Edition. Juba: Scripture Union Sudan, 2000.

USA for UNHCR. "What Is a Refugee?" *USA for UNHCR, the UN Refugee Agency*, August 12, 2013.

Wallace, Ian. "Bringing Good News to the Poor: Does Church-Based Transformational Development Really Work?" *Transformation* 19, no. 2 (April 2002): 133–7.

Weanzana, Nupanga. "Ezra." In *Africa Bible Commentary*, edited by Tokunboh Adeyemo. Nairobi: WordAlive Publishers, 2006.

———. "Nehemiah." In Africa Bible Commentary, edited by Tokunboh Adeyemo. Nairobi: WordAlive Publishers, 2006.

Williamson, Hugh G M. *Ezra and Nehemiah*. Old Testament Guides. Sheffield, England: Sheffield Academic Press, 1987.

———. *Ezra, Nehemiah*. Word Biblical Commentary 16. Waco: Word Books, 1985.

World Bank Group. "Poverty & Equity: Sub-Saharan Africa." *The World Bank: Working for a World Free of Poverty*, 2013. http://povertydata.worldbank.org/poverty/region/SSA.

———. "Poverty Overview." *The World Bank: Working for a World Free of Poverty*, 2013. http://www.worldbank.org/en/topic/poverty/overview

Wright, Christopher J H. *Old Testament Ethics for the People of God*. Leicester: Inter-Varsity Press, 2004.

Yongo-Bure, Benaiah. *Economic Development of Southern Sudan*. Lanham: University Press of America, 2007.

Lightning Source UK Ltd.
Milton Keynes UK
UKOW05f1234181213

223270UK00001B/1/P